THE PENAL LANDSCAPE

D1355108

The Howard League for Penal Reform is committed to developing an effective penal system which ensures there are fewer victims of crime, has a diminished role for prison and creates a safer community for all. In this collection of ten papers, the charity has brought together some of the most prominent academic experts in the field to map out what is happening in specific areas of criminal justice policy ranging from prison privatisation to policing and the role of community sentences.

The Howard League guide has two main aims: first it seeks to paint a picture of the current state of the penal system using its structures, processes and the specific groups affected by the system as the lens for analysis. However, each author also seeks to identify the challenges and gaps in understanding that should be considered to predicate a move towards a reduced role for the penal system, and prison in particular, while maintaining public confidence and safer communities. In doing so, we hope to inspire researchers and students alike to develop new research proposals that challenge the status quo and seek to create the Howard League's vision for the criminal justice system with *less crime, safer communities, fewer people in prison.*

Anita Dockley is Research Director of the Howard League for Penal Reform. She joined the charity in 1991 as its penal policy officer after completing her academic studies at the London School of Economics. Anita has had many roles at the Howard League, including as Assistant Director with responsibility for policy development, press and parliamentary work. Anita has undertaken research and written on a number of subjects including self-harm and suicide in the penal system, mothers and babies in prison, women lifers, and order and control in prisons. She is currently the managing editor of *The Howard Journal of Criminal Justice* and is a member of the law sub-panel in the 2014 Research Excellence Framework assessments.

Ian Loader is Professor of Criminology at Oxford University. He is author of six books: *Cautionary Tales* (1994, Avebury, with S. Anderson, R. Kinsey and C. Smith), *Youth, Policing and Democracy* (1996, Palgrave), *Crime and Social Change in Middle England* (2000, Routledge, with E. Girling and R. Sparks), *Policing and the Condition of England: Memory, Politics and Culture* (2003, OUP, with A. Mulcahy), *Civilizing Security* (2007, CUP, with N. Walker) and *Public Criminology?* (2010, Routledge, with R. Sparks). Ian is an editor of the *British Journal of Criminology*, Associate Editor of *Theoretical Criminology* and is on the editorial boards of *Policing and Society*, *Policing: A Journal of Policy and Practice*, *The Open Criminology Journal* and *International Political Sociology* (*IPS*). He is Chair of the Howard League's Research Advisory Group.

THE PENAL LANDSCAPE

THE HOWARD LEAGUE GUIDE TO CRIMINAL JUSTICE IN ENGLAND AND WALES

Edited by
Anita Dockley and Ian Loader

Routledge
Taylor & Francis Group

LONDON AND NEW YORK

First published 2013
by Routledge
2 Park Square, Milton Park, Abingdon, Oxon, OX14 4RN

Simultaneously published in the USA and Canada
by Routledge
711 Third Avenue, New York, NY 10017

Routledge is an imprint of the Taylor & Francis Group, an informa business

British Library Cataloguing in Publication Data
A catalogue record for this book is available from the British Library

Library of Congress Cataloguing in Publication Data
The penal landscape : the Howard League guide to criminal justice in England
   and Wales / [edited by] Anita Dockley and Ian Loader.
      p.   cm.
   Includes index.
   1. Criminal justice, Administration of – England.   2. Criminal justice,
   Administration of – Wales.   I. Dockley, Anita.   II. Loader, Ian.   III. Howard
   League for Penal Reform.
   HV9960.G7P46 2013
   364.942–dc23   2012039800

ISBN: 978-0-415-82328-9 (hbk)
ISBN: 978-0-415-82329-6 (pbk)
ISBN: 978-0-203-55009-0 (ebk)

Typeset in Garamond and Scala Sans by
Out of House Publishing

Printed and bound in Great Britain by MPG Printgroup

CONTENTS

LIST OF ILLUSTRATIONS

Contributors

Lol Burke is a Senior Lecturer in Criminal Justice at Liverpool John Moores University. He has worked as a Probation Officer and Senior Probation Officer and was involved in the delivery of probation training prior to his current appointment. Lol has written extensively on probation policy, practice and training issues and has spoken at both national and international conferences. He is co-author of *Redemption, Rehabilitation and Risk Management: A History of Probation* (2011), with Prof George Mair, and *Delivering Rehabilitation* (Routledge, 2013), with Steve Collett, which charts the changing face of the probation service under the New Labour and Coalition Governments. He is currently editor of the *Probation Journal* and a member of the editorial board of the *European Journal of Probation*. He is also a member of the Howard League for Penal Reform's Research Advisory Group, the European Society of Criminology Working Group on Community Sanctions and CREDOS (an international collaboration of researchers for the effective development of offender supervision). He is currently working on a three-year EU funded project with colleagues at Liverpool John Moores University, considering the implementation and potential transferability of Integrated Offender Management across three member states.

Neil Chakraborti is a Senior Lecturer in Criminology at the Department of Criminology, University of Leicester. He also holds an honorary position as an Adjunct Professor at the University of Ontario, Institute of Technology and is a Trustee of the Howard League for Penal Reform. He has published extensively in the fields of hate crime, victimisation, policing and diversity, and has conducted a wide range of research at a regional, national and international level, including projects commissioned by the Economic and Social Research Council, the European Commission, the Equality and Human Rights Commission, English local authorities and police forces. His books include *Responding to*

Hate Crime: The Case for Connecting Policy and Research (Policy Press, with Jon Garland, 2014), *Hate Crime: Concepts, Policy, Future Directions* (Routledge, 2010), *Hate Crime: Impact, Causes and Responses* (Sage, with Jon Garland, 2009) and *Rural Racism* (Routledge, with Jon Garland, 2004).

Anita Dockley is Research Director of the Howard League for Penal Reform. She joined the charity in 1991 as its penal policy officer after completing her academic studies at the London School of Economics. Anita has had many roles at the Howard League, including as Assistant Director with responsibility for policy development, press and parliamentary work. Anita has undertaken research and written on a number of subjects including self-harm and suicide in the penal system, mothers and babies in prison, women lifers, and order and control in prisons. She is currently the managing editor of *The Howard Journal of Criminal Justice* and is a member of the law sub-panel in the 2014 Research Excellence Framework assessments.

Stephen Farrall is Professor of Criminology at the University of Sheffield and Director of the Centre of Criminological Research. He is also a member of the Howard League for Penal Reform's Research Advisory Group. His most recent book is *Climate Change: Exploring the Legal and Criminological Consequences* as part of the Onati International Series in Law and Society (Hart Publishing, with T. Ahmed and D. French).

Elaine Genders is a Reader in Criminology in the Faculty of Laws at University College, London where she teaches Theoretical Criminology, Crime and Criminal Justice, Prison Ideology, Policy and Law, and Criminal Law. She is a long-standing supporter of the Howard League and is a member of their Research Advisory Group. Elaine has researched and published extensively on violent crime and on various aspects of imprisonment, including women in prison, race relations in prison, prison privatisation, therapeutic community regimes and human rights. She has advised the Ministry of Justice and currently serves on the Advisory Committees on the therapeutic regimes at HMPs Grendon, Dovegate and Send.

Barry Goldson currently holds the Charles Booth Chair of Social Science at the University of Liverpool, where he was previously Professor of Criminology and Social Policy. He is also Visiting Professorial Research Fellow at the Faculty of Law, University of New South Wales, Sydney, Australia and Professorial Fellow in Social Justice at Liverpool Hope University. He has researched and published extensively in the juvenile/youth justice fields. His most recent books include *Youth Crime and Justice* (Sage, 2006, with Muncie), *Comparative Youth Justice* (Sage, 2006, with Muncie), *Dictionary of Youth Justice* (Willan, 2008), *Youth Crime and Juvenile Justice* (an edited three-volume set of international 'major works', Sage 2009, with Muncie) and *Youth in Crisis? 'Gangs', Territoriality and Violence* (Routledge, 2011). He is the founding editor of *Youth Justice: An International Journal* (Sage). Professor Goldson has a long-standing professional association with the Howard League for Penal Reform.

Ian Loader is Professor of Criminology at Oxford University. He is author of six books: *Cautionary Tales* (Avebury, with S. Anderson, R. Kinsey and C. Smith, 1994), *Youth, Policing and Democracy* (Palgrave, 1996), *Crime and Social Change in Middle England* (Routledge, with E. Girling and R. Sparks, 2000), *Policing and the Condition of England: Memory, Politics and Culture* (Oxford University Press, with A. Mulcahy, 2003), *Civilizing Security* (Cambridge University Press, with N. Walker, 2007) and *Public Criminology?* (Routledge, with R. Sparks, 2010). Ian is an editor of the *British Journal of Criminology*, Associate Editor of *Theoretical Criminology* and is on the editorial boards of *Policing and Society*, *Policing: A Journal of Policy and Practice*, *The Open Criminology Journal* and *International Political Sociology* (*IPS*). He is Chair of the Howard League's Research Advisory Group.

Fergus McNeill is Professor of Criminology and Social Work at the University of Glasgow. Prior to becoming an academic in 1998, Fergus worked for a number of years in residential drug rehabilitation and as a criminal justice social worker. He is also a member of the Howard League for Penal Reform's Research Advisory Group.

Andrew Millie is Professor of Criminology at Edge Hill University. He is a member of the Research Advisory Group for the Howard League for Penal Reform. He has published widely on the topic of antisocial behaviour, including the book *Anti-Social Behaviour* (Open University Press, 2009) and edited collection *Securing Respect* (Policy Press, 2009). His broader research interests include policing, youth justice, criminological theory and philosophical criminology.

Nicola Padfield is a Reader in Criminal and Penal Justice at the University of Cambridge. A barrister by training, she has published widely on criminal law, sentencing and criminal justice. Her books include *The Criminal Justice Process: Text and Materials* (4th edn, 2008), *Criminal Law* (8th edn, 2012), *Beyond the Tariff: Human Rights and the Release of Life Sentence Prisoners* (2002) and *A Guide to the Proceeds of Crime Act 2002* (with S. Biggs and S. Farrell, 2002). She has edited other collections of essays, and is editor of the *Archbold Review*. She sits as a Recorder (part-time judge) in the Crown Court and is a Bencher of the Middle Temple.

Jill Peay is Professor of Law at the London School of Economics and Political Science and a member of the Mannheim Centre for Criminology at the LSE. She is an Associate Tenant at Doughty Street Chambers and also sat as a member of the Richardson Committee, the Expert Group established to advise Ministers on the future scope of the Mental Health Act 1983 (*Review of the Mental Health Act 1983*, Report of the Expert Committee, Department of Health 1999). She is the author of *Mental Health and Crime* (Routledge, 2010) and *Decisions and Dilemmas: Working with Mental Health Law* (Hart Publishing, 2003). In 2012, in honour of Professor Robert Reiner, she co-edited with Professor Tim Newburn *Policing: Politics, Culture and Control* (Hart Publishing, 2012).

Coretta Phillips is Senior Lecturer in the Department of Social Policy at the London School of Economics and Political Science. She has previously worked at Rutgers University and the Home Office, and was a member of Independent Advisory Group, HM Prison Service Race Equality Review Action Team. She is a member of the Howard League for Penal Reform's Research Advisory Group and Runnymede Trust's Academic Forum. Coretta's work is primarily within the fields of ethnicity, race and criminal justice. She is the author of *Racism, Crime and Justice* (Pearson Education, with Ben Bowling, 2001) and *The Multicultural Prison: Ethnicity, Masculinity, and Social Relations among Prisoners* (Oxford University Press, 2012). She is currently co-editing a book with Colin Webster, entitled *New Directions in Race, Ethnicity and Crime*, also for Routledge.

Jo Phoenix is Professor of Criminology, School of Applied Sciences, Durham University. Jo sits on the Howard League for Penal Reform Research Advisory Group. Her research interests include gender and justice, prostitution, sexual exploitation and youth justice, and she is currently working on an ESRC funded project, 'Implementing Policy Change in Youth Justice'. Jo is the author of *Making Sense of Prostitution* (Palgrave Macmillan, 2001) and, with Sarah Oerton, *Illicit and Illegal: Sex, Regulation and Social Control* (Willan, 2005). She is also the editor of *Regulating Sex for Sale: Prostitution, Policy Reform and the UK* (Policy Press, 2009). She is Director of the Centre for Sex, Gender and Sexualities at Durham University.

Lizzie Seal is Senior Lecturer in Criminology, School of Law, Politics and Sociology, Sussex University. Her research interests include gender representations of women who kill, cultural criminology and capital punishment. Her books include *Women, Murder and Femininity: Gender Representations of Women Who Kill* (Palgrave Macmillan, 2010) and, with Maggie O'Neill, *Transgressive Imaginations: Crime, Deviance and Culture* (Palgrave Macmillan, 2012). She is currently working on a monograph entitled *Capital Punishment in Twentieth Century Britain: Audience, Memory and Culture*, which will be published by Routledge. She also sits on the editorial board of the *British Journal of Criminology*.

Michael Rowe is Professor of Criminology at the University of Northumbria. Previously he was Director of the Institute of Criminology at Victoria University Wellington and Senior Lecturer in Criminology at the University of Leicester.

PREFACE

The Howard League for Penal Reform has been engaged in research, analysis and policy reform for almost 150 years. The aim of the charity's work has always been to make an impact and seek reform of the criminal justice system so that it is both humane and effective. Today the pegs that we hang our ideals on are: less crime, safer communities, fewer people in prison.

This guide has developed from the Howard League's commitment to 'stem the flow' of people into the criminal justice system. The concept of 'stemming the flow' is derived from our long-held reductionist beliefs that the size of the prison population, and ultimately the penal system, should and can be contracted while still ensuring the maintenance of order, the rule of law and safe communities with fewer victims of crime. This is a theme that runs strongly throughout the contributions in this book.

This collection has been the stimulus for a major Howard League initiative: The Symposium: What is justice? Re-imagining penal policy. The aim of What is justice? is to generate the climate and intellectual debate that can act as a springboard to contest the conventional role of the penal system and ultimately promote a new, achievable paradigm that will deliver a reduced role for the penal system while maintaining public confidence, fewer victims of crime and safer communities. Many of the authors in the guide will have a pivotal role in The Symposium (see http://www.howardleague.org/what-is-justice/ for more information), which the Howard League anticipates will be its vehicle for influencing the ethics as well as the underpinning beliefs, shape and dynamics for a future effective, efficient and humane criminal justice system.

The aims of the Howard League guide are twofold: to provide an up-to-date analysis, by some of the country's leading academics, that provides a base-level knowledge of what is actually happening now, but also to identify specific gaps in our understanding or what needs a greater

level of analysis or research. For that reason we asked our experts to identify areas for future research. The Howard League believes that research
and critical analysis as a stimulus for identifying pressure points and
ways of understanding the dynamics of criminal justice process would
ultimately allow for a stemming of the flow of people into the criminal
justice system. Second, this guide seeks to provide the spur to academics
and researchers to think about the ideas and issues raised in this guide
and take the metaphorical batonp to develop the research that can provide the knowledge base that may help the charity achieve its ultimate
aim to shrink the penal system.

This guide has been developed with the support of many people. First,
I must thank my co-editor, Ian Loader, for his support and enthusiasm for the project despite a burgeoning workload. I must also thank
all of the authors for their commitment to the Howard League and
providing us with the material for this book. At the Howard League,
there are too many people to mention that have guided, supported and
encouraged throughout, but thanks must go to the unstinting support
of Frances Crook, the guidance of Sue Wade and Penny Green, as well
as the patience and attention to detail shown by Vikki Julian and Jenny
Marsden in helping Ian and me prepare the text.

Anita Dockley
Research Director, the Howard League
for Penal Reform

INTRODUCTION

MAPPING THE PENAL LANDSCAPE OF ENGLAND AND WALES

IAN LOADER

The penal landscape of England and Wales is today marked – one might even say scarred – by three key features. The first of these is the sense of enduring *crisis* that has beset the criminal justice and penal system in England and Wales since the 1980s – a seemingly oxymoronic condition that shows few signs of abating. The second is the regime of permanent *revolution* that police and criminal justice agencies have been subjected to by successive governments over the last two decades – a form of governmental hyperactivity that continues in altered form under the Conservative-led Coalition. The third feature is an ongoing *expansion* in the numbers of people being processed through, or supervised or detained by, the agencies of penal control. There is little sign today that this is being brought to a halt, still less reversed.

In respect of the first feature – the sense of ongoing crisis – crime and its control continue to be a politically charged topic. Crime may in recent years have dropped down the list of public concerns – partly as a response to falling crime rates, partly due to the host of social anxieties generated by the global economic downturn. But questions of order and control now seem embedded in English political culture in ways which make crime both an ever-present threat to the political authority of elected politicians and a readily available and tempting means of shoring up that authority. In this hotter climate, the administration of justice by selected officials also becomes more precarious and subject to routine exposure, scrutiny and contestation. The police and criminal justice system has become an arena in which organisational failure and scandal – and the blame laying that attends them – are never very far away.

The second feature – the ceaseless governmental efforts to monitor, modernise, reform and reshape police and criminal justice agencies – also continues apace. It is true that, compared to the panoply of utterances, initiatives, institutions, orders and powers that marked the Blair years, the Coalition government is pressing down less hard on the gas. It is true also that there has been a shift in orientation – away from national targets towards localism, from bureaucratic to democratic accountability, and towards a pluralisation of service delivery in criminal justice. Reform of police and criminal justice nonetheless remains a high profile field of government policy. This is especially marked in the field of policing where the Coalition has embarked on what many see as a top-to-bottom overhaul in England and Wales. The arrival in November 2012 of 41 constitutionally novel and potentially powerful elected Police and Crime Commissioners is the flagship innovation. But it stands alongside a range of measures – cutting 'bureaucracy', direct entry to senior officer ranks, crime maps, a new college of policing – that seem designed to strip away the obstacles to the police becoming 'crime fighters'. The pace and scale of reform elsewhere in the criminal justice and penal system may be slower and less ambitious in scale. But here too – most obviously in respect of outsourcing to the private and voluntary sector and the advent of 'Payment-by-Results' – there are important and potentially far-reaching changes afoot.

In respect of the third feature – expansion – the picture is more mixed. We have clearly left behind an age in which increasing amounts of public money were given over to police and prisons, as they emphatically were during the 13 years of New Labour. We live now in austere times and the police, criminal justice, probation and prisons have not been spared significant cuts in their budgets. This is not a moment in which government is committed – as Margaret Thatcher once famously declared – to spending more on law and order while economising elsewhere. In this sense, we no longer live in an age of penal expansion. But the same cannot be said of the numbers being processed through, or detained within, the penal system. The prison population in England and Wales rose by 30 per cent between 2001 and 2011 – principally as a result of changes to sentencing practices (more people committing first time offences being imprisoned and those imprisoned receiving longer sentences), the introduction of Imprisonment for Public Protection and a stricter regime of recall for breach. In September 2012 86,553 men, women and children were held at great financial and social cost in for the most part overcrowded prisons in England and Wales. There has also – as Burke and McNeill (Chapter 6, this volume) observe – been a much less remarked upon drift during the period towards what they call 'mass supervision'. It is true that, in respect of prisons, the rate of increase has slowed since 2011. But the early efforts of the Coalition to try to reverse the upward trend faltered and it is not at all clear that there exists either the political will or any coherent plan for bringing penal expansion under control – save for the hope this will somehow be an effect of rehabilitation and reduced reoffending.

There has in recent years been a wealth of analysis of these penal developments – this topic has produced some of the most significant work in contemporary criminology (Simon and Sparks 2012). Some authors have analysed the punitive turn in macroscopic terms, situating it in the context of wider economic, social and cultural transitions named 'late modernity' (Garland 2001) or as an integral component of the political project of neo-liberalism (Wacquant 2009). Here the 'heating up' (Loader and Sparks 2010) of the criminal question is interpreted either as government's acting out in response to high crime rates and the exposure of the limits of the sovereign state, or else as a punitive upsurge required to deal with the effects of the withering of the social state and the deregulation of markets. In both cases political actors actively promise physical safety in the face of their inability or unwillingness to deliver social security. Another strand of enquiry has focused on the economies, political cultures and constitutional structures of different societies and sought to explain variation in the quantity and quality of punishment across different societies in these terms (Tonry 2007; Snacken and Dumortier 2012). In this vein, some authors have carefully and persuasively set out the ways in which political and legal arrangements can work either to drive penal excess or as factors shaping more moderate uses of punishment (Lacey 2008; Barker 2009). A recurrent theme of this work has been to identify England and Wales as one of the punitive outliers among western democracies.

The present volume aims to supplement this growing body of scholarship with a close institutional analysis of the penal landscape of England and Wales. As such, it has a distinctive provenance and some noteworthy ambitions. The book is the product of a deepening collaboration between academic criminologists and the Howard League for Penal Reform.[1] Such a collaboration has a long and distinguished history, but it has of late been revived and extended in various ways. The book is, in particular, the outcome of discussions within the Howard League's Research Advisory Group, of which most of the contributors are members. The basic aim of the volume is to describe the contours of the penal landscape of England and Wales today, and to this end the chapters that follow offer a close reading of the recent history and current state of the institutions of the police, criminal justice and penal system, and their interactions with certain key vulnerable groups. But the book aims to achieve more than this. The contributors to the volume were also invited to analyse in detail the reasons underlying the politically charged and volatile condition of the penal system, to think about the challenges and opportunities involved in trying to stem the flow of ever greater numbers into the penal system, and to set out agendas for future research.

The contributions in this volume are loosely organised into three strands. In the opening chapter, Stephen Farrall focuses on those aspects of wider society (including the economy) which operate in such a way as to influence aspects of individuals' and communities' experiences of crime and disorder. The chapter is geared in part to an examination of how such practices impede the desires of those individuals who wish to move away from crime. It starts by examining the relationship between crime and the economy, then considers the criminogenic effects of changes in social policies; then explores how social structures may impede desistance from crime. It concludes by reflecting on what the criminal justice system might consider doing to try to overcome some of these processes.

There then follow five chapters examining key institutional processes in criminal justice. In her account of the highly contested topic of prison privatisation, Elaine Genders examines the normative debates and empirical evidence used to evaluate the government's twin strategies of extending private sector provision of prison regimes and expanding the use of competitive practices in the management of prisons. The chapter raises questions which may help us better understand the consequences of the increasing privatisation of incarceration. At root, these questions concern (1) whether an arrangement founded on system interests can serve the needs of social as well as criminal justice; and (2) how the government could ensure penal policy is not derailed by the fiscal imperatives of private entrepreneurs.

Mike Rowe's chapter explores contemporary challenges facing the police services of England and Wales and the potential impact that some of these have in terms of imprisonment. It begins by reviewing trends in prison rates alongside data relating to policing to demonstrate that there is no clear relationship between police activity and imprisonment, before exploring the impact that cuts to police budgets will have on the internal organisation and delivery of policing. It concludes by examining how the wider recession might change the external landscape in terms of crime and disorder and concludes by identifying areas for further research.

Over recent years there has been growing policy and legislative focus on tackling antisocial behaviour, the most high profile measure being the Antisocial Behaviour Order (ASBO). In his chapter, Andrew Millie presents evidence that this expansion has led to an increased flow of people into the criminal justice system and, ultimately, into prison. In May 2012 the Coalition government published a White Paper on antisocial behaviour that promised the demise of the ASBO. Millie argues that the White Paper is an opportunity to stem the flow of people into the criminal justice system. However, while there are grounds for optimism, proposals for speedier and easier sanctions and increased discretionary powers for the police may further criminalise 'suspect' populations. Priorities for policy and research are outlined in conclusion.

In her chapter Nicola Padfield examines the role of sentencing practice in contributing towards, and potentially stemming, the flow of people into prison. Padfield shows that while courts are central to this process they are not the only institutional actors in play: the chapter also identifies decisions by others which add to the prison population, most obviously the power of the executive to recall people to prison (and then to re-release them, or not). The chapter concludes by identifying key issues and pressure points in the domain of sentencing, as well as potential areas for research.

In the context of the Coalition government's recent reviews of probation services and community sentences, Lol Burke and Fergus McNeill
explore the role that community sentences play in criminal justice and,
more specifically, the role they *may* play in stemming the flow of people
into custody. They begin by outlining the legal context of community
sentences in England and Wales, before going on to examine the relationship between the purposes of probation services and their credibility. They suggest that rather than trying to enhance their credibility by
promising to protect or to punish, credibility could be more effectively
secured by focusing on the potential of community sentences to deliver
justice constructively – particularly by working to support reparation.
They go on to discuss recent developments in ideas about probation
practice, inspired by evidence about desistance from crime, suggesting
that this evidence is consistent with a reparative approach to community sentences. Finally, they examine debates about structural reforms
to probation services and about the use of competition, commissioning
and 'Payment by Results'. In conclusion, Burke and McNeill argue that
constructive reforms of criminal justice cannot and will not be achieved
through market mechanisms; a deeper engagement with our penal politics and practices, visions and values is required.

The final four chapters focus on specific groups who are more vulnerable to entering into the criminal justice system and identify the reasons why this may be the case. Jill Peay's chapter examines the contribution made to the size of the prison population by those with mental
health problems, but observes that the fluidity of the concept of 'mental
disorder' makes this exercise problematic. The chapter poses a lengthy
series of questions about those areas that are either not known or not
sufficiently understood about the relationship between mental health
and imprisonment; the answers to which might help us to understand
why there appears to be a persistent problem of mental ill-health among
prisoners.

Neil Chakraborti and Coretta Phillips present an overview of
the key issues and pressure points surrounding minority groups
and the penal landscape. They consider factors which have contributed to the over-representation of ethnic minorities within the penal
system in England and Wales as well as factors that can make prisons
particularly challenging environments for prisoners who are gay, disabled, or from a minority ethnic or faith community. Their chapter also

discusses problems associated with using imprisonment as a default response to crimes committed against minority groups, and suggests areas which should be prioritised by researchers and policy-makers in the context of minority groups and the penal landscape.

Lizzie Seal and Jo Phoenix's chapter examines the expansion of penal control over women and girls in England and Wales since the 1990s, an expansion which has taken place despite no corresponding rise in their offending behaviour. They highlight positive lessons learned from using community-based and gender-specific services with women who offend. They also examine how trends of punitiveness and gender responsiveness in relation to criminal justice approaches to women and girls can become hybridised in ways that have increased sentencing severity. Finally, the chapter outlines gaps in our knowledge and suggests how further research could usefully address these.

In the final chapter, Barry Goldson reviews the impact of the contemporary penal landscape upon children and young people and explores the prospects for limiting their entry into the youth justice system per se and, in particular, into penal detention. The key implications for youth justice policy are considered and areas for future research are proposed. Goldson's principal aim is to offer a starting point from which to begin to imagine an alternative policy and practice framework directed towards diverting children and young people from a system of 'justice' that is frequently harmful and damaging and offers minimal practical comfort to a public desiring of crime reduction and community safety. It is a starting point that is shared broadly in common by all the contributors to this volume and one that gives shape and purpose to an informative, challenging and action-guiding tour of the current penal landscape in England and Wales.

Notes

1   www.howardleague.org/research.

References

Barker, V. (2009) *The Politics of Imprisonment.* Oxford: Oxford University Press.

Garland, D. (2001) *The Culture of Control: Crime and Social Order in Contemporary Society.* Oxford: Oxford University Press.

Lacey, N. (2008) *The Prisoners' Dilemma: The Political Economy of Punishment in Comparative Perspective*. Cambridge: Cambridge University Press.

Loader, I. and R. Sparks (2010) *Public Criminology?* Abingdon: Routledge.

Simon, J. and R. Sparks (eds) (2012) *The SAGE Handbook of Punishment and Society*. London: Sage.

Snacken, S. and E. Dumortier (eds) (2012) *Resisting Punitiveness in Europe?* Abingdon: Routledge.

Tonry, M. (ed.) (2007) *Crime, Punishment and Politics in Comparative Perspective*. Chicago: University of Chicago Press.

Wacquant, L. (2009) *Punishing the Poor*. Durham, NC: Duke University Press.

1

SOCIAL STRUCTURAL PROCESSES AND THE OPERATION OF THE CRIMINAL JUSTICE SYSTEM

STEPHEN FARRALL

This chapter will focus on those aspects of wider society (including the economy) which operate in such a way as to influence aspects of individuals' and communities' experiences of crime and disorder. The review is geared in part to an examination of how such practices impede the desires of those individuals who wish to move away from crime. It starts by examining the relationship between crime and the economy before looking at examples of changes in social policies; moving on to consider how social structures may impede desistance from crime. It concludes by reflecting on what the criminal justice system might consider doing to try to overcome some of these processes.

THE ECONOMY–CRIME LINK

There is an extensive and long-standing literature on the relationship between economic conditions and crime (see Chiricos 1987; Pyle and Deadman 1994). Studies often assume that shifts in the economy 'cause' variations in criminal behaviour. The literature suggests that lagged or coincident indicators of economic conditions (such as the unemployment rate, income inequality and GDP), contribute to increased rates of property crime either through economic need and criminal motivation or through the relative availability of 'stealable' commodities. There are, however, conflicting theories about this relationship. Of course, the relationship between the economy and crime interacts with effects of other social and criminal justice policies. Hale and Sabbagh (1991), for example, reported that the increase in police officers in Britain during the 1980s was nullified by the sizeable increases in unemployment experienced at that same time. Similarly, Reilly and Witt (1992) identified an association between unemployment and crime (this was mitigated by government spending), with housing expenditure associated with reductions in crime.

REVIEWING THE RECENT UK EXPERIENCE

In May 1979 a little over one million people were unemployed. This figure reached two million by November 1980 and rose to 2.5 million by June 1981. By March 1982, three million were unemployed, and the figure stood at 3.4 million in 1986, dropping to two million in February 1991, before rising again to three million in 1993. The result was that, in the early 1980s, many working-class young people left school in the north and midlands of England, Wales and Scotland with no prospect of finding work locally. The policy responses were to force young people into lower paid jobs which either failed to equip them with skills which were needed by the economy at that time or were simply jobs that their parents had done previously and been paid more for (see Carlen 1996: 46).

In the last 30 years, one of the most significant changes experienced by the UK economy has been a change in the nature of available employment. In particular, there has been a significant decrease in the manufacturing sector of the economy. *Social Trends* reports that:

> Over the last 25 years the UK economy has experienced structural change. The largest increase in employee jobs has been in the banking, finance and insurance industry, where the number of employee jobs has doubled between June 1981 and June 2006 from 2.7 million to 5.4 million. There were also large increases in employee jobs in public administration,

education and health (up by 40%) and in the distribution, hotels and restaurants industry (up by 34%). In contrast, the extraction and production industries, made up of agriculture and fishing, energy and water, manufacturing, and construction showed a combined fall of 43 per cent from 8.2 million jobs in 1981 to 4.7 million jobs in 2006. Manufacturing alone accounted for 81 per cent of this decline, with the number of employee jobs in this sector nearly halving from 5.9 million in 1981 to 3 million in 2006.

(Office for National Statistics 2007: 47)

Alongside the decrease in manual labour, there has been an increase in jobs in the knowledge economy (i.e. banking, finance and insurance). Such jobs, generally speaking, require graduate-level (or equivalent) skills, are highly competitive and essentially 'white collar' occupations. They are not usually jobs which those with few (or no) formal skills are able to either gain or even aspire to. In addition, there has been an increasing tendency for employers to ask prospective employees to undergo a Criminal Records Bureau check demonstrating no previous convictions which potentially creates difficulties for those with convictions seeking employment.

More broadly, the general tendency of recent structural change in employment in the UK is towards an increasing polarisation between two groups of potential employees: those who can evidence their skills on paper and as such are deemed 'employable' and those who have not sought, or have been unable to seek, such qualifications and as such are considered 'unemployable' (Furlong and Kelly 2005). Within such a context some of the effects of recent national educational policies, especially the introduction of 'league tables' of schools based on examination results, should also be noted. While such policies have raised aggregate performance levels, they also seem to have encouraged the practice of school exclusion for less successful pupils (seen as potentially disruptive). Thus the polarisation seen in the workplace is also refracted in the classroom (Willis 1977).

The social and economic change experienced in Britain in the 1970s and 1980s, in particular widespread unemployment, geographical concentration of social and economic deprivation via housing policies and the growth of inequalities coupled with real term reduction in social benefits, can be argued to have long-lasting legacies on the production of crime, public attitudes and criminal justice policies. The strengthening effect of the economy–crime link over time (Farrall and Jennings 2012), rising crime rates, increased public fear of crime and the increased salience of crime as a political issue led parties in government and opposition to emphasise punitive, 'hard line' thinking on crime in place of the social welfare model adopted by all British political parties before the 1980s. As such, the current 'imprisonment binge' owes much to shifts in the economy (themselves brought on in part by changes in macro-economic philosophy) rather than any sustained thinking on appropriate responses to crime.

The housing market

Sales of council houses were announced by Michael Heseltine in 1979 and homelessness began an immediate rise (Timmins 2001: 379). Murie (1997: 26) describes this process as one of 'residualisation' whereby council estates came to house the most disadvantaged. It is true that little new council housing stock has been built since the early 1980s (Murie 1997: 28), in some areas creating populations with high turnovers and therefore perhaps leading to higher levels of crime but less engagement with the police (Hope *et al.* 2002). Housing policies pursued in the 1980s created more people who were dependent upon the state, and ultimately created more 'sink' estates. Cardboard cities emerged in London (amongst other places) as a result of barring teenagers from benefits – one side effect of the new Youth Training Scheme. The results of the changes in housing provision, linked to economic recession and cutbacks in welfare provisions, are further documented by Carlen (1996).

Social security provision

Although the proportion of government spending on social security increased between 1980 and 1999, there were cutbacks to all forms of social security provision. Whilst the aim was to create greater responsibility on the part of individuals in the provision of their own social security, Family Credit operated in such a way as to trap more people in the worst paid jobs (Marwick 2003: 299). The running down of social services resulted in deprivation, neglect, increasing atomisation and social divisions (Marwick 2003: 372). The reforms undertaken in the mid 1980s had the net effect of reducing the benefits of those under 25 years of age, without children and the unemployed (Timmins 2001: 399). From April 1988, 16–17 year olds were no longer eligible for income support, instead needing to register for Youth Training Schemes (Timmins 2001: 447). However, the scheme ignored the fact that many young children had left home after abuse, were released from care, or could not be found a Youth Training Scheme place. These young people ended up on the streets (Timmins 2001: 447–8). As Andrews and Jacobs concluded in their review of poverty in the 1980s, for many, especially the more vulnerable members of society (such as single women with young children and those aged under 25), the changes in social security initiated by the Thatcher governments appeared only to have 'closed down the escape hatches from poverty' (1990: 282). As some have noted (e.g. Carlen 1996: 44) it was the New Right's own economic policies which led to increased spending on unemployment and furthered their own calls for cutbacks in public spending. Such cutbacks encouraged young people towards situations in which they became embroiled in crime (Carlen 1996: 47, 82). Similar policies stemming from the austerity measures of the current Coalition government relating to housing, the economy and social security in this respect are likely to lead to increases in crime, making desistance less attractive and harder to achieve.

Education and school exclusion policies

There is little doubt that the legislation enacted during the 1980s had profound effects upon the education system in the UK. Staff–student ratios went up during this time, arguably leading to greater disruption in classes, more exclusions and greater levels of staff absenteeism, not helped by the reduction in the status of teachers fostered by the government. In 1992 the first league tables of school exam results were published (Timmins 2001: 519). These had the unfortunate side effect of encouraging schools to exclude unruly children (school exclusions rose throughout the 1990s until reaching a peak of 12,668 in 1996–7 (DfES 2001)[1]), who, dumped on the streets, only served to cause further problems for other local residents and the police (Timmins 2001: 566).

The social, ethnic and geographical concentration of poverty

Standard, international measures of the distribution of wealth in a nation, such as the Gini coefficient, demonstrate growing inequalities

in the UK from the late 1970s (Stymne and Jackson 2000). These inequalities – in all likelihood due to shifts in taxation – increased dramatically from the early to mid 1980s at a time when other countries (e.g.
Sweden) saw declines in the Gini coefficient. Atkinson (2000: 364–5)
notes that between the end of the Second World War and the late 1970s
the trend in the distribution of wealth in the UK was strongly egalitar-
ian. However, after the end of the 1970s this picture changed dramatically. Between 1979 and 1985 widening inequality was due to many
families losing their incomes as unemployment rose (Atkinson 2000:
365). From 1985–90, however, the inequalities were due largely to government policies (Atkinson 2000: 365). As Garnett and Aitken note,
between 1977 and 1980 unemployment amongst black people in Bristol
(the scene of a riot in April 1980) had doubled, whilst it had declined for
white people (2003: 252).

Timmins (2001: 375) is not alone in noting the 'marked widening
in the gap between rich and poor during the Thatcher years', reporting
that as early as the late 1980s the first signs that the UK was becoming
a more unequal society were emerging (2001: 449). In 1948 only one
million people needed national assistance; by 1993, 5.6 million people
were living on income support as a result of increases in income inequality (Timmins 2001: 497–8). Walker (1990) reports that the number
of people reliant on income support increased by 45 per cent during
the period from around three million in 1979 to 4.35 million in 1989.
If one includes the dependants of claimants, as many as seven million
people were reliant upon income support during the 1980s. Further evidence in the mid 1990s suggested that the poor in the UK were getting
poorer (Timmins 2001: 507). With long-term unemployment endemic
in some parts of the UK, many residents found themselves reliant on
benefits for extended periods of time, making working cash-in-hand or
claiming and working more socially acceptable (Timmins 2001: 526).

Spillover and cascading influences

In a number of papers (Hay and Farrall 2011; Farrall and Hay 2010)
Colin Hay and I have outlined what we have called a 'cascade theory' of
radical social and economic policies. The argument is that radical policy
changes in one area (which may appear unrelated to crime) may well come
to have quite pronounced impacts on crime and the way in which it is

viewed and dealt with. Whilst the Thatcher governments were immediately radical in economic policy, few have seen them as being in any way radical in relation to crime policies. The ultimate consequences of that economic radicalism were a profound increase in levels of unemployment, social inequality and social polarisation that were reflected in a steep increase in rates of crime. Similarly, the radicalism associated with the changes to the housing market had significant consequences and spillover effects. The right to buy one's own council house, coupled with the requirement in the Housing Act 1985 that local councils house homeless people and the impact of the Social Security Act 1988 created a situation in which disadvantaged members of society were corralled together in particular estates in which low-level antisocial behaviour and crime became commonplace. This was to become an important element of the context in which crime and criminal justice policy would eventually be radicalised.

In a not unrelated set of processes, the changes in the social security system stemmed from the need to halt the rise in expenditure which followed the increase in unemployment in the early 1980s. These resulted in the creation of a series of traps which made escape from lifestyles in which offending and victimisation were common difficult. As has recently been shown, the reduction in social security spending and the increase in economic inequalities led to a steep rise in acquisitive crime during the 1980s (Farrall and Jennings 2011, 2012; Jennings *et al.* 2012).

The radicalism of the reform of the education system also served to alter experiences of crime. Reforming the education system made the management of schools harder by rising staff–student ratios and creating a series of spillover effects for communities and policing in terms of the numbers of young people excluded from schools. As with changes in the economy, housing provision and social security provision, the side effects included (but were not limited to) widening inequality; unemployment; 'sofa-surfing'; the creation of 'sink estates' and excluded pupils. All of these were to have significant ramifications for both crime and the criminal justice system.

THINKING ABOUT THIS IN RELATION TO DESISTANCE FROM CRIME

How important are the sorts of social and economic structures described above in enabling or hindering would-be desisters' attempts to become more integrated into society? A key focus is the relationship(s) between a potential desister's own actions and those structural properties of any social system which are important to desistance. A decade ago, Ben Bowling and I argued that 'the process of desistance is one that is produced through an interplay between individual choices, and a range of wider social forces, institutional and societal practices which are beyond the control of the individual' (Farrall and Bowling 1999: 261). The central premise is that desisting from crime, be it the sort of desistance which requires an all-encompassing reorganisation of the individual's sense of self (Maruna and Farrall 2004) or those more common and less dramatic pathways away from crime, is partly the result of wider social forces and practices, and as such changes in these may alter the ways in which individuals make the transition away from crime (see Farrall *et al.* 2010).

Changes in employment practices and the wider economy

Given the changes in the nature of the sorts of work on offer, it can be argued (Farrall *et al.* 2010) that exactly the type of employment which in the past assisted many men in making the move away from crime (manual labour) has largely disappeared, to be replaced either by posts which require formal qualifications or by lower-status white-collar jobs which have often, in the UK, had the image of 'feminised' work (and therefore might be culturally difficult for young males to consider). Given this context, would-be desisters, many of whom have no educational or trade qualifications and 'spoiled' pasts, may have a limited set of options. One option is to rely on casual employment or the informal economy (Shapland *et al.* 2003). However, even casual employment agencies may check the criminal records of potential employees and often the pay in casual employment is worse, making such employment relatively unattractive. An alternative route lies in self-employment. This too poses problems for people with criminal pasts. Building up sufficient business to secure a reasonable income may take many years, especially if the business is run legitimately and needs to pay the appropriate taxes. Alternatively, if the work is such that much of the business is run on a cash-in-hand basis, this creates no official record of employment, making the transition into mainstream employment harder. A third option is to seek retraining which will lead to employment in the knowledge economy, distribution or service sectors – but such training often requires at least some basic level of educational attainment, and sometimes higher qualifications, which may put it beyond the reach, given their low level of certificated, formal qualifications and education, of people who have previously offended. In addition to these structural factors, as several ethnographic studies have shown, a culture of low aspiration may often in effect rule out the more demanding of these options (MacLeod 1995; Willis 1977).

Such processes may, of course, also differ for different ethnic groups. Calverley (2012) has shown that the 'black British' would-be desisters in his sample had very poor experiences of and opportunities for employment whilst those from the Indian community were far better resourced. Bangladeshis were most likely to be assisted by family members, reorientating them to conventional goals. The potential role of families and friends in being able to act as a 'buffer', providing a start in employment for those who are hindered by their pasts is, however, not confined to any particular ethnic group, and can be invaluable.

In summary, it would appear that changes in the economy have restructured the legitimate routes out of crime and (together with changes in the educational system) have additionally influenced the availability of and access to such routes. In this respect, changes in the economy may have altered the speed, nature and timing of ways out of troubled pasts. Additionally, these processes may also be differentially mediated by the cultures of and opportunities available within different ethnic groups.

Changes in relation to housing and social security

It seems likely that the changes in housing tenure, together with recent financial crises, make it more difficult now for young people to set up house independently of parents and family. It will be particularly difficult where the families of origin do not have the financial means to contribute to the new family and/or where young adults are estranged from their families of origin. These conditions are particularly likely to occur amongst those with a significant history of adolescent offences, who will inevitably often find themselves looking for accommodation in the social housing sector. These institutional factors will, in turn, interact with the documented tension in early adulthood between the contrasting normative 'pulls' of (offending) peers and (non-offending) families and partners, as would-be desisters try to set up their own homes, often with partners who have much more pro-social attitudes in relation to offending (Bottoms and Shapland 2010). Reductions in social security spending have been found to be associated with increases in crime (see Reilly and Witt 1992; Farrall and Jennings 2011, 2012).

Changes in criminal policy and in conceptualisations of offending

It is impossible to discuss recent social-structural developments relevant to desistance in England and Wales without mentioning key shifts in criminal justice system thinking and in criminal policy. These are set out below.

The emergence of crime as a political issue   As many commentators (e.g. Downes and Morgan 1997) have noted, in the UK crime became a significant issue in national elections in the mid to late 1970s in a way that had not been true before that time. Part of the reason for this was that recorded crime had risen steadily from 1955 onwards, at an average rate of 5 per cent per annum, a trend that continued until the early 1990s. This shift from politically marginal topic to political 'hot potato' has occurred simultaneously with the rise of New Right economic policies in both the UK and the United States, though the causal connexions between the two trends are complex (Farrall and Hay 2010). In the UK, the 'law and order issue' was originally pressed politically by the Conservative Party, but more recently it has been strongly taken forward by Labour governments. The issue has also continued to be politically prominent despite decreases in recorded crime since the mid 1990s.

Increasingly punitive approaches to crime   A second major theme is the development of increasingly punitive policy approaches to crime. This 'punitiveness' has focused especially on violent and sexual offences, and on those who repeatedly offend. Its most obvious manifestation is the massive growth in the size of the prison population, which in England and Wales has risen from 49,500 in January 1995 to 87,501 in September 2011, a cumulative growth rate of 3.8 per cent per annum, despite the reduction in recorded crime for most of this period. The recent rapid population increase results from both an increase in the courts' use of imprisonment rather than non-custodial penalties, and from a lengthening of the average prison sentences imposed. Other features of the increasing punitiveness of recent criminal justice policy include the 'tightening up' of prison regimes in various ways and a general tendency to make community sentences more onerous.

The net effect of these developments has been to subtly redefine the relationship between the person who has offended and the state. Increasingly, the 'sin bin' analogy has been eroded. In the view of the classical jurists, during a period of punishment the state suspended various rights of the punished citizen; but, on completion of the punishment, the citizen resumed those rights. More and more, however, such a view is being replaced by an ideology in which the individual being punished becomes a sort of 'non-citizen' (Bauman 2004) or 'other', who is permitted to return to civil society either grudgingly or not at all.

The redefinition of rehabilitation   Not unrelated to the above, the period since the mid 1970s has seen some important changes in the way that the concept of rehabilitation has been understood and developed within the criminal justice system. This concept was, in the early post-war period, a cornerstone of the system, and at that time welfare was usually considered to be integral to rehabilitation. That version of 'the rehabilitative ideal' was dealt a severe blow by a series of research overviews (Martinson 1974) and controlled experiments (Folkard *et al.* 1974, 1976), which resulted in a marked diminution of confidence in rehabilitative approaches. Simultaneously, related developments led to the emergence of some sharp critiques of social work and the social work profession. Among the many consequences of these events, the training of probation officers in England and Wales has been drastically reshaped so that it is no longer associated with social work training. 'Rehabilitation', however, has not died; instead, since the 1990s it has been reborn in the so-called 'What Works?' agenda, where the primary theoretical focus has been on cognitive behavioural treatment approaches centred upon the modification of offending behaviour and the development of improved 'thinking skills'. This version of rehabilitation, only partially supported by empirical research (Harper and Chitty 2005), differs from the post-war rehabilitative approaches in that it places less emphasis on helping with practical obstacles to desistance (e.g. in employment and housing), and more emphasis on 'modifying the dynamic risk factors' in the criminal profile (Raynor and Robinson 2009).

The rise of the risk agenda   The concept of the 'risk society' has become familiar to sociologists in the last 20 years. In particular, Giddens (1990) has described a family of changes in which individualisation has to an extent been eroded and a new, more 'category-based' and security-focused approach has been adopted both by public agencies and the private sector. More specifically, within the criminological domain, Kemshall (2003), for example, has linked the rise of interest in risk with the demise of the 'modernist' welfare-oriented penal agenda. Such developments are arguably linked closely to the rise of an 'information' society, wherein the production and exchange of knowledge is central to the economic activities of contemporary societies. Information is stored, retrieved, analysed and exchanged in order to secure financial gains or, in some cases, to guard against losses or harms. In the context of this rise of the knowledge economy, the reconfiguration of rehabilitation and the increasingly punitive turn in criminal justice policies have arguably led to the notion of there being 'a public' which needs to be 'protected'; 'risks' which can be 'assessed' and sufficient information and actuarial accuracy to make such assessments. These ideas are obviously attractive for politicians mandated to control crime (see Lee 2007).

The rise of the 'risk management' style of thinking in the Probation Service has been charted by Robinson (2002), who notes that approaches to risk management are not 'imbued with a sense of transformative or rehabilitative optimism' (2002: 10). Indeed, more generally one might argue that the central message of the risk-based approach is not 'do good' but 'prevent harm'. Robinson's respondents reported some disturbing practices, such as the placing of all cases into high-risk teams for some of their sentences (2002: 15). In an era dominated by concerns with public protection, risk assessments can lead to a risk-averse mindset on the part of officials, and consequently to defensive or precautionary actions (such as refusing bail or parole).

In a review of the resettlement of prisoners, Maguire and Raynor (2006) point to developments within the practice of resettlement which, whilst being congruent with the suppression of risk, are in tension with elements known to be related to desistance. They report that a major focus on the enforcement of penalties and the emergence of rigid approaches to such enforcement has made it harder for individual probation officers to adapt their working practices to the needs of individuals as they try to resettle (2006: 33). Similarly, recalls to prison on the basis of minor offending or technical breaches tend to ignore the well-established 'zig-zag' nature of desistance, whereby – as with addictions – individuals tend to desist gradually rather than suddenly (Burnett 2004). Relapses are common even within a desisting pathway, and automatic harsh enforcement may create more problems in the longer term.

CONCLUSION

This analysis of national and regional structural changes in the UK in the last 30 years has suggested that, in principle, such changes could significantly affect would-be desisters' paths to desistance, so the case for desistance researchers to address social structures more fully than in the past is arguably strong. Social structures in the fields of employment, the family and housing, taxation policies and criminal policy have been examined. Relevant structural changes could readily be discerned; but of course other structural changes might also be relevant.

Finally it is important to reflect on what the criminal justice system might try to do to overcome some of the processes outlined above. Many of the processes discussed are beyond the immediate control of the system. However, schemes aimed at getting probationers into work have reported a positive impact on their lives (see Sarno *et al.* 2000), as did volunteering (Burnett and Maruna 2006). Meaningful working careers for those wanting to leave the education system at 16 also need to be provided (perhaps via apprenticeships). Schemes which seek to link employers to those being released from prison ought also to be explored. More and better housing (including social and council housing) would help to alleviate some of the accommodation problems faced by those leaving prison. Increasing social security payments has also been associated with reductions in property crime, and, as such, raising benefits across the board could serve to foster desistance at the individual level. Attempts to divert people from custody (or to reduce average sentence lengths) would also serve to make desistance more likely for some, especially those aged 35 to 40 (who, ironically, are likely to attract weightier sentences at that stage of their criminal careers). A criminal justice system which accepted that relapses are common and that change may take years for some people to achieve (and hence is not overly concerned about minor episodes of reoffending) would also reduce recalls and breaches. Any such initiatives will need to reflect the ethnic and cultural make-up of those in the system itself.

FURTHER RESEARCH

1. How have individuals who have committed offences responded to the sorts of changes described above? Have these changes meant that some routes away from crime have become blocked?
2. In what ways can criminal justice service providers (such as probation services) help those with a past or current involvement in crime make an orderly transition away from crime?
3. What else can the various branches of the criminal justice system do to acknowledge the difficulties inherent in leaving behind crime and aid those who wish to desist?
4. How might these processes unfold for different social groups and in different parts of the country?

Notes

1   See Bynner and Parsons (2003: 287) who show that those in school between 1975 and 1986 had twice the rate of temporary suspensions (15 per cent for males and 6 per cent for females) as the generation of children before them (7 per cent for males, 3 per cent for females).

References

Andrews, K. and Jacobs, J. (1990) *Punishing the Poor*. London: Macmillan.

Atkinson, A.B. (2000) 'Distribution of Income and Wealth' in A.E. Halsey and J. Webb (eds) *Twentieth-Century British Social Trends*. London: Macmillan, pp. 348–81.

Bauman, Z. (2004) *Wasted Lives: Modernity and its Outcasts*. Cambridge: Polity Press.

Bottoms, A.E. and Shapland, J. (2010) 'Steps towards Desistance among Young Adult Recidivists' in S. Farrall, R. Sparks, S. Maruna and M. Hough (eds) *Escape Routes*. Abingdon: Routledge.

Burnett, R. (2004) 'To Reoffend or not to Reoffend? The Ambivalence of Convicted Property Offenders' in S. Maruna and R. Immarigeon (eds) *After Crime and Punishment*. Cullompton: Willan, pp. 152–80.

Burnett, R. and Maruna, S. (2006) 'The Kindness of Strangers', *Criminology & Criminal Justice*, 6 (1), pp. 83–106.

Bynner, J. and Parsons, S. (2003) 'Social Participation, Values and Crime' in E. Ferri, J. Bynner and M. Wadsworth (eds) *Changing Britain, Changing Lives*. London: Institute of Education, pp. 261–94.

Calverley, A. (2012) *Cultures of Desistance: Ethnic Minorities and their Desistance from Crime*. Abingdon: Routledge.

Carlen, P. (1996) *Jigsaw: A Political Criminology of Homelessness*. London: Open University Press.

Chiricos, T. (1987) 'Rates of Crime and Unemployment: An Analysis of Aggregate Research Evidence', *Social Problems*, 34 (2), pp. 187–212.

DfES (2001) *Permanent Exclusions from Maintained Schools in England*. Issue 10/01 November 2001. Available at: www.education.gov.uk/research-andstatistics/statistics/allstatistics/a00193906/permanent-exclusions-from-maintained-schools-in-en [accessed July 2012].

Downes, D. and Morgan, R. (1997) 'Dumping the "Hostages to Fortune"?' in M. Maguire, R. Morgan and R. Reiner (eds) *The Oxford Handbook of Criminology*. Oxford: Clarendon Press, pp. 87–134.

Farrall, S. and Bowling, B. (1999) 'Structuration, Human Development and Desistance from Crime', *British Journal of Criminology*, 39 (2), pp. 252–67.

Farrall, S. and Hay, C. (2010) 'Not So Tough on Crime? Why Weren't the Thatcher Governments More Radical in Reforming the Criminal Justice System?', *British Journal of Criminology*, 50 (3), pp. 550–69.

Farrall, S. and Jennings, W. (2011) 'What did Mrs Thatcher do to Crime in the UK?', *Seminar on Exploring and Theorising the Long-Term Impacts of Thatcherite Social and Economic Policies*. British Academy, London, 10–19 July.

Farrall, S. and Jennings, W. (2012) 'Policy Feedback and the Criminal Justice Agenda: An Analysis of the Economy, Crime Rates, Politics and Public Opinion in Post-War Britain', *Contemporary British History*, 26 (4), pp. 467–88.

Farrall, S., Bottoms, A. and Shapland, J. (2010) 'Social Structures and Desistance from Crime' *European Journal of Criminology*, Special Edition entitled *European Criminal Careers Research: Showcasing Studies and Approaches*, edited by S. Farrall, 7 (6), pp. 546–70.

Folkard, S., Smith, D.E., Smith, D.D. and Walmsley, G. (1976) *IMPACT: Intensive Matched Probation and After-Care Treatment, Volume II: The*

Results of the Experiment. Home Office Research Study No. 36. London: HMSO.

Folkard, S., Fowles, A.J., McWilliams, B.C., McWilliams, W., Smith, D.D., Smith, D.E. and Walmsley, G. (1974) *IMPACT: Intensive Matched Probation and After-Care Treatment*. Home Office Research Study No. 24. London: HMSO.

Furlong, A. and Kelly, P. (2005) 'The Brazilianisation of Youth Transitions in Australia and the UK', *Australian Journal of Social Issues*, 40 (2), pp. 207–25.

Garnett, M. and Aitken, I. (2003) *Splendid! Splendid! The Authorized Biography of Willie Whitelaw*. London: Pimlico.

Giddens, A. (1990) *The Consequences of Modernity*. Cambridge: Polity Press.

Hale, C. and Sabbagh, D. (1991) 'Testing the Relationship between Unemployment and Crime: A Methodological Comment and Empirical Analysis Using Time Series Data from England and Wales', *Journal of Research in Crime and Delinquency*, 28 (4), pp. 400–17.

Harper, G. and Chitty, C. (2005) *The Impact of Corrections on Re-Offending: A Review of 'What Works'*, Home Office Research Study No. 291. London: Home Office.

Hay, C. and Farrall, S. (2011) 'Establishing the Ontological Status of Thatcherism by Gauging its "Periodisability": Towards a "Cascade Theory" of Public Policy Radicalism', *British Journal of Politics and International Relations*, 13 (4), pp. 439–58.

Hope, T., Karstedt, S. and Farrall, S. (2001) *The Relationship Between Calls and Crimes*. End of Award Report to Home Office.

Jennings, W., Farrall, S. and Bevan, S. (2012) 'The Economy, Crime and Time: An Analysis of Recorded Property Crime in England & Wales 1961–2006', *International Journal of Law, Crime and Justice*, 40 (3), pp. 192–210.

Kemshall, H. (2003) *Understanding Risk in Criminal Justice*. Buckingham: Oxford University Press.

Lee, M. (2007) *Inventing Fear of Crime*. Cullompton: Willan.

MacLeod, J. (1995) *Ain't No Makin' it*. Boulder: Westview Press.

Maguire, M. and Raynor, P. (2006) 'How the Resettlement of Prisoners Promotes Desistance from Crime: Or does it?', *Criminology and Criminal Justice*, 6 (1), pp. 19–38.

Martinson, R. (1974) 'What Works? Questions and Answers about Prison Reform' *The Public Interest*, 35, pp. 22–54.

Maruna, S. and Farrall, S. (2004) 'Desistance from Crime: A Theoretical Reformulation', *Kölner Zeitschrift für Soziologie und Sozialpsychologie*, 43, pp. 171–94.

Marwick, A. (2003) *British Society since 1945*. London: Penguin Books.

Murie, Alan (1997) 'Linking Housing Changes to Crime', *Social Policy and Administration*, 31 (5), pp. 22–36.

Office for National Statistics (2007) *Social Trends No. 37*. Basingstoke: Palgrave Macmillan.

Pyle, David J. and Deadman, Derek (1994) 'Crime and the Business Cycle in Post-War Britain', *British Journal of Criminology*, 34 (3), pp. 339–57.

Raynor, P. and Robinson, G. (2009) *Rehabilitation, Crime and Justice*. Basingstoke: Palgrave Macmillan.

Reilly, Barry and Witt, Robert (1992) 'Crime and Unemployment in Scotland: An Econometric Analysis using Regional Data', *Scottish Journal of Political Economy*, 39 (2), pp. 213–28.

Robinson, G. (2002) 'Exploring Risk Management in Probation Practice', *Punishment and Society*, 4 (1), pp. 5–25.

Sarno, C., Hearnden, I., Hedderman, C., Hough, M., Nee, C. and Herrington, V. (2000) *Working Their Way Out of Offending: An Evaluation of Two Probation Employment Schemes*. Home Office Research Study No. 218. London: Home Office.

Shapland, J., Albrecht, H.-J., Ditton, J. and Godefroy, T. (eds) (2003) *The Informal Economy: Threat and Opportunity in the City*. Freiburg: Max Planck Institute.

Stymne, S. and Jackson, T. (2000) 'Intergenerational equity and sustainable welfare', *Ecological Economics*, 3 (2), pp. 219–36.

Timmins, N. (2001) *The Five Giants*. London: HarperCollins.

Walker, A. (1990) 'The Strategy of Inequality: Poverty & Income Distribution in Britain 1979–89' in I. Taylor (ed.) *The Social Effects of Free Market Policies: An International Text*. London: Palgrave Macmillan, pp. 29–48.

Willis, P.E. (1977) *Learning to Labour*. Aldershot: Gower.

2

PRISONS AND PRIVATISATION

POLICY, PRACTICE AND EVALUATION

ELAINE GENDERS

INTRODUCTION

Private prisons are on the rise. The UK government praises their benefits – others question the vaunted success of these institutions. Thus evaluating the engagement of the private sector in the provision, management and administration of prisons becomes a key question in contemporary prison policy. However, adequate evaluation must adopt a binary approach: one that takes on board normative debates about whether it is legitimate to delegate the task of punishment to private organisations and an empirical investigation into its efficacy. Participants in these double-sided debates need to scrutinise the various evaluative criteria of incarceration, which include how well the routines of daily prison life are managed and whether policy objectives are met. Responses to any of these questions have also to take into account the structures and processes through which accountability and legality are negotiated.

This chapter takes the view that prisons aim to protect the public by segregating those who have committed grave offences and pose a serious risk to the safety of the community. Yet, it also recognises the negative impact that prison can have on the lives of those who are incarcerated. It follows that the use of imprisonment should be kept to an irreducible minimum. The inclusion of private sector providers and the embracing of competitive practices in the delivery of prison services reflect an ideological shift in conceptions of the role of the public sector. However, they have also been hailed as a means of easing the financial burden of providing the required prison places whilst driving up standards of service and performance. The fear is that whether or not it meets these objectives, the input of the private sector will lend pragmatic legitimacy to the practice of imprisonment and thereby endorse its maintenance as a dominant criminal justice intervention.

This chapter outlines the historical foundations of private entrepreneurship in the criminal justice system and describes the current arrangements of the penal economy. It examines the main arguments for and against prison privatisation, identifying key issues in the debate about the boundaries of legitimate and effective public–private collaboration. The chapter goes on to discuss important questions raised by the continued strategic development of a mixed penal economy and the increasing commercialisation of criminal justice with specific reference to the government's Green Paper *Breaking the Cycle: Effective Punishment, Rehabilitation and Sentencing of Offenders* (Ministry of Justice 2010). This leads to the ultimate question to be explored: whether an arrangement which is founded on system interests can serve the needs of social as well as criminal justice. The chapter concludes by identifying key questions to be addressed in order to evaluate the case for the privatisation of prisons.

BRIEF HISTORY OF PRIVATISATION IN THE CRIMINAL JUSTICE SYSTEM

Within much of the academic literature there is a widespread assumption that the punishment of criminals is, at root, a public function and, as such, an exercise of governmental power. Yet a brief consideration of penal history shows us that this has not always been the case (Lichtenstein 2001). Although criminal law was separated from the private law of torts and made an offence against the crown in the middle ages, most features of the administration of criminal justice remained in private hands until well into the eighteenth century.

Feeley (2002) argues that historical developments in the criminal just-ice system must be viewed in the context of commercial and industrial developments in society generally. His work examines the shift from feudalism to capitalism, charting the development of the criminal just-ice system from the inept and capricious arrangements overseen by the aristocracy and landed gentry, to the modern and more efficient system familiar today. He describes how the interests of the new commercial classes played an important role in this process, claiming that as the rising new business elite demanded more efficient and more effective criminal justice administration, private entrepreneurs stepped in. A key example of this is the development of transportation in the seventeenth century. Pioneered by merchant shippers, those who had committed offences were taken to the United States at low cost in exchange for the right to auction them off into limited-term slavery to the cotton and tobacco plantations. It was not until the Transportation Act 1718 that this system became institutionalised as a punishment and was controlled by means of Home Office contracts. Indeed, the private sector contin-ued its involvement in the administration of punishment even when the modern government-operated prisons such as Milbank (built in 1816) and Pentonville (built in 1844) took over from transportation as the major institution of punishment in the late nineteenth century.

Bentham's vision of the panopticon, where maximum surveillance is made possible at minimum cost, is a familiar concept. However, for 20 years Bentham also tried to obtain a contract from the government of the day to build and operate a self-financing 'prison factory' that would yield huge profits from the productive labour of the convicts. Bentham's business venture never came to fruition but his efforts did lend legitim-acy to the idea that prisoners could be put to profitable work to produce income for the government. Similar ideas gathered support in the United States where it was common in the nineteenth century for states to build prisons and then turn them over to private contractors to operate as a business, in the expectation that the state would share in any surpluses.

THE NEW WAVE OF PRISON PRIVATISATION

A new wave of state-led private sector involvement in the criminal jus-tice system has proliferated in the twentieth and twenty-first centuries.

In the UK, this has been largely restricted to prisons, court escort services, police detention, IT provision and other administrative and support services. This new trend should be understood as part of a much wider ideological shift that has recently taken place in several leading western democracies. There has been a rolling back of the state in many spheres of public life and a redesignation of the government's responsibilities to the regulation rather than provision of certain services. It started in the UK in the 1980s with the flotation on the Stock Exchange of a number of public utilities (gas, then electricity, then water). Since then there has been a continuing political commitment by successive British governments to privatisation as a means of reducing public spending.

The inclusion of prisons in the privatisation programme, as a result of the Private Finance Initiative (PFI) in 1992, was partly driven by the increasing remand population, which grew by a massive 76 per cent between 1979 and 1988. Since then, the prison population (both sentenced and remand) has continued to grow apace, and prisons have become an expensive business. The first modern privately run prison, the Wolds, opened in 1992 to house remand prisoners. Today, the UK has 14 privately run prisons, housing remand and sentenced prisoners, both adults and young people.

The first four privately run prisons were contracted out on a management-only basis, on agreements lasting five years. However, since 1995 most contracts have been issued for new build privately run prisons under the design, construct, manage and finance scheme (DCMF). DCMF means that the private contractor undertakes the whole range of activities that go into turning an empty site into an operational prison; from architectural planning and building through to staffing and running the prison. Legally, ownership of the land on which the prison stands remains with the government and the contractor receives a lease of the plot which has typically been set at 25 years. For this term the government pays the contractor a monthly fee to cover both set-up and running costs.

It is significant that the growth of private sector involvement in prisons closely followed the return to a 'just deserts' penal policy, evidenced in the Criminal Justice Act 1991. It also coincided with an expansionist prisons policy fuelled by the unprecedented public announcement by the Conservative government's Home Secretary,

Michael Howard, in 1993, that 'prison works'. The 'prison works' rhetoric underpinned the Conservative administration's Crime (Sentences) Act 1997 and led to a substantial increase in spending on prisons. Informed by principles of deterrence and incapacitation, the Act extended the use of mandatory life sentences and introduced compulsory minimum custodial terms.

The 'prison works' philosophy marked a radical departure in official thinking about penal policy, which up until then had emphasised the need to reserve imprisonment for only the most intractable cases. Despite two changes of government, there appears to be no significant change of direction. In 2008 the Labour Home Secretary, Jack Straw, endorsed Lord Carter's support for continued, albeit reined in, expansion of the prison estate. Whilst Kenneth Clarke, the Coalition government's former Minister of Justice, announced a planned reduction of 3,000 prisoners by 2014 (Hansard, 1 November 2010), after a forced U-turn on reduced sentences for guilty pleas in 2011, it is not clear how that will be achieved.

From a financial perspective, prisons are expensive capital items with high running costs. Thus, there is considerable attraction for government in any policy designed to reduce those costs. The proportion of the UK prison population held in private prisons is approximately 15 per cent (Prison Reform Trust 2012). This figure is set to rise with eight public sector prisons (Lindholm, Moorland, Hatfield, Acklington, Castington, Durham, Onley and Coldingley) being put up to competition. Currently, private prison contracts are shared between just three companies; Sodexo Justice Services operates three, Serco operates five and G4S operates six.

WHAT ARE THE ATTRACTIONS OF PRIVATE SECTOR PROVISION?

The purported benefits of private sector provision extend beyond a simple consideration of fiscal cost. Advocates of privatisation argue that private contractors are more efficient, more effective and represent better value for money than state providers. However, whether they are more cost-effective and whether they do deliver a better service is currently unclear. These issues are more complex than might be imagined and are discussed further below.

Better service

One quantitative measure to determine whether private prisons deliver a better service might be the official prison performance ratings. The National Audit Commission report (2003) found that privately contracted prisons were, on the whole, performing better than public prisons in areas related to the Prison Service decency agenda (for example, time out of cell, respect, etc.) but that, generally, they performed less well in areas such as safety and security. However, there have been problems of comparability related to the different ways in which data is collected for public and private sector prisons, and it is only in the past few years that a fairly reliable common measurement tool, the Prison Performance Assessment Tool (PPAT), has been developed.

Prison performance data is published quarterly and, according to this measure, the privately contracted estate has not fared well. Although there has been some variation over time, at the end of 2010 the average score for privately contracted prisons was lower (2.64) than for public prisons (2.90). Privately contracted prisons ranked about the same as public sector prisons on excellence: a similar proportion in each sector received the top rating. However, privately contracted prisons were over-represented amongst those requiring development or giving rise to serious concern, and this has been a consistent pattern until the last reported year of 2011–12.

Looking behind these figures, an inquiry under the Freedom of Information Act 2000 by More4 News revealed that in 2008–9, almost double the number of prisoner complaints were upheld in private prisons as in state-run institutions (5.8 per cent against 3.1 per cent). In addition, private prisons have held a higher percentage of their prisoners in overcrowded accommodation than public sector prisons every year for the last 14 years. In 2011–12 the private prisons average was 30.2 per cent, compared to an average of 23.3 per cent in the public sector (Ministry of Justice 2012a). Further evidence of poor performance by the private sector has been provided on an international scale with the revelation of riots, wrongful detention and high levels of self-harm in privately contracted detention centres in the United States, UK and Australia (*Observer* 2011).

Numbers of deaths in custody or instances of self-harm might constitute more specific measures to determine whether private prisons deliver a better service than public prisons. Between 2007 and 2009 there were 206 self-inflicted deaths in prison investigated and concluded by the Prison and Probation Ombudsman (PPO). Fewer than 5 per cent of these occurred in privately contracted prisons. Such institutions, at that time holding 11 per cent of the total prison population, were therefore under-represented in the PPO caseload (Prisons and Probation Ombudsman for England and Wales 2011). However, this type of measure can be misleading as some populations, such as remand prisoners and young people, have tended to produce higher rates of suicide and self-harm than others. Such simple statistical data also reveal nothing of the circumstances surrounding these deaths. Subsequent inquests are more enlightening: the second inquest in January 2011 into the death of 14-year-old Adam Rickwood in 2004 at Hassockfield Secure Training Centre found serious shortcomings in both the conduct of Serco and the exercise of the Youth Justice Board's responsibility, which, it was stated, reflected a failure of accountability and the structure of governance.

An alternative tactic might be to look at the reports of Her Majesty's Chief Inspector of Prisons (HMCIP) and at individual cases. For example, the Inspectorate's report on Rye Hill (a privately run prison) in June 2007 contained accounts of assaults, deaths, hostage taking and indiscipline as well as criticism of the high availability of drugs, drink and mobile telephones for prisoners. At Rye Hill alone, there were three deaths in the year 2005–6: two were self-inflicted and the third was caused by a stabbing by another prisoner. As a result of this report (and a subsequent investigation by *Panorama*), a Rectification Notice was served on GSL (the prison contractor) in August 2007. The Notice directed that GSL produce written proposals to be agreed by the authority and take remedial action on six key measures identified in an operational review.

This type of approach to evaluating the relative merits or demerits of different types of prison management is prone to the criticism of proof by selective instances. A number of HMCIP reports have been highly critical of private sector institutions, especially from a safety angle, but there are also problems at public sector prisons and immigration detention centres. Any study of such reports would need to be comprehensive and control for the type of establishment concerned.

More methodologically rigorous empirical research has been carried out on service delivery, physical conditions and the quality of life in privately and publicly managed prisons in the UK, Australia, New Zealand and the United States (Cooper and Taylor 2005; Harding 2001; Hatry *et al.* 1993; James *et al.* 1997; Moyle 1995; Logan 1992; Rynne *et al.* 2008). Most of the studies concur, highlighting the better facilities and more positive attitudes of staff on issues concerning fairness, respect and humanity in privately run rather than publicly managed prisons. Improved attitudes are attributed to the practice of private contractors recruiting staff with no prior experience of prison work. Hence staff in the privately managed prisons will not have been exposed to the negative influences of staff culture found within many prisons in the public sector. Yet, the research cautions that the relative inexperience of staff in privately contracted prisons can lead to negative consequences in the form of safety, well-being and institutional order.

A recent study in the UK examined the quality of life in two public and two private sector prisons, focusing on institutional cultures, interpersonal relationships and the respective experiences of prisoners and staff. The researchers found that the two public sector prisons scored higher than their private sector comparators on a number of measures and below them on none (Liebling and Crewe 2011). Yet in their evaluation of three further privately contracted prisons, they found that prisoner quality of life was higher in two of these than in the public sector prisons (ESRC 2011). Whilst these results are inconclusive, they highlight the importance of social relations in prisons. This is significant since custodial officers have the power to influence the quality of prisoners' lives on a daily basis, controlling their access to well-being, health and opportunities for risk reduction and release through the provision of structured programmes and routine interaction. As the researchers noted: 'where relationships have the right balance of control and respect almost all aspects of the prisoner experience are enhanced' (ESRC 2011). The research highlights the importance of experience and competence, as well as attitudes in determining how authority is exercised and experienced within public and private sector prisons (Crewe *et al.* 2011).

Cost-effectiveness

Many consider privately contracted prisons to be more cost-effective than their public sector counterparts. However, it has been suggested that whilst the strategy results in short-term gain it leads to long-term costs; and that the government could borrow money at better rates to build and run prisons themselves. It is further argued that the refinancing practices in which some of the contractors have engaged incur a potential long-term cost to the public sector because they expose the government to greater risk of the venture failing.

According to a parliamentary written answer, the costs of private prisons per place are higher than public sector prisons in most categories (Hansard, 9 January 2007). However, a real problem exists in comparing the price of public and private sector prisons in that the full public sector costs of PFI are difficult to evaluate. The task is compounded by the private sector's resort to claims of commercial confidentiality over matters relating to their competitive interests. Various studies have attempted to assess the relative costs of public and private prisons but their findings fail to provide conclusive evidence of financial efficacy (see, for example, Abt. Associates 1998; Park 2000; Pratt and Maahs 1999; Perrone and Pratt 2003).

A further fiscal issue is raised by the current drive for efficiency savings across prison services. In response to a question relating to budgetary cuts in 2009, Lord Bach stated that 'services provided by prisons run by private sector operators are stipulated and priced within a contract and therefore cannot be varied in the same way as public sector prisons, without agreement between the authority and the contractor' (Hansard, 14 December 2009). Yet, it has also been claimed that the private prison sector is not immune from the government's spending constraints and is being hit by a similar programme of efficiency savings. There is need for an independent and comprehensive research programme to look into the question of relative cost. This programme should include consideration of a wide range of social, economic and environmental factors and should examine how the privately contracted sector is affected by the financial cuts that are being imposed on the public sector.

Driving up standards in the public sector

It has been proposed that the introduction of privately run prisons has encouraged innovation and driven up standards in the public sector.

In July 2011 the Ministry of Justice stated that decisions about 'which prisons were selected for competition or closure [were] based on a wide range of criteria, including the potential for efficiency improvements, service reform and innovation' (Ministry of Justice 2011a). The ordering of the criteria is noteworthy. The importation of competitive practices to the public sector (e.g. performance management through target setting and the market testing of prisons) is said to have reduced the costs of public sector prisons largely by breaking down the power of prison officer unions and enabling more flexible staffing structures to be used (Carter 2007). There may well be something in this argument, as two of the originally privately managed prisons (Blakenhurst and Buckley Hall) have now returned to Prison Service management after retendering; the implication being that the public sector outperformed the private consortia in their bids. Yet, the Ministry of Justice's (2011a) own assessment tool (PPAT) shows no evidence of overall improvement in performance amongst public sector prisons. Indeed, returns have indicated a drop in performance by both public and private sector establishments.

ARGUMENTS AGAINST PRIVATISATION

Traditionally, those who argue against private prisons have done so on grounds other than cost-effectiveness. Some of the concerns relate to the effects of privatisation on the nature and form of imprisonment whilst others relate to issues of legitimacy and accountability. These are discussed in more detail below.

Effects on the nature and form of imprisonment

It seems reasonable to assume that the growth of privatised prisons will lead to an even greater expansion in the use of imprisonment as predicted by Lilly and Knepper's (1992) corrections-commercial complex thesis. This holds that because the privatisation of prisons satisfies both public and private sector interests, there will be an inevitable increase in the prisons estate and in the number of people held in them. England and Wales has one of the highest prison populations in the European Union at 153 per 100,000 (International Centre for Prison Studies). The need to contain the growth of the prison population has been acknowledged by the recent Carter report (Carter 2007) and by the government's Green Paper (Ministry of Justice 2010).

The danger of a commercially propelled upward drive in prison numbers should not be underestimated. Vivien Stern's disturbing study of imprisonment throughout the world uses the United States as a key example of potential trouble. In the United States, prisons are becoming big business. Small towns are 'queuing up' to get one built in their neighbourhood and advertising brochures describe the profits to be made from crime, urging investment managers to 'get in on the ground floor of this booming industry' (Stern 1998). In the UK there are also profits to be made from criminal justice investment. In evidence to the House of Commons Public Accounts Committee (2011), Dexter Whitfield reported that two sectors had higher than average profits from equity sales: health and criminal justice.

A further argument is that privatisation promotes an increased concern with security and militates against the rehabilitation of prisoners. Private companies have been involved in the development of community treatment programmes and the first purpose-built therapeutic community prison, Dovegate, is run by a private contractor (Serco). In theory, there is a tension between a penal policy aimed at rehabilitation and an operational policy that allows the private sector to formulate and run prison regimes. This is because the underlying force of rehabilitation is reductionist, the logical deduction of which would be that the profit motive would disappear in a shrinking market. By providing rehabilitative regimes, prisons would appear to be in the business of putting themselves out of business. In practice, the effects of a rehabilitative policy would be unlikely to have any great impact on the overall crime and imprisonment rate because it is only those who are caught and treated or trained who can be rehabilitated. However, privately operated institutions which have the declared aim of rehabilitation are left in the theoretical position where they have conflicting goals depending on whether success is defined in terms of penal policy values or commercial market interests.

There is, though, more than a simple theoretical issue here. Mona Lynch (2002) has argued that the involvement of the private sector in the penal market has coincided with an ideology of risk management and the commoditisation of security. Hence, prison is no longer designed to discipline the individual but has become a site of segregation and risk control, or as she puts it, prisons have become human warehouses for marginalised segments of the population. Lynch argues that the expansion of the penal commodities market is in keeping with a broader trend, involving the successful mass commoditisation of security throughout society over the past few decades, as seen in the increased reliance on hardware such as gates, barriers and alarms to promote safety in the home. To support her argument, Lynch analysed the advertisement columns of the US trade periodical *Corrections Today* between 1949 and 1999. She tracked how over this 50-year period advertisements by those in the corrections products and services industry showed less concern with the prisoner as an individual to be rescued or rehabilitated and more concern with institutional operations.

The relationship between supply and demand is complex and it is impossible to identify which came first: supply in the form of commercial innovation or demand, stemming from a new need based on a shifting ideology of risk and security. Nevertheless, Lynch's conclusion is that those in the corrections products and services industry appear to play at least a contributory role in the growing acceptance of the security-oriented 'warehouse' prison that has ascended in the United States over the past 20 years.

Accountability

Accountability in relation to prison privatisation needs to be assessed in two forms: (1) democratic accountability (sometimes linked to legitimacy); and (2) operational accountability.

Democratic accountability concerns the legitimate authority of the state and how much that authority can be delegated to private companies. Some argue that punishment, as a form of coercive force, is the quintessential function of government and should not under normal circumstances be delegated to private contractors. To do so, they warn, impoverishes the public sphere and weakens the moral bond between citizen and state (DiIulio 1990). Others argue that an important distinction can be made between the allocation of punishment (one of the core powers of government under social contract theory) and the administration of that punishment (which is not a core power and can therefore be delegated). The key questions are:

- How exactly does one distinguish between the allocation and administration of punishment?
- Does the allocation of punishment begin and end in the court?
- Are prisons only concerned with the administration of punishment?

The answers are not straightforward; for example, what about prison discipline, parole reports, sentence planning and classification? All of these processes affect the prisoner's experience of imprisonment and may be seen as part of the allocation and not simply the administration of punishment. In the UK, every privately operated prison has a controller, who is a crown servant. Under section 85(3) of the Criminal Justice Act 1991, the controller was charged with the duty to investigate and report on any allegations against custody officers in relation to the performance of their custodial obligations and with the task of inquiring into and adjudicating on all disciplinary charges brought against inmates. However, section 19 of the Offender Management Act 2007 repealed previous legislation and introduced measures to transfer to directors of privately contracted prisons the power to adjudicate, segregate and authorise the use of force against prisoners. Whilst they were in effect, the restrictions on the powers of directors went some way towards assuaging disquiet about both the formal and informal disciplinary procedures within prisons. But they did not address concerns relating, for instance, to the consequences of sentence planning or parole reports. The major objection here pertains to the chain of accountability within private sector prisons: beginning with custodial officers and ending with shareholders.

This can be explored further by examining the issue of operational accountability. All prisons, whether publicly or privately managed, are subject to performance testing by means of certain output orientated key performance indicators and targets. In the case of private prisons there is a supplementary method of accountability through the contract. Under the contract, the private company undertakes to provide a specified level of service in return for a monthly fee. The ultimate sanction for breach of contract is termination, but most common is the withholding of some portion of the monthly fee. This provides a powerful incentive to the contractor to meet the agreed performance standards. The knowledge that one can lose major profits creates a powerful pressure on the private sector to which the public sector has never been subject. There are two dangers in this. First, the threat of financial damage provides a strong incentive for the contractor to purport to have achieved specified targets when in reality they have failed to do so. This is made possible by the concern of key performance tools with ends rather than means. For example, should performance in a therapeutic community prison be measured by reconviction rates or time in therapy? If the measure is reconviction rates then this may lead to the selection of 'easy bets'. If the measure is time in therapy this may result in the prison retaining in therapy those who are unsuitable to continue (Genders 2003). Second, the overriding accountability of private contractors to their shareholders might result in the failing contractor making a commercial calculation to sustain the financial penalties imposed by the state rather than significantly increase investment to meet its performance targets. In both scenarios, the contractors could hardly be expected to behave otherwise: they have acted in accordance with the system set up to structure their operations and have behaved predictably in seeking to carry out their commercial obligations in ways which best accord with their own priorities and standards (Genders 2002). Such behaviour may result in the derailment of official policy objectives (Genders and Player 2007).

Although there is a need to explore new or additional methods by which private contractors might be held accountable for their behaviour, the prospect of the public authority being able to keep ahead of the game is bleak. At a structural level, the government operates as a nation state, whereas contractors operate at a global level. They are financed by international capital and engage in a diversified market. For example, it has been reported that Serco's $10 billion portfolio includes many businesses in addition to the prisons and immigration detention centres it operates in Australia, the United States and UK, from air traffic control and visa processing, to nuclear weapons maintenance, video surveillance and welfare to work programmes (*Observer* 2011).

CURRENT GOVERNMENT POLICY: THE STRATEGIC DEVELOPMENT OF A MIXED PENAL ECONOMY AND THE INCREASING COMMERCIALISATION OF CRIMINAL JUSTICE

Three features characterise the Coalition government's current strategy in respect of prison provision over the present spending period: (1) an increased commitment to competition and greater contestability; (2) the targeting of better outcomes in the form of a reduction in reoffending; (3) the introduction of an ideology of payment by results. As Secretary of State for Justice, Kenneth Clarke described how the use of contracting models where providers are paid by results would drive innovation, improve outcomes and ensure better value for money (Ministry of Justice 2011b). The current provisions apply to custodial services but will be developed and extended to non-custodial services. Hence, whilst the previous Labour government's policy appeared to favour a mixed economy of public and private provision (where competition was used as a means to select providers for new services or to address poor public sector performance), the new Coalition administration has pledged that competition will apply to all services not bound to the public sector by statute (Ministry of Justice 2011b).

This strategy marks a shift in the scale of contestability and the way in which competition is used in custodial and community services. At the same time, structural changes to the delivery of services have resulted in certain changes to the lines of accountability. Privately contracted prisons are no longer accountable to the Prison Service Agency (PSA) but to the Director General of the National Offender Management Service (NOMS), who is, in turn, accountable to the Ministry of Justice. Whilst the PSA continues to exist, it has essentially been subsumed within NOMS. Therefore, NOMS is now responsible for ensuring contestability in the provision of custodial and community based services, and for attracting new providers from the commercial and third sectors to the market through a planned programme of market testing. This new structure radically changes the role of the PSA, which now operates as a delivery arm of NOMS, placing it, at least theoretically, on a level playing field with private providers. One question that seems to arise from the new structural arrangements concerns the role of commercial confidentiality and the extent to which the ability of private sector organisations to withhold commercially sensitive information may place public sector providers at a disadvantage in bidding processes since public providers must, presumably, continue to submit to the process of transparency.

Michael Spurr, as Chief Executive Officer of NOMS, stated that the shift in the scale and way in which competition is to be used would enable the delivery of better outcomes for the taxpayer for less money, as contestability will be used to drive quality of service, value for money, innovation and market development (Ministry of Justice 2011b). The Ministry of Justice business plan additionally commits the department to creating an effective market in the provision of offender management and rehabilitation by ensuring that services are provided by whoever can most effectively and efficiently meet public demand. The application of payment by results (PbR) principles is designed to stimulate providers to focus on outcomes, giving them the freedom to offer new approaches to service delivery (Ministry of Justice 2011b).

The Green Paper *Breaking the Cycle: Effective Punishment, Rehabilitation and Sentencing of Offenders* (Ministry of Justice 2010) sets out plans for reducing reoffending without reducing punishment. It proposes the development of working prisons and drug rehabilitation programmes, with providers from all sectors (public, private and voluntary) to be paid by results. The Legal Aid, Sentencing and Punishment of Offenders Act 2012 incorporates provisions to give effect to the Green Paper's proposals that require primary legislation. A Ministry of Justice business plan details the strategies to be employed for the 'rehabilitation revolution', including paying private and voluntary organisations by results; working with the Department of Health to pilot and roll out drug recovery wings in prisons; and increasing the numbers of prisoners doing meaningful work for real wages. Eight publicly managed prisons were put up for competition in 2012; already, the first payment by results pilot scheme is under way at Serco-run Doncaster prison, with at least six further projects planned before 2015 (Ministry of Justice 2011b). The NOMS subsequently announced that a further nine prisons would be put out to competitive tender during 2012–13 (Ministry of Justice 2012b).

In its competition strategy document, the Ministry of Justice explicitly states:

- competition will be based on the required outcomes and the demand for services;
- competition activity should be focused on achieving mid- to long-term savings, not finding the cheapest solution at the expense of quality;
- competition should be used to deliver public sector reforms, ensuring providers are more effectively held to account for the outcomes they deliver;

- competitions should be run and regulated fairly;
- providers should work with each other to deliver the best outcomes for communities.

(Ministry of Justice 2011b)

These mandates raise a number of issues of interpretation and application, relating to the factors to be employed in evaluating 'the best outcomes for communities' and the indices to be used to calibrate performance and gauge success. Reconviction rates are the usual yardstick but are a poor choice as they count only offences for which the person has been caught and convicted. Softer measures such as getting a job or attending education might be attractive since they reflect current criminological understanding that desistance from crime is a gradual and multifaceted business built on integration into the community, employment and other social institutions. However, this type of approach may be criticised as reflecting more of a payments for 'process' than payments for 'results' scheme. More problematic is the issue of attribution. For example, since desistance may be influenced by numerous divergent factors and a variety of independent interventions, how might payment be fairly distributed amongst the different agencies involved? A collaborative scheme might provide the most equitable means but how would this synchronise with the competitive ethos of the private market?

Further questions should be asked of the strategy document, informed by what is already known about the involvement of private contractors in prison service provision. These should bear in mind contractors' access to global capital and business expertise; their commitment to the profit incentive; and the many issues associated with accountability, such as commercial confidentiality, lack of transparency and the inherent duty of private enterprise to its shareholders.

CONCLUSION

The most difficult question surrounding prison privatisation is how far structural arrangements rooted in system interests can serve the needs of criminal and social justice. The drivers of change propelling the increased commercialisation of criminal justice are informed less by concerns for the interests of justice or security and more by a commitment to a particular political ideology (evident in the transformation of the role of the state from service provider to service commissioner) and the exigencies of economic expediency (manifest in the pursuit of efficiency and cost-effectiveness). The dilemma is whether a mixed penal economy can meet the requirements of social and criminal justice whilst adhering to the dictates of market forces. For instance, the recognition that detainees are profitable not just for their labour, but also for their ability to generate payment by their very incarceration, generates disquiet about the nature of the investment by entrepreneurs in the production and commoditisation of prisoners. Particular concern might be raised when the structural relationships that designate prisoners amongst the most socially, economically and politically disempowered segments of society are acknowledged (see Mathiessen 2006; Bennett 2008; Wacquant 2005; Marchetti 2002). The influence of lobbying groups with a vested interest in the prison industry continues to be most evident in the United States (Leighton and Reiman 2010). Yet in the UK too, for example, private contractors raised objections, on grounds of cost, to the inclusion of prisons within the Corporate Homicide and Corporate Manslaughter Act (*Guardian* 2011), elevating considerations of profit over concern for human safety. This begs the question of how the government will manage the ostensibly competing objectives generated by market imperatives and the dictates of justice.

Finally, it must be questioned whether the current drive towards increasing commercialisation of prison management and the provision of a mixed economy of working prisons is likely to lead to a proliferation of the penal estate. The government's commitment to meting out tough criminal sanctions and its reductivist policy of driving down crime by delivering prisons that offer rehabilitation through hard work might accede to the demands of penal populism, but they raise an inherent contradiction. The policy of payment by results is designed to encourage service providers to deliver programmes that lead to desistance from crime. This appears to be a laudable aim since it aspires to reduce the risk of victimisation in the community whilst rebalancing social justice by providing enhanced opportunities for education, employment and social inclusion. Yet, from a reintegrative perspective, such efforts might be more effectively delivered through community schemes. From an economic perspective, too, community provision would be more cost-efficient.

Increasing private sector involvement in the provision of penal regimes is an attractive option for the government, enabling the realisation of its vision of encouraging desistance from crime whilst maintaining a tough stance on those who commit offences. The question is whether the meeting of these aspirations will succeed in providing rehabilitative opportunities to a reduced prison population comprising those who have committed the most serious offences; or trigger a net widening effect, whereby more people are drawn into the prison system for less serious offences, thus militating against the attainment of a reductionist prison agenda.

FURTHER RESEARCH

Analysis of these issues has identified a number of questions and directions for research, which, if pursued, could extend existing knowledge around prison privatisation. These include:

1. An extension of existing research on prisoner–staff relationships in publicly and privately managed institutions, incorporating:
   - an examination of staff attitudes and behaviours, and how these might influence prisoner outcomes;
   - an evaluation of management styles and practices, and how they shape the boundaries of staff action.

   To be comprehensive, it is imperative that such research take account of the issue of staff retention, in particular the ways in which retention rates contribute to the evolution of particular institutional cultures and how these may change over time.

2. An independent and comprehensive comparison of the relative costs of public and private sector prisons. This should include consultancy fees, the bidding process, borrowing arrangements, staff engaged in the competition process as well as risk transfer, since the cost of failure must ultimately be borne by the public purse. This type of analysis could be broadened out to incorporate social, economic, employment and environmental factors as well as community well-being. For example, questions could address the cost-effectiveness of operating privately contracted prisons with fewer and less experienced staff than in public sector prisons. In particular, research should examine:
   - how existing privately contracted prisons are affected by the financial cuts that are hitting the public sector;

- to what extent and in what ways they might be protected from fiscal clawback by the contractual arrangements that are already in place.

3. An investigation to identify innovations that have arisen from private sector management or PFI projects: whether these have been adopted by the public sector and to what effect. A prior question might be in what ways PFI contracts enable creativity and innovation and in what ways they constrain them.

4. An analysis of some of the concepts used in the Ministry of Justice's current strategy for competition, including the factors to be used in evaluating 'the best outcomes for communities'. At a more empirical level, the Ministry of Justice's payment by results projects will require ongoing critical and independent assessment, not least, a consideration of the indices that might be employed to calibrate performance and gauge success. Further questions include whether:

   - the level of risk entailed in the system of payment by results will deter smaller players or the voluntary sector from competing or might lead providers to mitigate potential loss by negotiating higher fees for their services;
   - the focus on payment by results might encourage contractors to manipulate outcomes or to play it safe by focusing their resources on easy targets;
   - the competitive ethos so intrinsic to the market model of service provision will lead to fragmentation and militate against the collaborative working practices required of a rehabilitative system.

5. A frank inquiry as to how the government will ensure that penal policy is not derailed by the fiscal imperatives of private contractors and that it is not outmanoeuvred as it has been before.

References

Abt. Associates (1998) *Private Prisons in the US: An Assessment of Current Practice*. Cambridge, MA: Abt. Associates.

Bennett, J. (2008) *The Social Costs of Dangerousness: Prison and the Dangerous Classes*. London: Centre for Crime and Justice Studies.

Carter, P. (2007) *Securing the Future: Proposals for the Efficient and Sustainable Use of Custody in England and Wales*. London: Cabinet Office.

Cooper, C. and Taylor, P. (2005) 'Independently verified reductionism: prison privatisation in Scotland'. *Human Relations* 58(4) pp. 497–522.

Crewe, B., Liebling, A. and Hulley, S. (2011) 'Staff culture, use of authority and prisoner quality of life in public and private sector prisons'. *Australian and New Zealand Journal of Criminology* 44(1) pp. 94–115.

Dilulio, J. (1990) 'The duty to govern: a critical perspective on the private management of prisons and jails' in McDonald, D. (ed.) *Private Prisons and the Public Interest*. New Brunswick: Rutgers University Press, pp. 155–78.

ESRC (2011) *Staff-Prisoner Relationships are Key to Prison Quality* – Press Release 17. Available at: www.esrc.ac.uk/news-and-events/press-releases/15594/staff-prisoner-relationships-are-key-to-prison-quality.aspx [accessed August 2012].

Feeley, M. (2002) 'Entrepreneurs of punishment'. *Punishment and Society* 4(3) pp. 321–43.

Genders, E. (2002) 'Legitimacy, accountability and private prisons'. *Punishment and Society* 4(3) pp. 285–303.

Genders, E. (2003) 'Privatisation and innovation – rhetoric and reality: the development of a therapeutic community prison'. *Howard Journal* 42(2) pp. 137–57.

Genders, E. and Player, E. (2007) 'The commercial context of criminal justice: prison privatisation and the perversion of purpose'. *Criminal Law Review*, pp. 513–29.

Guardian (2011) 'Privatisation will not rehabilitate our prisons'. Available at: www.guardian.co.uk/commentisfree/2011/apr/01/privatisation-prisons/print [accessed 6 May 2012].

Hansard HC, 9 January 2007, c546W.

Hansard HC, 14 December 2009, cWA179.

Hansard HC, 1 November 2010, C514W.

Harding, J. and Wortley, R. (2008) 'Market testing and prison riots: how public sector commercialisation contributed to a prison riot'. *Criminology and Public Policy* 7(1) pp. 117–42.

Harding, R. (2001) 'Private prisons'. *Crime and Justice* 28 pp. 265–346.

Hatry, H., Brounstein, P. and Levinson, R. (1993) 'Comparisons of privately and publicly operated corrections facilities in Kentucky and Massachusetts' in G. Bowman, S. Hakim and P. Seidenstat (eds) *Privatizing Correctional Institutions*. New Brunswick: Transaction Publishers, pp. 193–212.

House of Commons Public Accounts Committee (2011). Written evidence presented by Dexter Whitfield. Available at www.publications.parliament.uk/pa/cm201012/cmselect/cmpubacc/1201/1201we03.htm [accessed 25 January 2013].

International Centre for Prison Studies (2012) World Prison Brief. Available at: www.prisonstudies.org/info/worldbrief [accessed January 2013].

James, A., Bottomley, K., Liebling, A. and Clare, E. (1997) *Privatizing Prisons: Rhetoric and Reality*. London: Sage.

Leighton, P. and Reiman, J. (2010) *The Rich get Richer and the Poor get Prison*. Boston: Allyn and Bacon.

Lichtenstein, A. (2001) 'The private and public in penal history'. *Punishment and Society* 3(1) pp. 189–96.

Liebling, A. and Crewe, B. (2011) *Values, Practices and Outcomes in Public and Private Sector*. Available at: www.esrc.ac.uk/my-esrc/grants/RES-062–23–0212/outputs/Read/3e0fdcb7–238d-44e8-a54a-2d8cc7571c8c [accessed June 2012].

Lilly, J.R. and Knepper, P. (1992) 'An international perspective on the privatisation of corrections'. *Howard Journal* 31(3) pp. 174–91.

Logan, C.H. (1992) 'Well-kept: comparing quality of confinement in private and public prisons'. *Journal of Criminal Law and Criminology* 83(3) pp. 577–613.

Lynch, M. (2002) 'Selling securityware'. *Punishment and Society* 4(3) pp. 305–19.

Marchetti, A. (2002) 'Carceral impoverishment: class inequality in the French penitentiary'. *Ethnography* 3 pp. 416–34.

Mathiessen, T. (2006) *Prison on Trial*. Winchester: Waterside Press.

Ministry of Justice (2010) *Breaking the Cycle: Effective Punishment, Rehabilitation and Sentencing of Offenders*. Available at: www.justice.gov.uk/consultations/docs/breaking-the-cycle.pdf [accessed June 2012].

Ministry of Justice (2011a) *National Offender Management Service Annual Report 2009/10*. London: Ministry of Justice.

Ministry of Justice (2011b) *Competition Strategy for Offender Services*. Available at: www.justice.gov.uk/downloads/publications/moj/2011/competition-strategy-offender-services.pdf [accessed June 2012].

Ministry of Justice (2012a) *National Offender Management Service: Annual Report 2011/12*. London: Ministry of Justice.

Ministry of Justice (2012b) *National Offender Management Service: Business Plan 2012–13*. Available at: www.justice.gov.uk/downloads/publications/corporate-reports/noms/2012/noms-business-plan-2012–2013.pdf [accessed 20 December 2012].

Moyle, P. (2001) 'Separating the allocation of punishment from its administration'. *British Journal of Criminology* 41 pp. 77–100.

National Audit Commission (2003) *The Operational Performance of PFI Prisons Report by the Comptroller and Auditor General*. London: The Stationery Office.

Observer (2011) New York Times Supplement, Sunday 16 October.

Park, I. (2000) *Review of Comparative Costs and Performance of Privately and Publicly Operated Prisons, 1998–9*. Home Office Statistical Bulletin 6/00, London: Home Office.

Perrone, D. and Pratt, T. (2003) 'Comparing the quality of confinement and cost effectiveness of public v private prisons: what we know, why we do not know more and where to go from here'. *The Prison Journal* 83(3) pp. 301–22.

Pratt, T.C. and Maahs, J. (1999) 'Are private prisons more cost-effective than public prisons? A meta-analysis of evaluation research studies'. *Crime and Delinquency* 45(3) pp. 358–71.

Prison Reform Trust (2012) *Bromley Briefings Prison Fact File June 2012.* Available at: www.prisonreformtrust.org.uk/Portals/0/Documents/Fact%20File%20June%202011%20web.pdf [accessed January 2013].

Prisons and Probation Ombudsman for England and Wales (2011) *Learning from PPO Investigations: Self-Inflicted Deaths in Prison Custody 2007–2009.* Available at: www.ppo.gov.uk/docs/self-inflicted-deaths-in-prison.pdf [accessed June 2012].

Rynne, J., Harding, R. and Wortley, R. (2008) 'Market testing and prison riots: how public-sector commercialization contributed to a prison riot'. *Criminology and Public Policy* 7(1) pp. 17–142.

Stern, V. (1998) *A Sin against the Future: Imprisonment in the World.* London: Penguin.

Wacquant, L. (2005) 'The great penal leap backward: incarceration in America from Nixon to Clinton' in J. Pratt, D. Brown, M. Brown, S. Hallsworth and W. Morrison (eds) *The New Punitiveness; Trends, Theories, Perspectives.* Cullompton: Willan, pp. 3–26.

3

POLICING IN ENGLAND AND WALES

CHALLENGES AND PRESSURE POINTS

MICHAEL ROWE

INTRODUCTION

This chapter explores contemporary challenges facing the police services of England and Wales and the potential impact that some of these have in terms of imprisonment. It is argued that policing has only a marginal direct impact on imprisonment rates – not least because much of the police mandate relates to the provision of services only marginally associated with crime. Many of the service functions, community and reassurance activities, and other roles that the police undertake have little or no direct orientation to crime-fighting and no straightforward impact on imprisonment. Nonetheless, financial pressures that the service currently faces pose challenges that might erode the legitimacy of the police, and this raises significant concerns in terms of wider confidence in criminal justice and attitudes towards penology. This chapter identifies important pressure points faced by the police service and a number of areas where further research would be useful. It begins by reviewing trends in prison rates alongside data relating to policing to demonstrate that there is no clear relationship between police activity and imprisonment, and continues by exploring the impact that cuts to police budgets will have on the internal organisation and delivery of policing; before moving on to consider how the wider recession might change the external landscape in terms of crime and disorder.

POLICING AND THE FLOW OF PEOPLE
INTO PRISON: THE AGGREGATE DATA

A conundrum surrounds the role that the Police Service plays in relation to efforts to stem the flow of people into imprisonment. Clearly anyone who ends up sentenced to custody almost certainly began their journey through the criminal justice system in the hands of the Police Service. The police are often referred to as a 'gate keeper' agency in terms of the criminal justice system and it is difficult to think of any circumstances by which an individual moves from the primary to the tertiary sector of the system without some form of initial interaction with police officers. If a 'crime control' model of policing is adopted then it might be expected that the flow of individuals through the police gate plays an important part in determining the number of people in prison. Increases in expenditure on policing and the deployment of record numbers of police officers and other staff have continued over a relatively lengthy period during which prison numbers have also escalated and recorded crime has fallen in broad terms. A crime control model of policing would suggest that investment in the front end of the criminal justice system has paid dividends in terms of reductions in offending and the rise in prison numbers. While such a perspective might be comforting to senior police officers keen to promote the crime-fighting capacity of the service during a period of financial austerity, the broad statistical picture suggests that changes in the prison population cannot be linked to the activities and performance of the police.

Between 1995 and 2009 the prison population in England and Wales increased by 32,500 (66 per cent) (Ministry of Justice 2009). Three important measures of police performance suggest that there is no straightforward relationship between this increase and the activities of officers. One of the preliminary encounters between police and public that might open the gate towards later stages of the criminal justice system are Police and Criminal Evidence Act 1984 (PACE) stop and searches[1] which have risen over a comparable period (1999–2000 to

2009–10). However, the increase in the number of people stopped and searched by the police was much lower at 34 per cent (just over half the rise in the prison population). The value of stop and search is debated at greater length later in this section, but the rise in its use throughout the first decade of the twenty-first century cannot explain the increase in the prison population since only a small proportion (9 per cent in 2009–10) of those stopped and searched were arrested (Povey *et al.* 2011).

There is also no apparent relation in aggregate terms between the number of arrests affected by the police and the number of people subsequently entering prison. The significant recent increase in the prison population has occurred during a period when there has been only a modest increase in the overall number of people arrested: a rise of 9 per cent between 1999–2000 and 2009–10 (Povey *et al.* 2011). Police action post-arrest has an impact on the numbers of people entering the court system, who then form the population liable for custody. On this measure too, however, it seems unlikely that changes in the rate or nature of police activity could explain the rising number of people imprisoned. While the overall proportion of recorded crime that is classified as resulting in a 'sanction detection'[2] has risen from 19 to 28 per cent between 2002–3 and 2010–11, there has been a fall of 19 per cent in the number of charges/summons issued over the same period. What this suggests is that police performance has improved in terms of resolving crimes recorded – since a greater proportion is resulting in a sanction of some kind. However, a smaller proportion results in a sanction that requires a court appearance and might result in a prison sentence.

In broad terms, the rise in the prison population during the last 15 years or so has occurred during a period when the number of stop and searches carried out by the police has increased and the number of arrests has also grown (but both by a smaller proportion than the prison population). On the other hand, the number of people charged with offences or summoned to appear in court has fallen dramatically while the prison population has greatly expanded. The growth in prison population is not attributable to changes in police practice or resourcing. Instead the rise needs to be understood in terms of policy changes that have led to longer sentences and to changes in the types of offences being dealt with by the courts (namely that the courts are dealing with greater numbers of cases of violence against the person and drug offences: offence categories likely to lead to imprisonment) (Ministry of Justice 2009). In aggregate terms, it seems unlikely that efforts to reduce the flow of individuals into prison have much to gain from a focus on policing. Nonetheless, a number of developments in relation to the internal policing functions and resources and to the external landscape in which the police operate seem likely to shape future debates in criminal justice.

FINANCIAL AUSTERITY AND THE INTERNAL LANDSCAPE OF POLICING

A recent report by Her Majesty's Inspectorate of Constabulary (HMIC) (HMIC 2011a) reviewed police service plans in the light of reductions in the overall police budget. In broad terms the 43 police services of England and Wales have modelled future plans on the anticipation that gross revenue expenditure will decline 14 per cent over the period from 2010–11 to 2014–15. In terms of human resources (which account for 80 per cent of expenditure), forces estimate a reduction in police officers, police community support officers and police staff of 34,100 over the period March 2010 to March 2015. To some extent this reduction will be offset by a revival of the role of voluntary special constables, estimated to increase by 17 per cent to 22,600 over the same period. In overall terms, notwithstanding considerable differences between forces, the HMIC (2011a) study suggests that the planned cuts will mean that by 2014–15 police officer levels will be back to the position of 2001–2 and the total workforce will return to where it was in 2003–4.

Against this context, two considerations arise that are central to debates about public confidence in policing: the impact that such reductions might have on the 'frontline' of policing, and the implications that a reduction in human resources might have in terms of responding to crime. Defining what constitutes the frontline in policing terms is not straightforward, and forces have undergone a lengthy period of civilianisation and privatisation of 'back office', 'middle office' and administrative roles. HMIC (2011b) provided a working definition that characterised the 'frontline' in terms of staff 'in everyday contact with the public and who directly intervene to keep people safe and enforce the law'. While this is not an entirely satisfactory definition it does provide a tool to examine future prospects for routine visible policing. HMIC (2011a) found that in the immediate future (until March 2012) forces were focusing reductions on non-frontline activity. However, the report found considerable differences between services; unsurprisingly those that had already introduced cuts to non-frontline activities had less scope to target those areas in order to protect frontline services from future reductions. Conversely, those that had yet to introduce reductions to 'middle' or 'back' office functions were set to target overall reductions on those areas first, and so leave the frontline relatively intact in the medium term.

The link between police numbers and crime levels is among the most vexed debates about policing, and relates, in part, to broader questions about the value of routine police patrols in terms of crime prevention and detection, deterrence and public reassurance. The complexities of these debates cannot be reviewed in this brief section and it is clear that the political and policing imperative of maintaining the 'bobby on the beat' is rooted in symbolic value as well as effectiveness in terms of crime, law and order. Maintaining the number of officers on frontline patrol was a core pledge of many of the Police and Crime Commissioners (PCCs) elected to office in November 2012. The importance of PCCs to the future direction of local policing and the impact that they might have on the criminal justice and penal system is returned to later in the discussion. The quality of the research evidence examining the impact of increasing police numbers on crime rates is uneven, and is hampered by methodological and definitional problems.[3] A recent 'rapid review' of the extant research literature suggested that the balance of evidence suggests that increasing police officer numbers might have an impact on levels of property crime (estimating that a 10 per cent rise in the number of officers might yield a 3 per cent reduction in property crime) (Bradford 2011). However, there appears to be no relationship between police numbers and violent offending. In terms of current prospects, the research evidence is unhelpful since it has been focused on understanding relationships between increasing officer numbers and crime rates – there is little research into the consequences of a reduction in officer numbers on crime patterns. Even if some tentative conclusions can be drawn from existing studies it cannot be assumed that causal relations would work in reverse in the current climate in which a reduction in police numbers appears inevitable over the next few years.

One of the difficulties of forecasting the likely impact of a reduction in officer numbers on crime rates relates to how offending behaviour is understood. If a rational choice model is adopted then it might be assumed that fewer police effectively reduces the costs and risks of offending such that individual calculations are tipped in the direction of crime. On the other hand, if offending is understood in other terms, relating, for example, to strain theory or other factors influenced by socio-economic circumstances, then it might be that the recessionary climate that underlies cuts in police budgets might also exacerbate wider criminogenic conditions. Analysing the impact of reduced police numbers on crime rates is methodologically difficult in any context, but to measure any relationship in isolation from changes in socio-economic variables would be fraught with difficulty. Nonetheless, this is an important debate to which further research could usefully contribute.

A conceptual and methodological problem faced by studies seeking to establish if the number of police officers impacts upon crime rates arises from the many functions of patrol work not targeted at the prevention or detection of crime. Many aspects of police patrol work are related to the diverse range of service functions that officers perform, ranging from traffic control, assisting other emergency services, and responding to myriad public requests for help that are often unrelated to crime. The breadth and diversity of police tasks led Bittner (1974) to the acerbic view that 'when one looks at what policemen actually do, one finds that criminal law enforcement is something that most of them do with the frequency located somewhere between virtually never and very rarely'. Bayley's (1994) study of policing in Australia, Canada, England and Wales, Japan and the United States found that most officer time was dedicated to patrol work and that this was largely directed by calls from dispatchers receiving requests from the public. Only 7 to 10 per cent of such calls for assistance are estimated to be related to crime. The benefits of police patrol work are not solely or predominantly related to crime control, which suggests that looming cuts to the police frontline might have a deleterious impact in other terms such as public perceptions of police legitimacy and trust and confidence in the service.

Police legitimacy, procedural justice and the symbolic value of patrol

Recent British policing policy has valued foot patrol in terms of symbolic reassurance offered by officers on the beat; a reassurance that helps to assuage public insecurity and fear of crime that has risen even during a period where much of the evidence suggests that actual levels of offending have broadly fallen. A considerable body of research evidence has emerged in the United States and the UK to suggest that public support for the police is closely related to assessments of procedural justice (Tyler 2007; Hough *et al.* 2010). Police legitimacy is more closely related to perceptions that the police act fairly, ethically and in relation to agreed standards, rather than to effectiveness in terms of crime control. Hough *et al.* (2010) argued that procedural justice is important to developing trust in the Police Service but, moreover, underpins compliance with the law and wider support for the rule of law. Perceptions that the police are procedurally just might not be directly related to the extent to which frontline police provide a visible presence through foot patrol work. Prospective cuts to the frontline will not necessarily mean a decline in perceptions that the police act in a procedurally just manner, but analysis of British Crime Survey data suggests that public confidence in the police is strongly correlated to visibility of officers on foot patrol. Innes and Innes (2011) found that confidence in the police is most strongly associated with visibility; the more often people report that they see officers on patrol the more likely they are to report high levels of confidence. The link between visibility and confidence is stronger than the influence of familiarity (knowing officers by sight or by name). While this analysis suggests that a decrease in the visibility of police officers on routine patrol would erode public confidence in policing, further research is required into the prospects that public confidence could be secured through other means. The provision of a visible police presence, for example, through the deployment of special constables might maintain confidence even if fewer officers are on patrol.

The association between trust in the Police Service and procedural justice also requires further research. Crucially, understanding how 'procedural justice' is conceptualised in the public mind should be a priority during a period of police reform and restructuring. Recent debates about the police response to urban unrest – judged by some to be too 'soft' and by others to be too harsh – provide a good example of the limitations of seeking to ensure procedural justice as a means of shoring up trust in the police and a wider endorsement of the rule of law. Similarly, the use of stop and search powers, which disproportionally impact upon young males and some minority ethnic groups, raise questions about procedural justice to which there seem to be few answers that would secure widespread public support. The notion of procedural justice focuses attention on police adhering to legitimate established policies and procedures; concerns about stop and search practices are related to outcomes and impact. While some have called for stop and search powers to be significantly curtailed or even scrapped altogether (Bowling and Philips 2007), police and policy-makers tend to defend the totemic and practical value of stop and search. While the development of ethical policing is key to demonstrating procedural justice, the content of ethics is likely to remain contested in a period when financial austerity forces the role and mandate of police to be reconsidered.

In terms of stemming the flow of individuals into prison it seems unlikely that a reduction in police resources will, in and of itself, mean a reduction in the number of people brought to justice. The effect of removing officers from frontline, middle office or background duties on the detection of crime remains difficult to predict but the evidence suggests that this will not have an unintended consequence of reducing the flow of offenders through the courts and into the penal system. Studies that suggest that public support for policing is conditional upon the perception that the police act in a procedurally just manner note that this has implications for public cooperation with the police and the support for the rule of law more broadly. In many ways this reinforces an approach to policing that emphasises the symbolic presence that the police have in social, cultural and political identity (Reiner 2010; Loader and Mulcahy 2003). From such a perspective it seems that public support for the police brings with it significant positive externalities that shape wider perceptions of risks of crime and the popular politics of law and order that drive sentencing and penal policy. Current pressure points in terms of police resources might not be immediately related to efforts to stem the flow of individuals into custody but they seem likely to influence the broad direction going forward.

OPERATIONAL POLICING

If the legitimacy of policing rests on visibility, perceptions of procedural justice and an understanding that the police service are morally and socially aligned to the public, then aspects of operational policing will continue to be significant pressure points. A crucial challenge for policing will be to maintain frontline police service in terms of visible patrols and an appropriate response to public calls for assistance while engaging in activities that are 'backroom' or 'middle office' but nonetheless central to crime reduction. Changes in the nature of crime challenge the nature of modern policing. If offending becomes further displaced from local neighbourhoods into cyberspace, for example, then the territorial organisation of police services, at the level of constabularies, Basic Command Units and individual beats, makes less sense in terms of responding to crime. The use of 'backroom' intelligence analysts, crime mappers and Internet monitors will become increasingly significant to operational policing.

The 2011 summer riots further demonstrated the role of social media communications in crime and disorder and that the Police Service remains woefully unable to either monitor such services for pre-emptive purposes or to make use of them to communicate to the public (Silverman 2011). The challenge for the Police Service is to enhance capacity to respond to new modes of offending that are not easily tackled through the traditional frontline. The frontline is valuable in terms of encouraging public communication and cooperation with police such that intelligence and information can be gathered for the purposes of analysis and mapping. Nonetheless, current emphasis on protecting the frontline of policing (which clearly is valuable in terms of public trust and confidence) seems likely to be at the expense of other police functions that might be increasingly significant in terms of future types and trends in offending. Balancing the roles and functions of a plurality of police staff will continue to be a key pressure point for the immediate future.

In terms of stemming the flow of individuals into prison, the commitment to protecting the frontline of policing is likely to endanger police engagement in the range of multi-agency partnerships that have characterised community safety and crime control since the late 1990s. In 41 of the police service areas of England and Wales, Police and Crime Commissioners will influence – through funding provisions, for example – local criminal justice and community safety arrangements and the role that the police play within these networks. Police engagement with other criminal justice agencies to provide post-release support for prisoners and alternatives to custody, for example, entails a range of practices that might be considered far from the frontline but which have a huge potential in terms of preventing recidivism and future costs of offending and imprisonment. The use of community sentences has increased in the last decade, which has increased the requirement for police to work in partnership with offender managers on supervision in the community (Mills 2011). An expansion in schemes to support prisoners post-release also further embeds police officers in multi-agency partnerships.

A recent estimate suggested that investment in programmes such as the Diamond Initiative that ran in seven London boroughs or the Integrated Offender Management programmes that have developed in recent years might prove highly cost-effective in financial terms. Evaluation of one scheme in Camden suggested that the investment of £33 million per annum would yield savings of around £3 billion over a three-year period (Lanning *et al.* 2011). The role of the police is seen as central to models to divert those who have committed offences from prison, as has also been widely noted in the context of youth justice. As with their partner agencies, however, police leaders forced to make significant financial cuts might find it difficult to maintain investment in such activities. This problem is exacerbated since the costs incurred weigh upon institutional budgets whereas financial and other benefits accrue in less tangible form to the public purse in generic terms. If government commitments to reduce the use of short-term prison sentences in England and Wales are realised then the police role in providing robust and meaningful alternatives to custody will need to be enhanced. Reconciling this with demands to protect the frontline of police work will be an escalating challenge over the period of financial retrenchment set to last until at least 2014–15. The first PCC elections in 2012 saw many candidates commit to maintaining frontline police provisions. How these will be reconciled with developing innovative approaches to tackling offending remains to be seen in the era of PCCs.

THE WIDER LANDSCAPE

Much of the research evidence relating to the role of frontline policing in terms of the prevention and detection of crime and the provision of public reassurance assumes that policing is delivered against a steady state in terms of the external context of crime, disorder and other demands for police services. Most of the pressure points identified in the preceding discussion have related to the internal organisation and operational delivery of policing. Clearly, though, demands on policing and the wider social landscape are likely to be transformed in a period of financial austerity. The challenge facing the police service is widely articulated in terms of the need to 'do more, with less'. If the previous paragraphs reviewed the 'with less' part of this challenge then the discussion that follows examines various ways that the police might need to 'do more' in a recessionary climate in which other public services have been withdrawn. This is considered briefly in two respects: the impact of a reduction in other aspects of public sector provisions, and the likelihood that recession will cause crime rates to rise. In respect to both of these, there is also the potential that a period of austerity might increase public demands for tough policing and punitive criminal justice.

Police as the service of last resort

The same financial pressures that seem likely to impact negatively on the service delivered by the police will also affect other areas of public sector provision. Cuts in a host of social and public services are likely to significantly increase the police workload. Police services sometimes characterise themselves as the 'service of last resort' that has to respond to social problems that other agencies might not meet. Although in some respects a simplistic view, it draws attention to the 'downstream' impact that cuts to other social services might have in terms of crime and related demands on police. A retrenchment in youth service facilities, for example, will increase, in already stretched communities, the number of young people congregating in public areas who are then vulnerable to criminal behaviour (both as victims or perpetrators of crime). Such developments might also increase public perceptions of insecurity which will also raise demands for police responses to social problems and these demands might have been exacerbated by PCCs pledged to respond to local community concerns. Reductions in funding for emergency and social housing are likely to exacerbate the chaotic lifestyles of those who have offended and extend their criminal activities. While cuts to public sector provision will be implemented differently between local authorities and will not be uniform either in extent or terms of the focus of budget restrictions, it seems highly likely that they will have a disproportionate impact upon disadvantaged communities that do not have the social or other capital to withstand a withdrawal in services. The service role of police officers in responding to the needs of vulnerable and marginalised communities (which led Bayley (1994) to describe patrol officers as 'tour guides in the museum of human frailty') will be greatly extended in a recessionary period as other social and welfare services are diminished.

The impact of recession on crime rates

Related to cuts in public expenditure is the possibility that the recession will have an impact on crime rates. Previous attempts to research the extent and nature of the relationship between crime trends and the economic environment have been fraught with difficulty and there is little consensus on whether there is any relationship between, for example, unemployment and property crime (see Finklea 2010, for a recent overview of the literature). As Box's (1987) influential study noted, the evidence linking unemployment to crime is relatively weak and different conclusions might be reached in relation to different types of offending. While there might be a weak link between unemployment and property crime, such that a rise in the former leads to a much smaller increase in the latter, it might be that rising unemployment leads to a reduction in other types of offending that might be linked to consumption, such as violence associated with the night-time economy. A reduction in personal income that might prevent individuals socialising, and committing crime, in bars and city streets might, on the other hand, increase domestic violence if the consumption of alcohol is more likely to take place in the home. This echoes Field's (1990) analysis of long-term trends in the relationship between crime and the economy, which suggested that patterns and trends in consumption have a greater influence on offending than does unemployment. Hall et al (2008) have examined the criminogenic properties of consumerism but the impact of a consumerist society characterised by significant reductions in welfare and public spending remains to be seen. What the results of such analysis mean in terms of future demands on the police service is uncertain: while it might not be the case that a period of austerity will necessarily increase crime it might mean that the type and nature of offending will change if the pattern and extent of consumption is altered by the worsening economic climate.

As well as operating in a different environment in terms of crime, policing will be affected by heightened challenges in terms of maintaining public order. While the causes and consequences of the urban unrest of summer 2011 remain contested, if there are associations with social inequality then it seems likely that the police service will face a growing demand in terms of responding to relatively spontaneous incidents of public disorder as well as those associated with more organised political protests. The recent experiences of policing protest groups such as UK

Uncut and Occupy London (and equivalent) seem likely to loom larger on the horizon in a period of financial austerity.

Future pressure points in terms of the impact of a recession on crime and increasing challenges to public order remain difficult to predict with any certainty. Nonetheless, combined with cuts to public service provisions these suggest that internal changes within the police service will not be undertaken in a positive context in terms of the external services and functions of the police service.

FURTHER RESEARCH

The chapter has noted a number of areas on which future research activity could usefully focus. These are summarised below.

1. The nature and value of non-frontline aspects of policing in terms of their impact on offending and public trust and confidence needs to be better understood in a period in which such services are likely to face the brunt of reductions in expenditure. This could usefully include consideration of the appropriate blend of police officers, civilian staff, special constables and specialist expertise in the provision of 'middle' or 'back' office functions.
2. Studies of the impact of police numbers on offending rates have generally been conducted against a context of increasing resources. More needs to be known about the impact of trends in the opposite direction as the number of officers and other staff declines. Research in this area should include consideration of the implications for perceptions of procedural justice, police legitimacy and public trust and confidence.
3. The reassurance value of police patrol provided by staff other than fully sworn constables should be subjected to further research. It might be possible to secure public reassurance through the deployment of special constables and other staff. Positive externalities associated with patrol work – extending to trust and confidence in the criminal justice system and the rule of law in broad terms – can be better understood through research that examines public perceptions across a diverse range of communities.
4. The contribution of police to offender management, community sentences and a range of alternatives to custody needs to be further

researched. Qualitative fieldwork in this area would provide useful insight into aspects of police work that remain largely neglected in research terms.

5. The nature and extent of public demand for police services in a period of recession needs to be better understood through research work. This would provide for a body of evidence that would help the police service to make robust strategic decisions relating to ongoing expenditure cuts.

Notes

1 Although police have comparable powers under other pieces of legislation (most notably the Criminal Justice and Public Order Act 1994 and the Terrorism Act 2000) those conducted under PACE account for by far the greatest number of stop and searches.

2 Sanction detections include offences that are cleared up through a formal sanction to the offender: this includes a formal charge or summons, a caution, reprimand or final warning, an offence being taken into consideration, a Penalty Notice for Disorder, or a warning for possession of cannabis.

3 Among other things developing an effective measure of crime in areas patrolled by police is a significant challenge.

References

Bayley, D. (1994) *Police for the Future*. New York: Oxford University Press.

Bittner, E. (1974) 'Florence Nightingale in Pursuit of Willie Sutton: A Theory of the Police', in H. Jacob (ed.) *The Potential for Reform of Criminal Justice*. Beverly Hills: Sage Publications, pp. 17–40.

Bowling, B. and Philips, C. (2007) 'Disproportionate and Discriminatory: Reviewing the Evidence on Police Stop and Search'. *Modern Law Review* 70 (6) pp. 936–61.

Box, S. (1987) *Recession, Crime and Punishment*. London: Macmillan.

Bradford, B. (2011) *Police Numbers and Crime Rates – a Rapid Evidence Review*. London: HMIC.

Field, S. (1990) *Trends in Crime and their Interpretation*. Home Office Research Study 119. London: Home Office.

Finklea, K.M. (2010) *Economic Downturns and Crime*. Washington DC: Congressional Research Service.

Hall, S., Winlow, S. and Ancrum, C.(2008) *Criminal Identities and Consumer Culture: crime, exclusion and the new culture of narcissism*. Cullompton: William Publishing.

Her Majesty's Inspectorate of Constabulary (2011a) *Adapting to Austerity: A Review of Police Force and Authority Preparedness for the 2011/12–14/15 CSR Period*. London: HMIC.

Her Majesty's Inspectorate of Constabulary (2011b) *Demanding Times*. London: HMIC.

Hough, M., Jackson, J., Bradford, B., Myhill, A. and Quinton, P. (2010) 'Procedural Justice, Trust, and Institutional Legitimacy'. *Policing* 4 (3) pp. 203–10.

Innes, H. and Innes, M. (2011) *Police Presence and Public Confidence in Local Policing: An Analysis of the British Crime Survey*. Cardiff: Universities' Police Science Institute.

Lanning, T., Loader, I. and Muir, R. (2011) *Redesigning Justice – Reducing Crime Through Justice Investment*. London: IPPR.

Loader, I. and Mulcahy, A. (2003) *Policing and the Condition of England: Memory, Politics and Culture*. Oxford: Oxford University Press.

Mills, H. (2011) *Community Sentences – a Solution to Penal Excess?* London: Centre for Crime and Justice Studies.

Ministry of Justice (2009) *Story of the Prison Population 1995–2009 England and Wales*. London: Ministry of Justice.

Povey, D., Mulchandani, R., Hand, T. and Kaur Panesar, L. (2011) *Police Powers and Procedures, England and Wales 2009/10*. Home Office Statistical Bulletin 07/11. London: Home Office.

Reiner, R. (2010) *The Politics of the Police*. Oxford: Oxford University Press.

Silverman, J. (2011) *Crime, Policy and the Media – The Shaping of Criminal Justice, 1989–2010*. Abingdon: Routledge.

Tyler, T.R. (2007) *Legitimacy and Criminal Justice*. New York: Russell Sage Foundation.

4

REPLACING THE ASBO

AN OPPORTUNITY TO STEM THE FLOW INTO THE CRIMINAL JUSTICE SYSTEM

ANDREW MILLIE

INTRODUCTION

Over the past two decades there has been growing political and legislative emphasis in Britain on tackling antisocial behaviour. This chapter outlines this expanded focus on antisocial behaviour, which has resulted in a confusing array of enforcement powers, the most high profile of which was the Antisocial Behaviour Order (ASBO). Evidence is presented that a consequence of this expansion has been an increased flow of people – especially young people – into the criminal justice system and, ultimately, into prison. At a time when the prison population is at a record high the wisdom of sending people to prison for committing antisocial behaviour (rather than serious criminality) is questioned. In 2011 the Coalition government outlined proposals for a new approach to antisocial behaviour that would see legislative powers simplified and the ASBO replaced. In May 2012 the antisocial behaviour White Paper entitled *Putting Victims First* (Home Office 2012) was published. The proposals outlined in the White Paper are for England (and in some instances also apply to Wales).

In this chapter it is contended that the 2012 White Paper and the replacement of the ASBO could be an opportunity to stem the flow of people into the criminal justice system for committing antisocial behaviour. There are grounds for optimism; but the chapter also highlights areas of concern – in particular, with proposals for speedier and easier sanctions and increased discretionary powers that may result in further criminalisation of 'suspect' populations. The chapter concludes by outlining priorities for policy and research.

Antisocial behaviour has grown as an agenda, especially since the introduction of the ASBO with the Crime and Disorder Act 1998. However, it is clearly not a new problem, with records of the types of behaviours currently labelled as 'antisocial' – nuisance, unrest, incivility, persistent petty offending, etc. – stretching far back into history (e.g. Cohen 1972; Elias 1978; Pearson 1983). As Smith *et al.* (2010: 1) note, 'there has always been talk of poor public behaviour, of increasingly unruly streets and of the decline and fall of good manners'. Yet as a political construct, antisocial behaviour is a recent phenomenon (Burney 2005; Millie 2009a), occurring initially within the area of social housing policy but expanding substantially until, according to Crawford (2009: 5), 'education, parenting, youth services, city centre management, environmental planning, social housing and traditional policing increasingly [could all] be said to be governed through a preoccupation with "antisocial behaviour"'. This expansion was tracked by Waiton:

> in the 1980s a couple of articles a year were printed in the UK discussing antisocial behaviour, whereas in January 2004 alone, there were over 1000 such articles. Not even the most pessimistic social critic would suggest a parallel increase in problem behaviour.
>
> (2005: 23)

Indeed, by the mid 2000s Britain was described as an 'ASBO Nation' (Millie 2008; Squires 2008).

The origins of antisocial behaviour as a legislative and policy focus lie with the Public Order Act 1986 introduced by the then Conservative government. The label antisocial behaviour was not used in this instance; however, the Act talked of words or behaviour likely to cause 'harassment, alarm or distress'. The first time the term 'antisocial behaviour' appeared in legislation was in the Housing Act 1996 (again, brought in by the Conservative government of the time) where it was equated with 'nuisance or annoyance'. For New Labour's Crime and Disorder Act 1998, antisocial behaviour had become defined as 'harassment, alarm or distress':

> that the person has acted ... in a manner that caused or was likely to cause harassment, alarm or distress to one or more persons not of the same household as himself.
>
> (Crime and Disorder Act, 1998, section 1(a))

The term 'harassment' had only recently been covered by criminal legislation under the Protection from Harassment Act 1997, yet was seen as a constituent element of antisocial behaviour. The Crime and Disorder Act definition formed the legal basis for ASBO applications despite being both broad and vague. The vagueness was seen by some as an advantage. For instance, according to influential New Labour government advisor Louise Casey[1] (2005), 'the legal definition of antisocial behaviour is wide. And rightly so'. That said, this lack of clarity has also been criticised widely (Ashworth *et al.* 1998; Ramsey 2004; Macdonald 2006; Millie 2009a), as what causes one person harassment, alarm or distress might be different for someone else, and what is considered to be antisocial may change depending on context. For the legal definition of antisocial behaviour the phrase 'likely to cause' emphasises the subjectivity of the behaviour in question. Various influences on perceptions of antisocial behaviour have been suggested, including: direct or personal experience (Mackenzie *et al.* 2010); media influence (Wisniewska *et al.* 2006); location (Millie 2007); experiences and/or perceptions of harm (von Hirsch and Simester 2006); aesthetic expectations for the look and feel of public spaces (Millie 2008) and moral beliefs concerning civility and respect (Millie 2009b).

Behaviours commonly regarded as antisocial have been divided into three overlapping types (Millie *et al.* 2005: 9); these being 'interpersonal or malicious' (such as threats to neighbours or hoax calls), 'environmental' (such as graffiti, noise nuisance or fly-tipping) and 'restricting access to public spaces' (such as intimidation by groups of young people on the street, aggressive begging, street drinking and open drug use). The same categories are adopted in the current White Paper (Home Office 2012: 14), simplified as: personal threat antisocial behaviour, environmental antisocial behaviour and public nuisance antisocial behaviour. They are behaviours on the boundaries of criminality including some obvious crimes (e.g. drug use) and some less clearly criminal behaviours, perceived as antisocial (e.g. being intimidated by groups of youths). What seems to make these behaviours antisocial is their repetition and cumulative impact (Campbell 2002; Millie *et al.* 2005; Bottoms 2006).

NEW LABOUR LEGISLATION AND POLICY HISTORY

The New Labour government introduced a wide range of measures designed to tackle antisocial behaviour. The measures included what the 2012 White Paper (Home Office 2012: 23) has called an 'alphabet soup' of legislative powers, including ASBOs; DOs (Dispersal Orders); POs (Parenting Orders); ASBIs (Antisocial Behaviour Injunctions); DPPOs (Designated Public Place Orders); FPNs (Fixed Penalty Notices); PNDs (Penalty Notices for Disorder) and NANs (Noise Abatement Notices), etc. New Labour actively promoted the use of these powers through centrally coordinated campaigns and taskforces including: the Together campaign (2002–6); the Respect Taskforce (2006–7); the Youth Taskforce (2007–9); and the Tackling not Tolerating campaign (2009–10). The initial focus for New Labour policy was to promote the use of the various enforcement tools. As Tony Blair (2003) put it: 'We've given you the powers, and it's time to use them'. It was the language of action, of getting things done. (See Millie *et al.* 2005.)

For Blair (2003) antisocial behaviour was 'for many the number one item of concern right on their doorstep'. Yet there is evidence that the problem was overestimated (Millie 2007). While antisocial behaviour could certainly be a major concern for some and was apparent in many deprived and/or inner city neighbourhoods, for the rest of the country it was less of an issue. According to the British Crime Survey[2] only a minority saw antisocial behaviour as a major problem where they lived. When asked about seven different measures for antisocial behaviour, in 2001–2 only 18.7 per cent perceived them to be a 'fairly big' or 'very big' problem in their area. In 2002–3 this was up to 20.7 per cent, but by 2010–11 had fallen to 13.7 per cent (Innes 2011). Clearly, for the majority, antisocial behaviour was not the major concern we had been told. Furthermore, New Labour's focus on enforcing standards of behaviour through legislation may have missed the public mood. In a national survey of public opinion on antisocial behaviour respondents were asked:

> If there was more money to spend in your local area on tackling antisocial behaviour, should this be spent on tough action against perpetrators, or preventive action to deal with the causes?
>
> (Millie *et al.* 2005: 13)

Only a fifth opted for 'tough action' whereas two-thirds chose prevention (and 11 per cent said both prevention and tough action). The conclusion of this research was that there needed to be a more balanced approach to tackling antisocial behaviour and that enforcement should only be part of any solution.

Since the initial push for enforcement there has been increasing awareness among many local practitioners that a balanced approach is preferable (Hodgkinson and Tilley 2007; Clarke *et al.* 2011; Hoffman and Macdonald 2011). Often a tiered approach is adopted, with the ASBO regarded as a last resort (Millie 2009a; Hoffman and Macdonald 2011; Home Office 2011a; Crawford *et al.* 2012). Central government was also shifting in its view that enforcement was the best way to deal with antisocial behaviour. For New Labour, Ed Balls stated:

> It's a failure every time a young person gets an ASBO. It's necessary – but it's not right ... I want to live in the kind of society that puts ASBOs behind us.
>
> (Cited in Blackman 2007)

Yet, with this softer rhetoric came parallel talk of getting tough with perpetrators. Soon after Ed Balls' statement, the New Labour government was again declaring it would get tough:

> We are ... sending a clear message that the behaviour of the minority will not be tolerated at the expense of the majority. All young people should play by the rules and will be dealt with appropriately when they do not.
>
> (HM Government 2008: 17)

When the current Coalition government took office in 2010 it was clear that a new approach to antisocial behaviour was to be adopted (Millie

2011). The Home Secretary Theresa May (2010) declared that 'it's time to move beyond the ASBO'; and in the White Paper the need for a balanced approach was acknowledged:

> Practitioners have told us what works in tackling antisocial behaviour ... they know that a balanced response, incorporating elements of both enforcement and prevention is essential ... especially for the most persistent perpetrators.
>
> (Home Office 2012: 23)

Yet, emphasis was also on speedier justice and what the Home Secretary had earlier called '[s]impler sanctions, which are easier to obtain and to enforce' (May 2010). There would also be increased police discretion.

Fitting in with broader 'big society' and 'localism' agendas (e.g. Newlove 2011), the Coalition promised greater 'bottom-up' influence on policy, with local communities having greater say. For Theresa May (2010), 'as with so much [New Labour] did, their top-down, bureaucratic, gimmick-laden approach just got in the way of the police, other professionals and the people themselves from taking action'. In February 2011 the Coalition presented their plans for consultation, followed by the White Paper in May 2012.

THE ASBO

At the time of writing, in England and Wales an ASBO can be granted for anyone aged ten or above.[3] The ASBO acts as a two-step prohibition: in the first instance it is a civil order, yet breach of the order is a criminal offence (Simester and von Hirsch 2006). Following House of Lords' ruling,[4] a criminal standard of proof is required despite the ASBO being a civil order (Macdonald 2003). That said, hearsay evidence is also admissible. The mixing of civil and criminal law was controversial from the start, with, for example, Gardner *et al.* (1998) calling it 'hybrid law from hell'. The ASBO was introduced as civil law as the New Labour government saw the criminal justice system as slow and ineffective (Millie 2009a). It was assumed the complexities of the system could be bypassed, leading to speedier justice. A major concern was that by making breach a criminal offence the universality of criminal law was ignored.

Despite being in response to behaviour deemed to be antisocial, the ASBO was designed to prevent future antisocial behaviour (rather than to punish the past). In order to prevent behaviour, powerful restrictions on liberty are given in the form of various geographical, temporal, non-association and other behavioural conditions on each order issued. For instance, an ASBO recipient may be restricted on what streets can be visited and at what times. There may be restrictions on whom the recipient may associate with, or maybe on using certain forms of public transport if this is relevant to patterns of antisocial behaviour. The result is that using public transport, visiting certain streets or being out after a certain hour becomes criminalised for that individual when for the rest of society it is entirely legal activity. According to the European Commissioner for Human Rights (Gil-Robles 2005), 'such orders look rather like personalised penal codes, where non-criminal behaviour becomes criminal for individuals who have incurred the wrath of the community'. The significance of these 'personalised penal codes' is that the punishment for breach is such that adults can receive up to five years in prison, and those under 18 can be given a Detention and Training Order of up to two years. The high maximum tariff has attracted criticism for being disproportionate to the original behaviour (Ashworth 2005; Hewitt 2007). Someone on an ASBO can be imprisoned for behaviour that is legal for everyone else.

Following the Police Reform Act 2002 and the Serious Organised Crime and Police Act 2005, the scope of the ASBO was expanded with the introduction of interim ASBOs that acted as a stop-gap measure put in place prior to a full hearing, and ASBOs granted post-criminal conviction in order to prevent future criminal behaviour (also known as criminal ASBOs or CrASBOs). In effect, three main forms of ASBO were created:

- interim ASBOs;
- standalone ASBOs (also known as ASBOs on application);
- post-conviction ASBOs, or CrASBOs (there are also interim CrASBOs).

The ASBO system is supposed to include support for the perpetrator, especially if they are a young person. Following the Criminal Justice Act 2003, courts are obliged to grant an Individual Support Order (ISO) alongside an ASBO for young people aged between 10 and 17 years providing certain conditions are met. Yet since 2004, only 11 per cent of ASBOs granted to those aged 10–17 have had an ISO attached (Home Office 2011b).

THE ASBO AND IMPRISONMENT

As noted in the introduction, the extent to which ASBOs have led to imprisonment is considerable (Home Office 2011b). Evidence of this is given in Table 4.1, which shows that between 2000 and 2009, 59 per cent of adults who breached their ASBO were given custody. This represented over 4,000 people entering an already overcrowded prison system. In terms of young people on ASBOs, according to the Sentencing Guidelines Council (2008: 10), 'in most cases of breach by a young offender convicted after a trial, the appropriate sentence will be a community sentence'. However, while 46 per cent of 10–17 year olds received a community sentence as their maximum penalty, 40 per cent received custody for breach of their ASBO. This amounted to over 1,300 young people entering custody. The average sentence length for juveniles given custody was 6.3 months and 4.9 months for adults.

It is possible that some of these breaches were for criminal activity that would ordinarily receive a custodial sentence, especially following the introduction of post-conviction ASBOs or CrASBOs. In 2002 just one CrASBO was issued; however, from 2003 to 2009, on average 62 per cent of ASBOs issued were CrASBOs. From 2002 to 2009 there were over 900 standalone ASBOs per year and 1,600 CrASBOs per year (Home Office 2011b). From the available data it is not known which form of ASBO is more likely to be breached, and what the breach is for.[5] That said, a survey of Youth Offending Teams by Brogan and PA Consulting (2005) provides some limited information on reason for breach. According to this survey, for young people on ASBOs, 'in terms of the named reasons, the principal restrictions breached [were] non-association and the geographic restrictions' (Brogan and PA Consulting 2005: 26). What the available evidence shows is that many ASBOs were being breached and a large proportion of these breaches resulted in custodial sentences. Furthermore, many breaches were for behaviours that would otherwise be non-criminal (such as breaking non-association and geographic restrictions).

Table 4.1   ASBOs proven at court to have been breached by type of sentence received and age, 1 June 2000* to 31 December 2009

Age at appearance in court		By severest type of sentence received during period					Total ASBOs breached
		Discharge	Fine	Community sentence	Custody	Other**	
10–17	N=	83	158	1,505	1,332	220	3,298
	%	3	5	46	40	7	
18+	N=	114	558	1,215	4,187	1,008	7,082
	%	2	8	17	59	14	
All ages	N=	197	716	2,720	5,519	1,228	10,380
	%	2	7	26	53	12	

Note: Figures for England and Wales – excludes data for Cardiff magistrates' court for April, July and August 2008.
* 104 ASBOs were issued prior to June 2000 – however, full details of these were not recorded.
** 'Other' includes: one day in police cells, Disqualification Order, Restraining Order, Confiscation Order, Travel Restriction Order, Disqualification from Driving, and Recommendation for deportation and other miscellaneous disposals.

Source: Home Office (2011b: Table 12).

CRIMINALISING THE COMPARATIVELY TRIVIAL AND TRIVIALISING THE SERIOUSLY CRIMINAL

The imprisonment of people for behaviour that is legal for the rest of society leads to some confusion over seriousness of offences. Furthermore, the use of ASBOs and CrASBOs to cover a range of behaviours from the upsetting (but not criminal) through to the seriously criminal has stretched the term 'antisocial behaviour'. At its extremes 'antisocial behaviour' has been used to describe littering through to serious harassment and violence. In effect, the term criminalises the comparatively trivial yet also trivialises the seriously criminal (Millie 2009a).

In media and political discourse two cases are frequently cited as examples of how serious a problem antisocial behaviour is; yet both are examples of serious harassment and criminality and perhaps ought not be seen as merely 'antisocial' behaviour. These are the cases of Garry Newlove and Fiona Pilkington. In 2007 Newlove was murdered after he confronted a group of young people who had been vandalising his car. The vandalism was the type of behaviour often regarded as antisocial behaviour, although also criminal damage. The subsequent murder was clearly something more serious. In the case of Fiona Pilkington, she and her family had been repeated targets for harassment and intimidation, with 33 related calls to local police from 1997 to 2007 – with calls coming from Fiona Pilkington, her mother and from other local residents (IPCC 2009: 23). The police classed most of these incidents as antisocial behaviour or assault. Many were targeted at Pilkington's disabled daughter. According to a typical police incident log for 24 June 2004:

> The police received a call from Fiona Pilkington who reported an ongoing problem with local youths ... who were currently outside her house and were taunting her 15 year old disabled daughter. Fiona Pilkington informed the call taker she had asked the youths to move on but was verbally abused, one youth was carrying a house brick and she was unsure of the youth's intentions.
>
> (IPCC 2009: 41–2)

In 2007 Fiona Pilkington killed herself and her disabled daughter. The harassment that led to this incident was reported as antisocial behaviour (e.g. *Daily Mirror* 2009) and soon after the inquest the then Home Secretary for New Labour, Alan Johnson, stated:

> Fiona Pilkington and her daughter weren't rescued and despair led to the terrible events we've been hearing about. It's an exceptional case but it's one that should never have happened ... this case tragically exposes the insufficient response to public anxiety that still exists in some parts of the country and we need to guarantee consistent standards for dealing with antisocial behaviour everywhere.
>
> (Johnson 2009)

Rather than describing such cases as antisocial behaviour, they ought to be seen as the serious criminality that they are – in the Pilkington case, criminal harassment.[6] Furthermore this is the kind of case that ought to be flagged as 'disability hate crime' (IPCC 2009). According to the

Crown Prosecution Service (2007: 7) disability hate crime is defined as 'any incident, which is perceived to be based upon prejudice towards or hatred of the victim because of their disability or so perceived by the victim or any other person'.

Politicians still link these cases to antisocial behaviour. For example, the Coalition Home Secretary Theresa May has cited both the Newlove and Pilkington cases to demonstrate that antisocial behaviour can have serious consequences:

> Antisocial behaviour ruins neighbourhoods and can escalate into serious criminality, destroying good people's lives. People like ... Garry Newlove, who was attacked and brutally murdered after having the courage to confront a group of drunken vandals. People like Fiona Pilkington, who was terrorised and tormented by a gang of youths for many years, crying out for help on no fewer than 33 occasions before, finally, she could take no more.
>
> (May 2010)

Fortunately these cases are uncommon. The danger is that, by linking such cases to antisocial behaviour – by saying they are examples of antisocial behaviour (Alan Johnson) or that antisocial behaviour leads to more serious crime (Theresa May) – it trivialises serious crime. Conversely, the response to more frequent but less serious cases of antisocial behaviour may become ever more punitive.

COALITION PLANS FOR ANTISOCIAL BEHAVIOUR

In the foreword to the Coalition's White Paper on antisocial behaviour, Theresa May claims 'the current powers do not work as well as they should' (Home Office 2012: 3). The question is whether the proposed changes are any better. There are a number of proposals in the White Paper. Following antisocial behaviour call-handling trials (Home Office and ACPO 2012) one priority is better call handling to identify vulnerable and repeat victims in an attempt to address issues raised by the Pilkington case.[7] The White Paper also proposes the use of 'Community Harm Statements' in court and the introduction of a 'Community Trigger' for intervention, giving 'victims and communities the right to require action' (Home Office 2012: 7). Action will be guaranteed if there have been:

- three or more complaints from one individual about the same problem, where no action has been taken; or
- five individuals complaining about the same problem where no action has been taken by relevant agencies (Home Office 2012: 19).

The proposal fits in with the Coalition's emphases on the 'big society' and localism and is also a clear response to the Pilkington case. In the case of vulnerable victims, 'the trigger can be initiated by a third party' (Home Office 2012: 19) such as a carer or relative. Further emphasising the Coalition's focus on local solutions, the White Paper promises use of restorative approaches in new 'Neighbourhood Justice Panels' involving community representatives[8] in cases where a criminal sanction is not required. The aim of the panel is to agree an outcome, including reparation to the victim (Home Office 2012: 22). Other proposals include tackling underlying issues of antisocial behaviour, improved measurement of antisocial behaviour, increased police discretion and speedier evictions for antisocial tenants.

In 2011 the Coalition also promised a 'radical streamlining' of antisocial behaviour powers (Home Office 2011a: 5). According to the 2012 White Paper, this simplification will result in replacing 19 enforcement measures with six. The headline is the demise of the ASBO (and associated CrASBO). The standalone ASBO will be replaced by a 'Crime Prevention Injunction' (CPI) whereas the CrASBO will become a 'Criminal Behaviour Order' (CBO). There are elements of political rebranding (Millie 2011), in that the ASBO was New Labour's baby and therefore anything that was not an ASBO was required. However, just a glance at New Labour's 'alphabet soup' of measures hints that simplification may be a good thing. The full list of changes is outlined in Table 4.2.

REPLACING THE ASBO WITH A CRIME PREVENTION INJUNCTION (CPI)

The replacement for the standalone ASBO is the proposed 'Crime Prevention Injunction' (CPI). The CPI also replaces the Antisocial Behaviour Injunction (ASBI).[9] Similar to the ASBI, the test for antisocial behaviour will be whether 'the person has engaged in conduct

Table 4.2   Proposed coalition government changes to ASB enforcement

Existing system	Proposed changes
ASBO on conviction (CrASBO) Drinking Banning Order (DBO) on conviction	Criminal Behaviour Order (CBO)
ASBO on application (standalone ASBO) Anti-Social Behaviour Injunction (ASBI) Drinking Banning Order (DBO) on application Individual Support Order (ISO) Intervention Order	Crime Prevention Injunction (CPI)
Litter Clearing Notice Street Litter Control Notice Defacement Removal Notices	Community Protection Notice (CPN)
Designated Public Place Order (DPPO) Gating Order Dog Control Orders	Community Protection Order (CPO Open Space)
Premises Closure Order Crack House Closure Order Noisy Premises Closure Order s161 Closure Order	Community Protection Order (CPO Closure)
Dispersal Order (DO) (s30 of the 2003 ASB Act) Direction to leave (s27 2006 Violent Crime Reduction Act)	Direction Power

Source: Home Office (2012: 46–7).

which is capable of causing nuisance or annoyance to any person' (Home Office 2012: 48). It is a shift from the ASBO's focus on 'harassment, alarm or distress'; however, 'nuisance or annoyance' are similarly difficult to define and highly subjective.

Like the ASBI and the ASBO, the CPI will be a civil power. According to the White Paper, civil law is useful as it gives the police 'an alternative to criminal charges in cases where it is difficult to prove that an offence had been committed or where victims are afraid to give evidence' (Home Office 2012: 24). This is very much like the justification originally given for the ASBO. However, as noted, following the House of Lords' ruling, a criminal standard of proof is required for an ASBO (despite being civil law). The CPI will be secured using a civil burden of proof (balance of probabilities rather than beyond reasonable doubt). The aim is for CPIs to be granted quickly, 'in a matter of days or even hours' (Home Office 2012). For an ASBO, a breach is a criminal offence requiring a criminal standard of proof. For the CPI, breach will be treated as contempt of court, again in an attempt to provide speedy justice. The emphasis on speed may be problematic as it puts in danger procedural checks that make a fair and proportionate response more likely. For instance, according to Tyler (2006) the benefits of procedural justice are in processes that are seen to be both fair and respectful resulting in greater trust in the justice system. Emphasising speedy justice may make this more difficult.

A benefit of the approach adopted for the CPI is that it will – ordinarily – be civil throughout. Breach of an ASBO leaves the perpetrator with a criminal record and the prospect of imprisonment. According to the 2012 White Paper, 'sanctions for breach [of a CPI] are civil not criminal, which prevents people getting a criminal record unnecessarily' (Home Office 2012: 46). Confusingly, it is also claimed that 'breach by an adult would be contempt of court, punishable in the usual way for the County Court by up to two years in prison or an unlimited fine'[10] (Home Office 2012). Presumably, receiving a prison sentence will be for criminal contempt rather than civil? For juveniles aged 10 to 17, the punishment options for breach would include:

> curfew, activity or supervision requirement, or as a very last resort, repeated breach causing serious harm could result in custody for up to three months for someone aged 14 to 17 years old.
>
> (Home Office 2012: 49)

Again, custody is presumably restricted to breaches that will be classed as criminal contempt rather than civil. It was acknowledged that the appropriateness of custody for breach was an issue raised during con-sultation. However, it was stated that the government 'is committed to ensuring the judiciary have tough powers at their disposal on breach, but also that custody is used in a proportionate way' (Home Office 2012).

To make the injunctions widely available a long list of state and non-state agencies will be able to apply for a CPI, including the police, British Transport Police, local authorities, NHS Protect, Transport for London, the Environment Agency and 'private registered providers of social housing'. This is similar to an ASBO (and ASBI); and the inclu-sion of private companies/charities – such as social housing providers – continues to blur boundaries between state and non-state organisations that may have quite different priorities. Ease of use is further emphasised by minimising need for wider consultation with other agencies, with for-mal consultation being restricted to cases involving under-18s – which will need to involve the local Youth Offending Team. Interim injunc-tions will be available requiring no consultation.

Despite maybe too much emphasis on ease of use, speed and tough-ness, the proposals are encouraging as they should result in fewer people entering the criminal justice system and will hopefully result in prison being restricted to those committing criminal (rather than merely anti-social) activity. Furthermore, positive requirements attached to the CPI will include support for the recipient – replacing the underused Individual Support Order (ISO). However, just like the ASBO, the CPI will have powerful restrictions on the person's liberty in the form of 'any prohibitions or requirements that assist in the prevention of future anti-social behaviour' (Home Office 2012: 48). As with the ASBO (Macdonald 2006), the risk is that these will be disproportionate or ill thought through.

REPLACING THE CrASBO WITH A CRIMINAL BEHAVIOUR ORDER (CBO)

The Criminal Behaviour Order (CBO) is very similar to the CrASBO it is designed to replace,[11] in that it will be a civil order available following criminal conviction. Like the CPI, the only formal consultation required will be with the local Youth Offending Team for someone under 18. An interim order will also be available and, like the CrASBO, powerful restrictions on liberty will be available if it is thought the order 'will assist in the prevention of harassment, alarm or distress being caused to any member of the public' (Home Office 2012: 49). Presumably 'harassment, alarm or distress' defines a CBO, whereas 'nuisance and annoyance' defines a CPI as an indication of more deleterious behaviour. Being more serious, breach of the order will be a criminal offence, making it a two-step prohibition (Simester and von Hirsch 2006), with all the problems of blurring civil and criminal law as identified for the ASBO and CrASBO. The maximum sentence will be five years in custody (Home Office 2012: 50). An improvement on the old system is that positive requirements will be integral to the Order. However, it seems likely the Order will be used in similar circumstances to the CrASBO and will have minimal impact on reducing the use of imprisonment. That said, by labelling it a Criminal Behaviour Order (rather than merely antisocial) the issue of trivialising criminality identified earlier is potentially lessened. Yet by restricting a person's liberty and imposing various spatial, temporal, associational and other conditions, the CBO applies also to wider behaviour that is not necessarily criminal. The blurring of criminal and antisocial behaviour continues.

INCREASED POLICE DISCRETION

When introduced in 2003 the Dispersal Order was controversial. The Order defines geographical boundaries where antisocial behaviour is thought to be particularly problematic and where a police officer in uniform can disperse groups of two or more people if their 'presence or behaviour ... resulted, or is likely to result, in any members of the public being intimidated, harassed, alarmed or distressed (Antisocial Behaviour Act 2003 section 30(3)). The restrictions are not only on behaviour, but also on *presence* which is deemed unacceptable, or *likely* to be problematic. The police officer's perception is clearly important. The focus on presence also has clear human rights concerns. According to Crawford (2009: 19), Dispersal Orders 'escalate intervention and draw young people more rapidly into the orbit of formal youth justice processes'.

With the 2012 White Paper, the Dispersal Order will be replaced by increased police discretion by strengthening 'Direction to Leave' powers. The Coalition's consultation document claimed the new power would 'be dependent on actual behaviour, rather than an individual's presence in a particular area' (Home Office 2011a: 22). The Dispersal Order's emphasis on 'presence' was removed for the 2012 White Paper; however, subjectivity remains with a focus on behaviour that is 'contributing or is likely to contribute' (Home Office 2012: 50) to problematic behaviour. According to the White Paper:

> [the test would be] that the constable has reasonable grounds for suspecting that the person's behaviour is contributing or is likely to contribute to antisocial behaviour or crime or disorder in the area and that the direction is necessary.
>
> (Home Office 2012: 50)

The new power will apply for 48 hours. It shifts from the Dispersal Order's control of groups (two or more people) to control of any individual deemed likely to be problematic. The power also broadens to any public location with '[n]o designation or consultation' (Home Office 2012: 50) required, thereby having the potential to criminalise even more young people. The power would similarly apply to 'common areas of private land with the landowner's consent' (Home Office 2012: 51). Further powers include the handover of items such as alcohol and the return of children under 16 to their home. The power to return children to their home was in the original Dispersal Order legislation (section 30(6)), although many forces have been reluctant to use the power[12] (Crawford and Lister 2007; Millie 2009a).

The risk with the Coalition plans is in the extension of an already controversial power to remove any individual in any location at any time. Failure to comply with the police's 'Direction to Leave' will be a criminal offence with the prospect of a fine or three months in custody. Failure to hand over confiscated items will also be a criminal offence, with failure to comply possibly leading to a fine or one month in custody. Usage date will be recorded, so some monitoring of implementation will be possible; however, the disproportionate targeting/profiling of certain populations is a distinct possibility. The police do not have a great record with the use of existing stop-and-search powers, being more frequently used against black and minority ethnic groups (Bowling and Phillips 2007). The risk is that 'usual suspect' populations will be targeted, moved on or banished from public spaces (Beckett and Herbert 2010), including groups of young people, black and minority ethnic populations, the street homeless and street sex workers. This becomes even more likely as the power will be available, not only if the person's behaviour 'is contributing', but also if it is thought 'likely to contribute to anti-social behaviour or crime or disorder' (Home Office 2012: 50). Following the August 2011 riots the temptation to give the police such a power must have been strong. However, the risks of disproportionate use are also strong.

CONCLUSION

The focus for this chapter has been antisocial behaviour legislation and the Coalition government's proposals for change. It is argued that a result of New Labour's antisocial behaviour legislation has been an increased flow of people – especially young people – into the criminal justice system by criminalising behaviour that for the rest of society is legal. That many ASBO recipients have ended up in custody for breaching their conditions is cause for concern, especially when the prison population is at a record high. Other antisocial behaviour interventions have worked in a similar criminalising fashion.

The Coalition's 2012 White Paper and plans to replace the ASBO are an opportunity to stem this flow of people into the criminal justice system. There are some grounds for optimism. The White Paper proposes that 'custody is used in a proportionate way' (Home Office 2012: 49) and a balanced approach is emphasised incorporating prevention, restorative approaches and support. The replacement of the standalone ASBO with the CPI is also encouraging as it is ordinarily civil throughout and, according to the White Paper, 'prevents people getting a criminal record unnecessarily' (Home Office 2012: 46). However, the emphasis on speedier and easier sanctions is a concern, especially when powerful restrictions on liberty that come with a CPI are considered. The continued muddling of civil and criminal law in relation to breach – as criminal or civil contempt of court – would also need to be clarified. As for the replacement of the CrASBO (the CBO), the relabelling as 'criminal behaviour' rather than 'antisocial' marks the more serious nature of such offences. However, the minimal other changes to this order will likely result in at least as many people gaining custody through breach of conditions.

The other major development is the increase in police discretion with the introduction of universal police 'Direction to Leave' powers (rather than the spatially restricted Dispersal Orders). If Dispersal Orders were controversial on human rights grounds, then the 'Direction to Leave' powers are going to be even more so. There is a strong risk that 'usual suspects' will be targeted as being '*likely to* contribute to antisocial behaviour or crime or disorder in the area' (Home Office 2012: 50, emphasis added). In daily confrontations between suspect populations and the police – or on occasion between protestors and the police – it is not difficult to imagine cases where the direction to leave an area will be refused – leading to arrest, a criminal record and possible imprisonment.

The 2012 White Paper contains some good news in that it is a simplification of the existing system and that it is claimed the CPI will 'prevent people getting a criminal record unnecessarily' (Home Office 2012: 46). However, other proposals – in particular the CBO and universal direction powers – continue the criminalisation process and will likely result in many people being drawn into the criminal justice system and ultimately into prison. It is worth remembering that, according to the British Crime Survey, it is only a minority of people who see antisocial behaviour as a major problem where they live. The criminalisation and imprisonment of people for criminal activity (as is the case for the CBO) is at least understandable. It is less justifiable for cases where the behaviour is not criminal but antisocial, or for that matter where someone is thought likely to contribute to antisocial behaviour (or crime or disorder) in an area. When the 2012 White Paper becomes law, these are issues that need consideration.

FURTHER RESEARCH

As the new antisocial behaviour policy and legislative landscape evolves, areas for policy development and further research will become apparent. However, some important priorities can already be identified:

1. If the flow of people into the criminal justice system is to be stemmed then one important area for policy development and research is an informal restorative justice approach to tackling antisocial behaviour. This is proposed by the 2012 White Paper for low-level

antisocial behaviour. It will be useful to identify where lessons can be learnt and whether there is scope to adopt such an approach more broadly.

2. The Coalition has emphasised local solutions to problems through the 'big society' and localism agendas. As part of this approach, voluntary and community groups are encouraged to be more proactively involved in local issues. A policy and research priority will be to assess the efficacy of such an approach for tackling antisocial behaviour and whether there is a risk that certain 'outsider' populations might be disproportionately targeted.

3. When ASBOs were introduced, Ashworth *et al.* (1998: 9) were concerned that they could be used as 'weapons against other unpopular types. Such as ex-offenders, "loners", "losers", "weirdoes", prostitutes, travellers, addicts, those subject to rumour and gossip, those regarded by the police or neighbours as having "got away" with crimes, etc.' It is important to consider which groups are most likely to be recipients of antisocial behaviour interventions and to identify any criminalising consequences. There has been limited research that has considered the ethnicity (Isal 2006) and social and mental health (BIBIC 2007; Matthews *et al.* 2007; Nixon *et al.* 2007) backgrounds of ASBO recipients. A comprehensive investigation will be needed for the new powers when introduced.

4. As noted, one of the motivations for introducing the ASBO was for speedy justice, as a way of bypassing 'protracted court process, bureaucracy and hassle' (Blair 2003). The Coalition plans are similarly for speedy justice; yet much of the 'bureaucracy and hassle' is there to ensure fairness. A procedural justice approach may be a useful policy alternative to be investigated, including a procedural justice approach to police encounters with young people.

5. The Coalition proposes increased emphasis on police discretion through greater use of 'Direction' powers. In relation to Dispersal Order powers, Crawford (2009: 17) has noted that 'the discretionary nature of the powers leaves considerable scope for inconsistent implementation which further served to undermine young people's perceptions of fairness'. With such an emphasis on police officers' subjective interpretation, research into police perceptions of antisocial behaviour will be useful for policy.

Notes

1   Casey went on to head New Labour's antisocial behaviour-centred Respect Task Force (Millie 2009b). Although New Labour left office in 2010, Casey's influence continues, initially employed by the Coalition as 'victim's tsar', but more recently in 2011 to head the government response to the August 2011 riots and looting in a somewhat stigmatising Troubled Families Programme (see Casey 2012).

2   The BCS has since been more accurately renamed as the Crime Survey for England and Wales (CSEW).

3   In Scotland it is anyone aged 12 or above.

4   Clingham and McCann [2002] UKHL 39.

5   Breach could be for breaking ASBO conditions and/or committing a criminal offence.

6   The 1997 Protection from Harassment Act has already been mentioned.

7   Multi-Agency Risk Assessment Conferences (MARACs) are also proposed to improve inter-agency working.

8   It is not clear who will sit on these panels and who the 'community representatives' will be.

9   Also replacing the Drinking Banning Order on application, Intervention Order and Individual Support Order.

10   Contempt of Court Act 1981.

11   The CBO will also replace the Drinking Banning Order (on conviction).

12   The power was also legally challenged, albeit unsuccessfully (Dobson 2006).

References

Ashworth, A. (2005) *Sentencing and Criminal Justice* (Fourth Edition). Cambridge: Cambridge University Press.

Ashworth, A., Gardner, J., Morgan, R., Smith, A., von Hirsch, A. and Wasik, M. (1998) 'Neighbouring on the oppressive: the government's "Anti-Social Behaviour Order" proposals'. *Criminal Justice* 16(1) pp. 7–14.

Beckett, K. and Herbert, S. (2010) 'Penal boundaries: banishment and the expansion of punishment'. *Law & Social Inquiry* 35(1) pp. 1–38.

BIBIC (2007) *BIBIC Research on ASBOs and Young People with Learning Difficulties and Mental Health Problems*. Bridgwater: British Institute for Brain Injured Children.

Blackman, O. (2007) 'Asbos are a failure'. *Daily Mirror*, 27 July. Available at: www.mirror.co.uk/news/top-stories/2007/07/27/asbos-are-a-failure-115875 19528541 [accessed July 2012].

Blair, T. (2003) *PM Speech on Anti-Social Behaviour*. QEII Centre, London, 14 October.

Bottoms, A.E. (2006) 'Incivilities, offence and social order in residential communities', in A. von Hirsch and A.P. Simester (eds) *Incivilities: Regulating Offensive Behaviour*. Oxford: Hart Publishing pp. 239–80.

Bowling, B. and Phillips, C. (2007) 'Disproportionate and discriminatory: reviewing the evidence on police stop and search'. *Modern Law Review* 70(6) pp. 936–961.

Brogan, D. and PA Consulting (2005) *Anti-Social Behaviour Orders: An Assessment of Current Management Information Systems and the Scale of Anti-Social Behaviour Order Breaches Resulting in Custody*. London: Youth Justice Board.

Burney, E. (2005) *Making People Behave: Anti-Social Behaviour, Politics and Policy*. Cullompton: Willan.

Campbell, S. (2002) *A Review of Anti-Social Behaviour Orders*. Home Office Research Study 236. London: Home Office.

Casey, L. (2005) (debate with Shami Chakrabarti) 'Mob justice or yob control?'. *Guardian*, 19 March. Available at: www.society.guardian.co.uk [accessed March 2012].

Casey, L. (2012) *Listening to Troubled Families*. London: Department for Communities and Local Government.

Clarke, A., Williams, K., Wydall, S., Gray, P., Liddle, M. and Smith, A. (2011) *Describing and Assessing Interventions to Address Anti-Social Behaviour: Key Findings from a Study of ASB Practice*. Home Office Research Report 51, London: Home Office.

Cohen, S. (1972) *Folk Devils and Moral Panics: The Creation of Mods and Rockers*. London: MacGibbon and Kee Ltd.

Crawford, A. (2009) 'Criminalising sociability through anti-social behaviour legislation: dispersal powers, young people and the police'. *Youth Justice* 9(1) pp. 5–26.

Crawford, A. and Lister, S.C. (2007) *The Use and Impact of Dispersal Orders: Sticking Plasters and Wake-Up Calls*. Bristol: Policy Press.

Crawford, A., Lewis, A. and Traynor, P. (2012) *Anti-Social Behaviour Interventions with Young People*. Leeds: University of Leeds.

Crown Prosecution Service (2007) *Disability Hate Crime: CPS Policy for Prosecuting Cases of Disability Hate Crime*. London: CPS.

Daily Mirror (2009) 'Police apologise after Fiona Pilkington inquest verdict criticises their failure'. Available at: www.mirror.co.uk [accessed July 2012].

Dobson, N. (2006) Government: anti-social behaviour – removing young persons, Pinset Masons Update, June. Available at: www.pinsetmasons.com/mediafiles/244814425.pdf [accessed July 2012].

Elias, N. (1978) *The Civilising Process, Vol. 1: The History of Manners* (translated by E. Jephcott). Oxford: Blackwell.

Gardner, J., von Hirsch, A., Smith, A.T.H., Morgan, R., Ashworth, A. and Wasik, N. (1998) 'Clause 1 – the hybrid law from hell?'. *Criminal Justice Matters* 31 pp. 25–7.

Gil-Robles, A. (2005) *Report by Mr Alvaro Gil-Robles, Commissioner for Human Rights, on His Visit to the United Kingdom*, 4–12 November 2004. Office of the Commissioner for Human Rights, 8 June 2005, CommDH(2005)6, Strasbourg: Council of Europe.

Hewitt, D. (2007) 'Bovvered? A legal perspective on the ASBO'. *Journal of Forensic and Legal Medicine* 14(6) pp. 355–63.

HM Government (2008) *Youth Crime Action Plan*. London: HM Government.

Hodgkinson, S. and Tilley, N. (2007) 'Policing anti-social behaviour: constraints, dilemmas and opportunities'. *Howard Journal of Criminal Justice* 46(4) pp. 385–400.

Hoffman, S. and Macdonald, S. (2011) 'Tackling youth anti-social behaviour in devolving Wales: a study of the tiered approach in Swansea'. *Youth Justice* 11(2) pp. 150–67.

Home Office (2011a) *More Effective Responses to Anti-Social Behaviour*. London: Home Office.

Home Office (2011b) *Anti-Social Behaviour Order Statistics – England and Wales 2009*. Available at: www.homeoffice.gov.uk/publications/science-research-statistics/research-statistics/crime-research/asbo-stats-england-wales-2009/ [accessed July 2012].

Home Office (2012) *Putting Victims First: More Effective Responses to Anti-Social Behaviour* Cm8367. London: The Stationery Office.

Home Office and ACPO (2012) *Focus on the Victim: Summary Report on the ASB Call Handling Trials*. London: Home Office.

Innes, J. (2011) 'Public perceptions', in R. Chaplin, J. Flatley and K. Smith (eds) *Crime in England and Wales 2010–11: Findings from the British Crime Survey and Police Recorded Crime (2nd Edition)*. Home Office Statistical Bulletin 10/11. London: Home Office pp. 83–100.

IPCC (2009) *IPCC Report into the Contact between Fiona Pilkington and Leicestershire Constabulary 2004–7*. London: Independent Police Complaints Commission.

Isal, S. (2006) *Equal Respect: ASBOs and Race Equality*. London: Runnymede Trust.

Johnson, A. (2009) *Alan Johnson's Speech to Labour Conference*, 29 September. Available at: www.labour.org.uk/alan-johnson-speech-conference [accessed July 2012].

Macdonald, S. (2003) 'The nature of the Anti-Social Behaviour Order – R (McCann & Others) v Crown Court at Manchester'. *The Modern Law Review* 66(4) pp. 630–9.

Macdonald, S. (2006) 'A suicidal woman, roaming pigs and a noisy trampolinist: refining the ASBO's definition of "anti-social behaviour"'. *The Modern Law Review* 69(2) pp. 183–213.

Mackenzie, S., Bannister, J., Flint, J., Parr, S., Millie, A. and Fleetwood, J. (2010) *The Drivers of Perceptions of Anti-Social Behaviour*. Home Office Research Report 34. London: Home Office.

Matthews, R., Easton, H., Briggs, D. and Pease, K. (2007) *Assessing the Use and Impact of Anti-Social Behaviour Orders*. Bristol: The Policy Press.

May, T. (2010) *Moving Beyond the ASBO – Speech at the Coin Street Community Centre in London*, 28 July. Available at: www.homeoffice.gov.uk/media-centre/speeches/beyond-the-asbo [accessed July 2012].

Millie, A. (2007) 'Looking for anti-social behaviour'. *Policy & Politics* 35(4) pp. 611–27.

Millie, A. (2008) 'Anti-social behaviour, behavioural expectations and an urban aesthetic'. *British Journal of Criminology* 48(3) pp. 379–94.

Millie, A. (2009a) *Anti-Social Behaviour*. Maidenhead: Open University Press.

Millie, A. (ed.) (2009b) *Securing Respect: Behavioural Expectations and Anti-Social Behaviour in the UK*. Bristol: The Policy Press.

Millie, A. (2011) *Big society, small government: The British coalition government and tackling anti-social behaviour*. Crime Prevention and Community Safety, 13(4) pp. 284–87.

Millie, A., Jacobson, J., McDonald, E. and Hough, M. (2005) *Anti-Social Behaviour Strategies: Finding a Balance*. Bristol: The Policy Press.

Newlove, Baroness H. (2011) *Our Vision for Safe and Active Communities*. London: Department for Communities and Local Government.

Nixon, J., Hodge, N., Parr, S., Willis, B. and Hunter, C. (2007) 'Anti-social behaviour and disability in the UK'. *People, Place & Policy Online* 2(1) pp. 37–47.

Pearson, G. (1983) *Hooligan: A History of Respectable Fears*. Basingstoke: Macmillan.

Ramsay, P. (2004) 'What is anti-social behaviour?'. *Criminal Law Review*, pp. 908–25.

Sentencing Guidelines Council (2008) *Breach of an Anti-Social Behaviour Order: Definitive Guidance.* London: SGC.

Simester, A.P. and von Hirsch, A. (2006) 'Regulating offensive conduct through two-step prohibitions', in A. von Hirsch and A.P. Simester (eds) *Incivilities: Regulating Offensive Behaviour.* Oxford: Hart Publishing pp. 173–94.

Smith, P., Phillips, T.L. and King, R.D. (2010) *Incivility: The Rude Stranger in Everyday Life.* Cambridge: Cambridge University Press.

Squires, P. (ed.) (2008) *ASBO Nation: The Criminalisation of Nuisance.* Bristol: The Policy Press.

Tyler, T.R. (2006) *Why People Obey the Law.* Princeton NJ: Princeton University Press.

von Hirsch, A. and Simester, A.P. (2006) *Incivilities: Regulating Offensive Behaviour.* Oxford: Hart Publishing.

Waiton, S. (2005) 'The politics of antisocial behaviour', in C. O'Malley and S. Waiton (eds) *Who's Antisocial? New Labour and the Politics of Antisocial Behaviour*, Institute of Ideas Occasional Paper No. 2. London: Academy of Ideas Ltd pp. 23–36.

Wisniewska, L., Harris, L. and Oliver, C. (2006) *The Voice behind the Hood: Young People's Views on Anti-Social Behaviour, the Media and Older People.* London: YouthNet and the British Youth Council.

5

THE INFLUENCE OF SENTENCING AND THE COURTS ON THE PRISON POPULATION

NICOLA PADFIELD

INTRODUCTION

The Howard League's ambition to 'stem the flow' of people into prison is to be welcomed: prison may have certain useful functions (protecting individuals or the public from dangerous people, punishing people, sometimes even giving people time to address issues in their lives which have led to offending, etc.) but it is also very expensive and damaging. It is widely accepted that helping or training people to lead law-abiding lives within a custodial setting is often less effective than offering similar support within the community. This chapter explores the journey that suspects take through the criminal justice system towards prison, identifying key decisions and stages. Clearly the courts are central in this – indeed, most people are sent to prison by the courts. However, this chapter also identifies decisions by others which add to the prison population, most obviously the power of the executive to recall people to prison (and then to re-release them, or not). The chapter concludes by identifying the key issues and pressure points, as well as potential areas for research. Such a focus may help to identify ways to 'stem the flow', or indeed to identify alternative outcomes which could not only reduce the prison population but also more effectively reduce reoffending.

GATEKEEPING DECISIONS

Both the police and the Crown Prosecution Service (CPS) have an important role in the sentencing process. This is due not only to their huge discretionary powers in relation to deciding who to arrest and who to charge, but also in relation to decisions about how to collect and present the evidence and which charges to pursue. The subject of plea bargains has been under-explored in the English literature but it is clear that a system which measures the CPS's 'successful' outcomes as those which lead to a guilty plea or a conviction may result in many negotiated pleas.[1]

Whilst 'stemming the flow' of people into prisons, the wider picture also needs to be explored – for example the role of preliminary players in shaping the courtroom decision-making. In practice, a 'basis of plea' (BOP) can be offered at an early stage in an investigation, or 'at the door' of the court. The judge or magistrate has no involvement.[2] When it comes to sentencing, it must be made clear to the court on what basis any plea has been advanced and accepted. Where a defendant pleads guilty to a charge or charges, the court should always seek a written basis of plea.[3] If the prosecution disputes this version, and different versions of the facts may significantly affect sentence, then the court is entitled to (indeed, should) hear evidence to determine what happened, and then sentence on that basis. This has resulted in a complex case law (*Newton* (1982) 4 Cr App R (S) 388; *Underwood* [2005] 1 Cr App R 13). These preliminary negotiation processes have not been subject to detailed research in recent times in England and Wales.

Prosecutors also make vital decisions about multiple offending: how to divide up the offending behaviour into various charges, how many charges to put on an indictment, whether to include additional offences as 'TICs' (offences taken into consideration) and so on. The prosecution role at sentencing hearings has also shifted subtly in recent years, largely as a result of gentle pressure from the Court of Appeal (see, for example, *James* [2007] EWCA Crim 1906). Most notably, prosecutors now have a duty to offer assistance to the sentencing court in reaching its decision as to the appropriate sentence by drawing the court's attention to the following:

1. the aggravating or mitigating factors in the prosecution case;
2. any Victim Personal Statement;[4]
3. where appropriate, evidence of the impact of the offending on a community;[5]
4. any statutory provisions, sentencing guidelines or guideline cases which may assist;[6] and
5. any relevant statutory provisions relating to ancillary orders (such as antisocial behaviour orders, compensation orders, disqualifications, etc.).

Prosecutors often now also make submissions, in the light of all the above factors, as to the sentencing range within which the current offence falls. The Code for Crown Prosecutors goes so far as to say that:

> in all complex cases or where there is the potential for misunderstanding, the prosecutor must set out in writing the aggravating and mitigating factors that he or she will outline when informing the court of the case in the sentencing hearing. In all other cases, this approach should be considered and undertaken if it will be of benefit to the court or the public to understand the case.

There has been no recent research into how often this is done in practice. It would also be interesting to see the different role of different prosecutors: it is likely that the CPS's own staff perform these functions differently from agency prosecutors, and the senior QC differently from junior counsel. Practice in magistrates' courts is very different from practice in the Crown Court. Are there regional and local variations? As well, many people are prosecuted by non-CPS agencies (see Padfield 2008: chapter 4) and the sentencing process in these cases may well be subtly different.

Defence solicitors also have a pivotal role here, particularly in helping a client 'negotiate' a sensible plea. When it comes to the sentencing hearing, they have traditionally played a greater role than the prosecution, but often it appears, somewhat paradoxically, that, as the prosecutor's role appears in recent years to have grown, so the defence case often seems to have fossilised into a rather routine 'plea in mitigation'. Shapland (1981) gave a very useful analysis, but there has been little later work. Different barristers and solicitors are likely to influence sentences in different ways. Also very important is the role of the Probation Service, in particular by way of pre-sentence reports, which may have a strong influence on decision-making. But there are other 'players' too, such as the rather invisible but increasingly influential Multi-Agency Public Protection Arrangements (MAPPA) (see Wood and Kemshall 2007).

I have so far (as do most commentators and practitioners) ignored the role of the defendant. Clearly, their culpability is likely to be judged in many ways by their demeanour on arrest, in interview and in court (as well as, of course, by what they have actually done). More research here, in particular into perceptions of the system by those who have committed offences, would be invaluable.

WHICH COURT AND WHICH SENTENCERS?

Since magistrates' sentencing powers are limited (currently up to a six-month sentence of imprisonment for a single offence, and in most cases a maximum fine of £5,000), it is highly relevant to consider which court will decide someone's sentence. If a case is decided in the Crown Court, a judge can sentence people to anything up to and including life imprisonment and/or an unlimited fine. All crimes are divided into one of three categories: summary crimes are dealt with in the magistrates' court and indictable-only offences in the Crown Court. A surprising number of cases are 'either way' (burglary, theft, etc.), and may be tried in either the Crown or magistrates' courts. It is important to notice the way these cases are allocated between the two courts. First, the defendant has a right to trial by jury. His decision whether to opt for trial by jury (doubtless heavily influenced by his solicitor or barrister) will have a large impact on any future sentence: whilst the jury may be more likely to acquit than a magistrates' court, the ultimate sentence if he is convicted is likely to be higher in the Crown Court. Second, magistrates may refuse jurisdiction even if the defendant would prefer trial by magistrates. The Sentencing Council has recently drafted a guideline designed to encourage a consistent approach to decisions as to allocation to ensure that each person is tried and, in the event of conviction, 'tried at the appropriate level' (see page 18C of the updated Magistrates' Courts Sentencing Guidelines, effective from 11 June 2012). The Guidelines suggest that:

in general, either way offences should be tried summarily unless it is likely that the court's sentencing powers will be insufficient. Its powers will generally be insufficient if the outcome is likely to result in a sentence in excess of six months imprisonment for a single offence. The court should assess the likely sentence in the light of the facts alleged by the prosecution case, taking into account all aspects of the case including those advanced by the defence.

This is a significant change in emphasis, moving away from the previous position of taking the prosecution case at its highest and instead directing courts to take all aspects of the case into account. Clearly designed to keep even more cases in the magistrates' court, this development should be monitored.

The vast majority of sentences continue to be imposed by the lay magistracy. Lay magistrates sit without juries, normally in panels of three, and decide guilt as well as sentence. There have been numerous studies of the lay magistracy (see, for example, Morgan and Russell 2000; Seago *et al.* 2000; Liberty 2002) but this work needs to be updated to be particularly useful for current debates. Particularly worrying is the poor retention rate for ethnic minority magistrates (Vennard 2004). Recent decades have seen the closure of many magistrates' courts and the advantages of so-called 'local' justice need to be carefully scrutinised. On 1 April 2011, there were 26,966 magistrates in post. Any study of sentencing decisions must of course study the sentencer. The characteristics of the typical magistrate have remained relatively unchanged over the years, and as long as they remain unpaid, they are likely to remain middle-class and middle-aged. There are also a certain number of salaried lawyer District Judges (Magistrates' Court) sitting in the magistrates' courts: 137 in 2011, as well as 143 Deputy District Judges (Magistrates' Court). The District Judges (formally known as stipendiary magistrates) are enormously powerful, sitting on their own and deciding guilt as well as sentence.

In the Crown Court, sentencing is likely to be done by a circuit judge (there were 665 circuit judges in post in April 2011) though Crown Court trial and sentencing work is also carried out by many part-time judges (Recorders). The sentencing decisions of the 1,221 Recorders would be interesting to analyse: most of them are practising barristers or solicitors who usually sit as judges between three and six weeks a year, and their usual professional practice may not be in criminal law at all. Finally, very serious crimes such as murder may well be tried by High

Court judges, and these senior judges are responsible for a significant number of the lengthiest sentences imposed every year. It is of course worth questioning the characteristics of these judges, as well as their gender and ethnicity, in order to consider how and if this affects their decision-making.

THE LEGAL FRAMEWORK

The current framework of English sentencing law is too complex and changes too frequently. Many people think that the judge has a wide uncontrolled discretion but the reality is very different: this discretion is constrained by a very detailed mixture of law and other guidelines. Indeed, the judge or magistrate has much less discretion than is often imagined. There are a few mandatory sentences, set about with complex details: not only murder, but also a seven-year mandatory sentence for repeat Class A drug dealing, three years for repeat burglars, etc. Parliament has legislated the maximum sentence for offences created by Parliament and a statutory maximum for magistrates' courts, where, as we have seen, the vast majority of cases are tried. There are many statutory rules (for example, section 143(3) Criminal Justice Act 2003, which provides that it is mandatory to treat the commission of an offence on bail as an aggravating factor in assessing the seriousness of that offence; or section 144 Criminal Justice Act 2003, which is the current formulation of the discount for guilty pleas). There was an excellent attempt at consolidation on the Powers of the Criminal Courts (Sentencing) Act 2000, but it was significantly amended within weeks. The Criminal Justice Act 2003 brought huge changes but no codification, and there have been many changes since then, made in the Violent Crime Reduction Act 2006, the Criminal Justice and Immigration Act 2008 and the Legal Aid, Sentencing and Punishment of Offenders Act 2012, for example. Sentencers have to make sense of a plethora of different provisions in a wide variety of different Acts of Parliament.

Then there is the guidance from the Court of Appeal, whose judgments give important guidance on the interpretation of the law. This in itself can be confusing. It is difficult not to smile at the example provided by the unfortunate Mrs Noone (*R. (Noone) v Governor of Drake Hall Prison* [2010] UKSC 30), though the reality from her point of view was doubtless not remotely funny. Her case was appealed first to the Court of Appeal (see [2008] EWCA Civ 1097) who expressed a certain outrage at the state of the law. This is a 'simple' case on short-term sentence calculation, complicated by the imposition of a short consecutive sentence. The Master of the Rolls explicitly agreed with Wall L.J.'s comment that:

> I cannot, however, leave the case without expressing my sympathy both for the 'despair' which the judge felt when considering the statutory provisions in the case, and for the view which he expressed in paragraph 2 of his judgment:
> 'It is simply unacceptable in a society governed by the rule of law for it to be well nigh impossible to discern from statutory provisions what a sentence means in practice'. The argument in this court lasted for the best part of a day, and the respondent's correct release date has only emerged in a careful reserved judgment (at [60]).

But astonishingly, the Supreme Court concludes two years later that the Court of Appeal and the Master of the Rolls were quite wrong in their interpretation of the law. Lord Judge (in the Supreme Court) concluded that:

> It is outrageous that so much intellectual effort, as well as public time and resources, have had to be expended in order to discover a route through the legislative morass to what should be, both for the prisoner herself, and for those responsible for her custody, the prison authorities, the simplest and most certain of questions – the prisoner's release date.
>
> (para. 87)

Quite so. If the senior judges cannot construe this law with any certainty, what hope for the prisoners on the receiving end of these sentences, or the administrative staff with the duty to calculate release dates? But the guidance in individual cases is invaluable in developing consistency. It is perhaps not surprising that David Thomas QC's huge and encyclopaedic *Current Sentencing Practice* (Thomas, 2010) has now expanded into five enormous loose-leaf volumes: students will find his digest (the Sentencing Referencer) an easier guide to the law. But a flavour of the guidance can be gained by reading key decisions such as *Millberry* [2003] 2 Cr App R (S) 31 (on rape) or *Myers* [2009] EWCA Crim 119 (on distraction burglaries), or *Blackshaw* [2011] EWCA Crim 2312 (on the riots of 2011).

Then there is the guidance from the Sentencing Council,[7] which was created by the Coroners and Justice Act 2009. The Sentencing Council has continued the work of its predecessor, the Sentencing Guidelines Council, in trying to encourage consistent and transparent sentencing, but there remain very many barriers beyond their control (Roberts 2008, Ashworth 2010).

One example of a 'problem' is the so-called 'custody threshold'. A recent article argued that, although the 'custody threshold' is usually seen as short-hand for the (statutory and common sense) principle that no one should be sent to prison unless their offence is serious enough to justify a custodial sentence, in practice it can work very differently (see Padfield 2011c). First, it is a dangerous concept because the expression gives a false sense of security by implying clarity where there is no exact threshold to be crossed. It can be used to justify custodial sentences for those who perhaps should be sentenced to penalties served in the community. Second, a 'threshold' test, or a line or a pyramid approach, encourages sentencers to take too rigid an approach to the hierarchy of available sentences. A judge is actually seeking out the 'tipping point to custody' through a fog of aggravating and mitigating factors. A tipping point is all about balance, about balancing considerations:[8]

> The custody threshold, conceived as a hurdle, a barrier to the inappropriate use of imprisonment, is not useful because the issues exceed the carrying capacity of the metaphor. Perhaps we should replace the pyramid with a diagram which looks more like this, which provides a vague hierarchy of penalties but which overlap. A tough community sentence may be higher up the ladder than a short custodial sentence; a tough fine may well be more punitive than a low-level community penalty, depending upon the circumstances. The judge has to assess aggravating and mitigating factors to form a judgement about whether they tip the offender one way or the other in the particular case.

Those interested in 'stemming the flow' might like to look at the way trial courts use individual sentences (see for example www.sentencing.justice.gov.uk for local data). The growing number of indeterminate sentences is well known, and a huge cause of concern (Ministry of Justice 2009). When imposing sentence, the judge usually specifies a minimum term. The concerns surround the very low rate of release for 'lifers' and those serving IPP (imprisonment for public protection), even when they

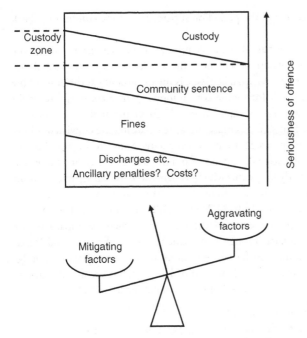

Figure 5.1   Avoiding the sentencing pyramid (taken from Padfield 2011c: 593–612).

are post-tariff. Less often discussed is the growing number of extended sentences, which also result in lengthy times in prison. These sentences are designed as a fixed-term sentence, combined with an extended period of supervision in the community. When the judge decides to impose an extended sentence, he or she will present it in some way like this:

> Having decided that the risk you present to the public is great even though the actual harm caused on this occasion was relatively low, I shall impose on you an extended sentence, made up in this case of a custodial period of two years, and an extended period of supervision in the community of five years.

This sentence, known informally as a '2 + 5', means that, under the current version of the law, the sentenced person will, like others, come out of prison on licence after one year (at half time) but he or she is liable to recall at any stage and once they have been recalled, they may in fact spend the entirety of the period of 'supervision in the community' back in custody.

There are numerous other 'problem areas' in sentencing: when to impose consecutive or concurrent sentences; the totality principle; the role of previous convictions. Perhaps a key issue is the uncertainty at the heart of the sentence: what is it for? Some constitutions grant a constitutional right to rehabilitation: for example, article 27(3) of the Italian Constitution provides that punishments must aim at resocialising the convicted. Other countries have legislated the aims of sentencing. Some distinguish the aims of the implementation of sentences from the aims of sentencing more generally, particularly in systems which recognise the formal separation of the administration of sentences from the initial imposition of a sentence (as in France or Italy: see Padfield 2011c). Different aims may have priority at different stages in the sentence: for example, when the initial sentence is imposed and later during its implementation. In England and Wales, where there is no such formal separation, on the other hand, the judge must have regard to the following broad and often inconsistent purposes of sentencing (see section 142 of the Criminal Justice Act 2003):

- the punishment of offenders
- the reduction of crime (including its reduction by deterrence)
- the reform and rehabilitation of offenders
- the protection of the public, and
- the making of reparation by offenders to persons affected by their offences.

Without clear objectives, it is well nigh impossible to assess the 'efficacy' of a penal system (Walker 1999). In penal theory, there has been a long-standing debate between retributivist and utilitarian aims. Empirical research could valuably analyse what sentencers actually say about the aims of individual sentences.

WHAT DO SENTENCERS ACTUALLY DO?

We don't know very much about decision-making by sentencers in this country, in large measure because much data-gathering in recent years has been quantitative and not qualitative. Useful statistical data is published in the annual *Sentencing Statistics*, but these statistics do not allow comparison of individual decisions. Dhami and Souza (2009) assessed the feasibility of what would have been a major study, collecting data from court records in order to help understand the reasons behind individual sentence decisions. Perhaps unsurprisingly, the pilot revealed that much crucial information was not readily obtainable from court records, making it difficult to achieve the study's objectives, and so the Sentencing Guidelines Council and Ministry of Justice decided not to continue funding it. The Sentencing Council launched the Crown Court Sentencing Survey in 2010, but this one-page questionnaire given to sentencers to complete seems unlikely, on its own, to gather very much useful and usable data.[9] Judges are strongly encouraged to complete the form: in the first year, there was an overall national response rate of 61 per cent. However, response rates by location vary from 20 per cent to 95 per cent. It is doubtful whether in the current climate the Sentencing Council has the resources to ensure that meaningful (qualitative as well as quantitative) data on sentencing decisions is collected and independently analysed.

We know how many people have been sent to prison and for what principal offences, but little about the reasons for these decisions. Judicial variations may often turn on the sentencers' perceptions of culpability. Two useful studies of the role of mitigation on sentencers' decisions were Shapland (1981) and Rumgay (1998) (see also Padfield 2011a). Jacobson and Hough's (2007) study of mitigation also revealed the vital importance of personal mitigation in actual sentencing decisions. This study was carried out across five crown court centres, and involved the observation of 132 cases involving 162 defendants and 52 sentencers, as well as interviews with 40 sentencers. Hough *et al.*'s study of sentencers' perceptions concluded:

> It was evident from the ways in which the sentencers described their borderline cases that sentencing as currently practised is an unavoidably value-laden process, reflecting the fact that the court process as a whole, especially where there is a trial, centres on the complex human stories of the accused and those affected, as much as on the law. In both studies sentencers' accounts of borderline decisions involved social and moral reasoning as well as expertise in applying the law. Decisions were framed within a set of explicitly ethical – and subjective – concepts, assessments of an offender's intentions and capabilities, as well as attitudes towards the offence and signs of remorse.
>
> (Hough *et al.* 2003: 256–7)

Thus, research can seek to study either actual decision-making or perceptions of decision-making. It can usefully be enriched by work which has studied the role of 'discretion'. Socio-legal explorations have sought to identify the variables that may influence the exercise of discretion, such as process, environment, context, and indeed illicit considerations (for example, the social class, ethnicity or sex of the accused) (see Gelsthorpe and Padfield 2003: chapter 1).

GETTING OUT – AND RECALL

The rules on release from prison are clearly hugely important. For example, no one interested in reducing the prison population can ignore the role of the Probation Service, the Ministry of Justice and the Parole Board in getting prisoners who have been released subsequently recalled to prison and in then keeping them in prison. Most prisoners serving a determinate length sentence will be released at the halfway point in their sentence, or earlier on Home Detention Curfew (HDC) (see Padfield 2009a for a summary of release rules). The number of determinate sentence prisoners who were recalled to prison in the second part of their sentence during 2009–10 was 13,919 (as compared with only 2,457 prisoners recalled in the year 2000–1).[10] The numbers of lifers recalled, compared with the number released, is even more striking. In 2009, 124 lifers (and 21 prisoners serving IPP) were recalled. Given that the Parole Board only directed the release of 172 of the 1,530 eligible lifers whose cases were considered, it is clear that it is not only difficult to 'earn' release, but that, once out, it is difficult to resist recall to prison. In 2006, more lifers were recalled to prison (164) than were released (135): see Appleton (2010). In 2009, 21 IPP prisoners were recalled (a total of only 52 IPP prisoners had ever been released by the end of 2008, although by that time there were already 4,500 offenders serving IPP). The problem has been growing for a number of years (see HMIP 2005; Prison Reform Trust 2005; Padfield and Maruna 2006; Padfield 2007; House of Commons Justice Committee 2008).

The numbers still seem to be rising: during the quarter ending March 2011, 3,821 offenders had their licence revoked and were recalled to prison (Offender Management Statistics, Quarterly Bulletin). But these statistics do not tell us any details about who exactly is recalled, for what reason, and for how long they stay in prison. There is a shortage of published research: little empirical work has been done on the Parole Board in the last ten years, though its annual reports provide plenty of material to be mined for information.

A key issue is whether courts should be involved in these decisions. At present, most decisions to release are taken administratively, by those who run prisons. The Parole Board decides only on the release of those serving indeterminate sentences, and reviews and decides on the cases of those who have been (administratively) recalled to prison. It is difficult to conclude that the Parole Board is a 'court' in any real sense of the word. Indeed, in *R. (on the application of Brooke) v Parole Board* [2008] EWCA Civ 29 the Lord Chief Justice stated that:

> Neither the Secretary of State nor his Department has adequately addressed the need for the Parole Board to be and to be seen to be free of influence in relation to the performance of its judicial functions. Both by Directions and by the use of his control over the appointment of members of the Board the Secretary of State has sought to influence the manner in which the Board carries out its risk assessment. The close working relationship between the Board and the unit acting as its sponsor has tended to blur the distinction between the executive role of the former and the judicial role of the latter.
>
> (para. 78)

He was also critical of the funding restriction which stopped the Board from interviewing prisoners, contrary to its wishes:

> While this did not threaten the Board's impartiality it was interference that exceeded what could properly be justified by the role of sponsor.
>
> (para. 80)

Yet despite a Consultation Paper on the *Future of the Parole Board* in 2009 (see Padfield 2009b, 2011d) nothing has been done to make the Board truly independent.

On recall, a small research project conducted in the summer of 2011 raised many concerns about the fairness of recall processes and the uncertainties surrounding a prisoner's journey towards rerelease (Padfield 2012). These findings were compatible with Digard's conclusion that:

> disregard for procedural fairness may decrease offender's levels of mental well-being, engagement in their management, motivation to forge new

> lives, and respect for authorities and the civic values they represent. It may inhibit the maintenance of an effective probation/client relationship and increase resistance.
>
> (Digard 2010)

There is widespread misunderstanding of the process by both prisoners and prison staff: for example, the criteria for the somewhat rare 'fixed term' recall; or whether a 'standard' recall is for a fixed or indefinite term. Once recalled, prisoners often face a lengthy and unpredictable period of time awaiting rerelease. The recall process is seen by many people as unfair, especially with the growing power of the executive to control the gateway to rerelease.

PRESSURE POINTS

An organisation such as the Howard League, committed to trying to reduce the use of imprisonment, rightly focuses on pressure points which tip those who have committed offences into prison, and then keep them there for what appear to be ever lengthening periods (Bennett 2008). The courts are largely responsible for the size of the remand (unconvicted and unsentenced) population and the size of the sentenced prison population. But as this discussion has shown, there are many other players within the process who may control the 'tipping' points. Key pressure points include:

- gatekeeping decisions: who gets prosecuted, and for what offences;
- 'out-of-court' penalties and breach proceedings;
- whether too many people receive community orders, or a community order with unnecessary requirements;
- the role of the probation officer, prosecutor and defence advocate before and at the sentencing hearing;
- the decision to imprison (a crucial sentencing decision);
- length and type of sentences of imprisonment;
- decisions to release, and to recall, and to rerelease.

It may be trite to suggest that, currently in England and Wales, too many people appear to be imprisoned for too long a period of time. But this is the 'bottom line' on which the Howard League should focus.

POTENTIAL AREAS OF RESEARCH

Research is needed in many related areas and only a few are identified here:

- theoretical research (on, for example, the importance of proportionality as a limit on sentence lengths);
- analytical reviews of policy;
- empirical research on sentencing practices (not only focused on sentencers, but also other key 'players' within the process: police, Crown Prosecution Service, lawyers, probation officers, prison staff, multi-agency arrangements, Parole Board, etc.).

We noted earlier the Sentencing Council's Crown Court Sentencing Survey, commenting that this one-page questionnaire given to sentencers is of only limited utility. The Howard League may be able to help by adding its authoritative voice to argue for much more data collection and analysis.

There is also a huge need for comparative work in this area, particularly in the European context where the 27 members of the European Union seem to be rushing fast into the compulsory transfer of prisoners between jurisdictions without any fundamental understanding of how our various systems can co-exist fairly (see Padfield et al. 2010). Nor should sentencing law and practice be seen as the exclusive preserve of legal or socio-legal scholars. There is plenty of work for the political scientist and for the historian. The courtroom is an excellent place for both the anthropologist and for the psychologist. In recent years, English judges and magistrates have not always welcomed the critical eye of the academic researcher, but there is reason to hope that this might be changing.

Sentencing law shapes sentencing practice. This chapter has sought to show something of the complexity of the practical reality: Parliament may have created a complex legal framework of rules, which heavily influence decisions to imprison and to release and to re-imprison. But this framework is applied in practice by a number of key decision makers who are influenced by many legal and extra-legal factors. Attempts to reduce the prison population are more likely to be successful if we have much greater understanding of these processes.

Notes

1   In my work as an Independent Legal Advisor to a Hate Crime Scrutiny Panel in 2008–11, it was not rare for files to show that a plea to a

> lesser offence had been accepted, even at court, in order to ensure a successful outcome. These decisions provided material for lively discussion about whether the lower charge adequately reflected the seriousness of the offence.

2   This non-involvement should be distinguished from a procedure whereby a judge may be asked to give an advance indication of sentence when the defendant is considering a guilty plea: see *Goodyear* [2005] EWCA Crim 888 and many other cases.

3   An area worthy of research: how often in fact are written BOPs not available? How often is the judge sentencing without a clear understanding of the factual basis of the offence(s)?

4   www.cps.gov.uk/legal/v_to_z/victim_personal_statements/index. html.

5   It is not clear how often this happens, but the requirement is found in Attorney General's Guidelines on the Acceptance of Pleas and the Prosecutor's Role in the Sentencing Exercise (the Attorney General's Guidelines) (paragraph B4).

6   *Reynolds and others* [2007] EWCA Crim 538.

7   Their excellent website is well worth exploring: www.sentencingcouncil.org.uk.

8   The following quotation and figure are taken from Padfield (2011: 611).

9   See sentencingcouncil.judiciary.gov.uk/docs/CCSS_Annual_2011.pdf.

10   See Table 9.10, National Offender Management Caseload Statistics (this excludes Home Detention Curfew which in 2009–10 amounted to another 1,441 recalls: see Table 9.9).

References

Appleton, C. (2010) *Life after Life Imprisonment*. Oxford: Oxford University Press.

Ashworth, A. (2010) 'Sentencing guidelines and the Sentencing Council'. *Criminal Law Review* pp. 389–401.

Bennett, J. (2008) *The Social Costs of Dangerousness: Prison and the Dangerous Classes*. Available at: www.crimeandjustice.org.uk/dangerousness.html [accessed August 2012].

Dhami, M. and Souza, K. (2009) *The Study of Sentencing and its Outcomes: A Pilot Report* (MoJ Research Series 2/09). London: Ministry of Justice.

Digard, L. (2010) 'When legitimacy is denied: offender perceptions of the prison recall system'. *Probation Journal* 57 pp. 43–61.

Gelsthorpe, L. and Padfield, N. (eds) (2003) *Exercising Discretion: Its Uses in Criminal Justice and Beyond*. Cullompton: Willan.

Her Majesty's Inspectorate of Prisons (2005) *Recalled Prisoners: A Short Review of Recalled Adult Male Determinate-Sentenced Prisoners*. London: HM Inspectorate of Prisons.

Hough, M., Jacobson, J. and Millie, A. (2003) *The Decision to Imprison: Sentencing and the Prison Population*. London: Prison Reform Trust.

House of Commons Justice Committee (2008) *Towards Effective Sentencing*. Available at: www.publications.parliament.uk/pa/cm200708/cmselect/cmjust/184/184.pdf [accessed August 2012].

Jacobson, J. and Hough, M. (2007) *Mitigation: The Role of Personal Factors in Sentencing*. London: Prison Reform Trust.

Liberty (2002) *Magistrates' Courts and Public Confidence – a Proposal for Fair and Effective Reform of the Magistracy*. Available at: www.liberty-human-rights.org.uk/policy/reports/magistrates-court-review-february-2003.pdf [accessed August 2012].

Ministry of Justice (2009) *Story of the Prison Population 1995–2009 England and Wales*. London: Ministry of Justice.

Morgan, R. and Russell, N. (2000) *The Judiciary in the Magistrates' Courts*. London: Home Office.

Padfield, N. (ed.) (2007) *Who to Release? Parole, Fairness and Criminal Justice*. Cullompton: Willan.

Padfield, N. (2008) *The Criminal Justice Process: Text and Materials (4th edn)*. Oxford: Oxford University Press.

Padfield, N. (2009a) 'Parole and early release: the CJIA 2008 changes in context'. *Criminal Law Review* pp. 166–87.

Padfield, N. (2009b) 'The future of parole'. *Archbold News* 9 (6) pp. 6–9.

Padfield, N. (2010) 'Discretion and decision-making in public protection' in M. Nash and A. Williams (eds) *Handbook of Public Protection*. Cullompton: Willan, pp. 103–32.

Padfield, N. (2011a) 'Intoxication as a sentencing factor: mitigation or aggravation?' in J.V. Roberts (ed.) *Aggravation and Mitigation at Sentencing*. Cambridge: Cambridge University Press, pp. 81–101.

Padfield, N. (2011b) 'Time to Bury the Custody "Threshold"?'. *Criminal Law Review* pp. 593–612.

Padfield, N. (2011c) 'An entente cordiale in sentencing?'. *Criminal Law and Justice Weekly* 175 pp. 239–41, 256–8, 271–3 and 290–2.

Padfield, N. (2011d) 'Amending the Parole Board rules: a sticking plaster response?'. *Public Law* October pp. 691–8.

Padfield, N. (2012) 'Recalling conditionally released prisoners in England and Wales'. *European Journal of Probation* 4 (1) pp. 34–45.

Padfield, N. and Maruna, S. (2006) 'The revolving door at the prison gate: exploring the dramatic increase in recalls to prison'. *Criminology and Criminal Justice* 6 pp. 329–52.

Padfield, N., van Zyl Smit, D. and Dünkel, D. (eds) (2010) *Release from Prison: European Policy and Practice*. Cullompton: Willan.

Prison Reform Trust (2005) *Recycling Offenders through Prison*. London: Prison Reform Trust.

Roberts, J. (2008) 'Aggravating and mitigating factors at sentencing: towards greater consistency of application'. *Criminal Law Review* pp. 264–76.

Rumgay, J. (1998) *Crime, Punishment and the Drinking Offender*. Basingstoke: Palgrave Macmillan.

Seago, P., Walker, C. and Wall, D (2000) 'The development of the professional magistracy in England and Wales'. *Criminal Law Review* pp. 631–51.

Shapland, J. (1981) *Between Conviction and Sentence: The Process of Mitigation*. London: Routledge.

Thomas, D.A. (2010) *Current Sentencing Practice*. Available at: www.sweet-andmaxwell.co.uk/Catalogue/ProductDetails.aspx?productid=5892&recordid=153 [accessed August 2012].

Vennard, J., Davis, G., Baldwin, J. and Pearce, J. (2004) *Ethnic Minority Magistrates' Experience of the Role and of the Court Environment* (DCA Research Series 3/04). Available at: http://webarchive.nationalarchives.gov.uk/+/http://www.dca.gov.uk/research/2004/3_2004.htm [accessed August 2012].

Walker, N. (1999) *Aggravation, Mitigation and Mercy in English Criminal Justice*. London: Blackstone.

Wood, J. and Kemshall, H. (2007) *The Operation and Experience of MAPPA* (Home Office Online Report 12/07). Available at: www.caerdydd.ac.uk/socsi/resources/MAPPA1207.pdf [accessed August 2012].

6

THE DEVIL IN THE DETAIL

COMMUNITY SENTENCES, PROBATION AND THE MARKET

LOL BURKE AND FERGUS MCNEILL

INTRODUCTION

In March 2012 the government published its consultation paper *Punishment and Reform: Effective Community Sentences* (Ministry of Justice 2012a) outlining its plans to overhaul the delivery of community sentences as part of its 'rehabilitation revolution'. Alongside this, another consultation document *Punishment and Reform: Effective Probation Services* (Ministry of Justice 2012b) further promoted the belief that opening up the work of the Probation Service to the private sector would encourage new innovations and bring about greater efficiencies. Whilst the consultations do not seek to replace short prison sentences with community penalties, they propose a clear punitive element in every community order and the creation of an intensive punitive community disposal for those on the cusp of custody. In this respect the tone of the consultation papers reflects a long-standing hope that credible and effective community sentences would enable judges to channel many more people away from prison.

The reality has of course often been different; in many jurisdictions, significant growth in the use of community sanctions has accompanied increasing use of custody (see McNeill and Whyte 2007: chapter 2). Though this does not preclude the possibility that growth in the use of community sentences has moderated or decelerated prison growth, critical criminologists and sociologists of punishment have long since argued that through the mechanisms of 'net-widening' and 'mesh-thinning' community sentences can and often do draw more people into the 'carceral' net of supervision and sometimes, through default and breach, into custody itself (Cohen 1985), sometimes including people who would never have received custodial sentences in the first place. And of course, when the intent is to make community sentences more 'punitive' or more 'robust', these risks are exacerbated.

The emergence of what some have termed 'mass supervision' (i.e. in the community) can be seen as representing *both* opportunities and threats. Yet as a new network of European scholars has argued:

> [mass supervision] has largely escaped the attention of legal scholars and social scientists more concerned with the 'mass incarceration' reflected in prison growth. As well as representing an important gap in critical research and scholarship, the neglect of community sentences and offender supervision means that research has not delivered the knowledge that is urgently required to engage with political, policy and practice communities grappling with delivering justice efficiently and effectively in fiscally straitened times, and with the challenges of communicating the meaning, legitimacy and utility of community sentences to an insecure public.[1]
>
> (COST 2012)

In this short chapter, which focuses on England and Wales, we aim to explore the conditions under which and mechanisms through which community sentences might indeed serve to 'stem the flow' of imprisonment, but we also aim to encourage all those with an interest in penal reform to develop and maintain a properly critical perspective on community sentences themselves, and how they may come to be configured and delivered in an increasingly marketised environment.

COMMUNITY SENTENCES IN ENGLAND AND WALES AND THEIR USAGE

The use of community sentences by the courts increased by 28 per cent between 1999 and 2009 (Ministry of Justice 2010a). A key driver behind this expansion has been the desire to use community sentences as a mechanism for controlling the prison population. The *Breaking the Cycle* Green Paper estimates that the 'vicious cycle' of reoffending by ex-prisoners costs the UK economy between £7 billion and £10 billion per year (Ministry of Justice 2010b). The potential role of community sentences in reducing these costs has become a key interest of contemporary penal policy; particularly in relation to using community sentences to displace shorter custodial sentences which have higher costs per day and are typically associated with high reconviction rates. For example, a recent enquiry has calculated that diversion from custody to residential drug treatment produces a lifetime cost saving of approximately £60,000 per person (Make Justice Work 2011).

Some argue (somewhat more controversially) that, as well as being much less expensive than imprisonment, community sentences can produce lower reoffending rates. According to the government's own figures, proven reoffending of those individuals receiving community orders in 2008 was 8.3 percentage points lower than for those who had served prison sentences of 12 months or less, even after controlling for differences in terms of offence type, criminal record and other significant characteristics (Ministry of Justice 2012c: 10).

The Criminal Justice Act 2003 legislated for a new framework for the delivery of community sentences. The existing community sentences were replaced with a generic community order with 12 possible requirements. At the same time, a suspended supervision order (SSO) was introduced with the same 12 requirements. The SSO, however, is, in a legal sense, a custodial sentence and is intended to be used when the court is considering the imposition of a sentence of imprisonment. These new orders were intended to increase the credibility of community sentences; the pursuit of credibility was seen as requiring that they would be more punitive and demanding than their predecessors. It was also intended that they would give sentencers greater flexibility and also rationalise what was perceived as being a confusing array of penalties that had existed beforehand.

Research into the workings of the new orders has however highlighted wide disparities in the use and availability of requirements that can be attached to the community order. The National Audit Office (2008) found that many of the 12 requirements formally available to the courts are not in fact available in certain areas. Thus, the options available to sentencers are restricted and vital requirements are often not received because they are not available locally. Specialist programmes for drug users, alcohol abusers and mentally disordered people were found to be particularly patchy, but of course, the provision of these services is not solely the responsibility of, or under the control of, criminal justice agencies. These, and various other reasons, have been put forward to attempt to explain different patterns of usage of community sentences in different places. The explanations include: a lack of availability; lack of knowledge on the part of both sentencers and probation staff; a desire by probation staff to work within their comfort zone; confusion on the part of sentencers and probation officers as a result of the potential duplication of some requirements; uncertainty about how some requirements are monitored; and problems in assessment (Mair 2011). In addition, the recent report into the future of the Probation Service by the Justice Affairs Select Committee (2011) has also drawn attention to the poor targeting of people for particular orders and requirements, linked to the increasing use of fast delivery reports by the Probation Service.

Despite these challenges and variations, the increase in the use of community sentences has been more marked than that of the use of custody. However, the 'shape' or content of community sentences has also changed; there has been a decline in the use of supervision and accredited programmes (both measures aimed at facilitating the rehabilitation of offenders) within the orders (see Figure 6.1).

This may suggest a displacement of traditional notions of rehabilitation by a more fragmented set of requirements designed to appeal to other purposes of sentencing, such as punishment and reparation. With these shifting purposes and priorities also come a wider range of different providers in the mixed economy of corrections that the government is keen to promote and encourage (Mair 2011).

Whatever the purpose and whoever the provider, the intensity and potential intrusions of community sentences – what we could call 'the pains of probation' (Durnescu 2009) – have also developed considerably in recent decades, moving beyond traditionally rehabilitative supervision to include unpaid work, medical, psychological or substance misuse treatment, mandatory drug or alcohol testing, exclusion orders and residence conditions, curfews, as well as other innovations such as electronic monitoring. The consultation paper on community sentences (Ministry of Justice 2012a) seeks to further extend the punitive weight

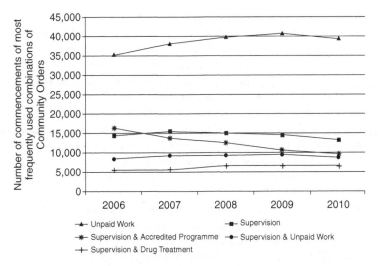

Figure 6.1   Volume of community order starts by top requirement combinations (Ministry of Justice 2012c)

and surveillant control of community orders through the harnessing of new location monitoring technologies such as GPS (Global Positioning System) and GSM (Global System for Mobile Communications). These technologies are seen as a means of monitoring certain requirements in relation to exclusion areas, alcohol abstinence, foreign travel and residence. The government also suggests that, as well as enforcing restrictions, tracking through the use of 'cyber-tags' would also be used to develop and reinforce positive behaviour.

Napo – the Probation Workers' Union and Professional Association – has recognised that there is potential for such measures where there is a risk of repeat offending in relation to certain types of crime such as domestic violence or other predatory sexual offending, stalking and harassment, as well as suggesting that such measures could be used more frequently in order to reduce remands (Napo 2012). However, others argue that 'current evidence suggests that electronic monitoring has at best a neutral effect on reoffending and there was no significant difference in compliance levels of electronically monitored curfew orders compared to a comparison group serving other community penalties' (Criminal Justice Alliance 2012). Perhaps, therefore, the harnessing of new technologies should be used to complement other community interventions that are designed to challenge behaviour and address the underlying issues behind offending. Simply restricting a person's liberty is unlikely to be successful at reducing reoffending in the longer term.

Recent research into the impact of curfews and electronic monitoring as experienced by youth gang members in the West of Scotland (Deuchar 2012) has found that such measures often had a number of unintended negative consequences and led to additional strains between the young men and their families leading to further criminality. Where such measures had a limited success in reducing antisocial behaviour and criminality, they were complemented by additional mechanisms for rehabilitation and care. As such they were largely used to augment and support broader offender management and other interventions in order to reduce the risk of serious harm and/or to reduce the likelihood of reoffending. Nellis (2010), in reviewing the global literature on the use of electronic monitoring (EM) in offender supervision, bemoans the tendency (especially in England and Wales) for probation and EM to develop along 'parallel tracks', suggesting that the disintegration of EM from wider processes of offender management may undermine the utility of both. Others have similarly argued that '[t]echnological solutions are not an adequate replacement for the face-to-face supervision and the relationships that underpin effective interventions with offenders' (Humberside Probation Trust 2012). In its response to the consultations, Napo (2012: 7) has raised concerns about the uncoordinated manner in which electronically monitored curfews operate with other community order requirements and the fact that the current contracts in England and Wales are operated completely independently of the Probation Service. This contrasts sharply with other countries where this provision is operated in-house by some European Probation Services. As Nellis (2010) notes, this seems to offer a less complicated and more effective integration of EM into community sentences, though not necessarily a cheaper one.

Whether relying on the use of new technologies or not, the displacement, diversification and intensification of community sentences has ultimately had limited success in reducing the use of custody, as has been highlighted in recent research:

- Sentences introduced as explicit alternatives to custody have failed to act as like for like replacements for prison sentences.

- Community sentences do not appear to have leveraged a sustained reversal in the numbers sentenced to short-term custody.
- Reforms have produced tougher community sentences without the desired reduction in the use of custody and with unintended 'up-tarrifing' consequences.
- Efforts to reform community sentences in this period appear, at best, to have been a mechanism for *maintaining* the size of the short-term custodial population by putting a hold on possible future growth (Mills 2011).

In many respects, one simple lesson to take from these enduring problems is that it is not possible to reform sentencing just by changing the type, tone or availability of community sentences. Reducing the prison population requires a more direct engagement with fundamental questions about what punishment is for, and how we define and delimit the role of imprisonment with our conception of punishment (see Scottish Prisons Commission 2008). However, rather than getting into these broader questions of penal policy, and staying with our focus on Community sentences, we move on to examine what lies behind their supposed problems of credibility.

THE PURPOSES OF COMMUNITY SENTENCES AND THEIR CREDIBILITY

Lack of knowledge and understanding is a fundamental problem in relation to community sentences, not least because the mix of ignorance and reliance on media (mis)representation seems to be toxic to probation's credibility. The most recent British Crime Survey, for example, suggests that only 20 per cent of people surveyed thought that probation in England and Wales was doing a good job and it was the only criminal justice agency whose rating had decreased since 2002–3 (Smith 2010). These figures may reflect, at least in part, the consequences of political and media criticisms of probation that have arisen in high profile cases where supervision has been seen as having failed to protect the public. Conversely, research suggests that public confidence in the use of community penalties can and does increase where the public come to know more about them. As the Justice Affairs Select Committee (2011) has stated recently, public confidence is arguably most likely to be gained by setting out clearly what community sentences attempt to achieve.

Probation managers and staff may be surprised by such perceptions. For them, public protection has become a key purpose and even a 'meta-narrative' in recent times (Robinson and McNeill 2004). Building the service around public protection carries both benefits and threats. Offering the promise of managing and reducing risk would seem to make sense in times of insecurity, given probation's political position and its need to justify and defend its claims on limited public resources. However, a fundamental problem with public protection as a narrative for probation is that it tends to dichotomise the interests of those who have committed offences and the interests of victims and communities in a zero-sum game where to be 'pro-offender' is to be 'anti-victim' and vice versa, despite the empirical reality that these are overlapping social groups (McCulloch and McNeill 2007). Moreover, probation's traditional mechanisms for generating protection or security are more likely to be found in the support of long-term change processes. However, these rehabilitative processes provide relatively little security and little reassurance to the public in the short term (McNeill 2011). The problem of 'over-promising' has been compounded by unrealistic political and public expectations regarding what can be achieved and refusal to accept the evidence of the inherent limitations of supervision's capacity to reduce reoffending and protect the public *in all cases and all of the time*.

So, what alternative narratives might be imagined for community sentences? Attempting to persuade people that community sentences can compete with incarceration on the grounds of toughness is both extremely challenging and ultimately counter-productive because '[if] punitiveness is the currency, then imprisonment has a higher value' (McNeill 2012b). Indeed adding punitive weight to sanctions purely for the sake of general deterrence and increasing public confidence has shown to have very limited positive effects (Criminal Justice Alliance 2012). Making community orders more punitive in a misguided attempt to match the damaging impact of imprisonment can also undermine their legitimacy, without which securing compliance from those subject to community sentences, and even ultimately supporting their desistance from crime are jeopardised (see McNeill and Robinson 2012). As one of us has noted elsewhere:

> Community punishment makes sense as a way of securing *positive* [author's emphasis] payback that benefits communities; it can't compete

with prisons when it comes to imposing penal harm. When community punishment tries to do that, it also undermines its capacity to secure a positive contribution from reforming citizens.

(McNeill 2012b)

Emphasising positive forms of restitution could also maximise the potential to expand the use of reparative approaches, including restorative justice. In Scotland, for example, recent policy developments have encouraged 'paying back' in the community as the default position for those who have committed less serious offences. In principle, 'paying back' can be achieved through restorative justice practices, through financial penalties, through unpaid work and, perhaps most interestingly in the Scottish context, through 'working at change' (McNeill 2011).

For such an approach to work, it would need to put people under supervision at the centre of the process; it implies higher expectations of what people can do to 'make good', both through their own rehabilitation and through contributions to restoring or enhancing the well-being of others, including victims, communities and their own families. The case for pre-sentence restorative justice has been strongly demonstrated in the government's own evidential findings (Ministry of Justice 2010b), which recognise that it has the potential to lead to greater victim satisfaction at less cost and that it helps those who have committed offences develop a better sense of remorse over their criminal activities. Estimates from Victim Support and the Restorative Justice Council suggest that using restorative justice pre-sentence, with 70,000 adults convicted of burglary, robbery and violence, would produce cost-savings to the Criminal Justice System of £185 million from reductions in reoffending alone (Prison Reform Trust 2012). Section 2 of the consultation document on community sentences would seem to acknowledge the potential of reparation and restorative approaches and the limitations of punishment as a means of repairing the damage caused by crime to victims and communities. However, its analysis is somewhat superficial and inconsistent with the general tone of the rest of the document.

Though restorative and reparative approaches have perhaps never become mainstream in probation, a stronger focus on these themes may therefore have much to offer in dealing with the vexed and vexing question of credibility. For example, there is some evidence, at the local level, that communities are more likely to be less punitive towards those who have committed offences and perhaps less exclusionary where they feel that their crime and justice-related problems are being recognised and taken seriously by the relevant public authorities (Bottoms and Costello 2010; Bottoms 2008). This implies that, just like police services, probation trusts need to think carefully not just about their *technical effectiveness* (for example in reducing reoffending), but also about what 'signals' they send to communities in and through their work; perhaps the signals that matter most here are not so much about public protection as they are about justice being done constructively. Reparation, restoration and reintegration signals are likely to be very important in this regard. Seeing and hearing about people who have previously committed offences 'making good' in, to and for their communities (Maruna 2001) is arguably much more likely to build public confidence than the inevitably weaker and ultimately less credible claims that probation can make about community punishment or public protection (Maruna and King 2008).

CHANGING PRACTICE APPROACHES

These arguments about new approaches to seeking public credibility also have the advantage of resonating with recent developments in approaches to probation practice. It has been argued by many commentators that, in the recent past, there has been an excessive focus on getting those who have offended into treatment and keeping them engaged at the expense of a commitment to getting them out of treatment and moving them on with their lives through rebuilding family relationships, accessing accommodation and enhancing employment, training and other meaningful activities. A 'desistance-based' perspective still leaves room for programmes that aim to constructively address the risks and needs of those who have offended, but it attempts to move from a 'treatment-centric' worldview. It suggests a shift in emphasis; away from thinking first of the intervention or programme and towards thinking first about the change process that the person is experiencing; what it means for them and to them; and how its personal, social and cultural contexts impel or impede it. Support services revolve around the individual, but they also look outward at the community, and ask how the relationships between individuals and communities can be rebuilt so that desistance and reintegration can be achieved. In other words, a desistance perspective drives us to ask what reintegration (or integration) in communities actually means and what might permit and obstruct it practically, psychologically, politically (McNeill 2012a).

Our developing understanding of desistance suggests that it is an inherently individualised and subjective process. Those subject to community-based sanctions do not make up a homogenous group and have varied and complex needs. As such, approaches to community sentences must accommodate and exploit issues of identity and diversity (McNeill 2011). Women are particularly badly affected by supervision processes that focus primarily on risk management instead of providing help, support and guidance. The report into the future of the Probation Service by the Justice Affairs Select Committee found that 'the importance of positive relationships for women's ability to engage well with supervision tends to be overlooked by probation services, except in probation areas where women's centres provide holistic help and supervision for female offenders' (Justice Affairs Select Committee 2011). Yet, research has shown that the experience of community sanctions can be an empowering process for women, giving them a renewed sense of self-belief and self-efficacy (Malloch and McIvor 2011). It is disconcerting that the consultation papers make little reference to the implications for addressing diversity of contracting out services and the potential loss of the public sector equality duty. Neither is it clear whose responsibility it would be to monitor practice in this regard.

The problems presented by many people who have offended are not only complex but interdependent and require careful assessment and well-planned interventions. Professional expertise and judgement is crucial in this process and depends on a well-trained workforce. The *Bradley Report* (2009) for example has highlighted the need for better training as regards mental health awareness. Research into recently qualified probation officers would seem to suggest that most practitioners were motivated to offer 'help' in the broadest sense to their supervisees in order to guide/assist/facilitate or even teach them to overcome personal and structural issues that were at the root of their offending. Although they had undoubtedly taken on the language of evidence-based practice, public protection and enforcement, this was underpinned by a commitment to an individualised approach to assessment and intervention (Gregory 2007; Annison *et al.* 2008; Deering 2010). But the capacity to respond creatively and thoughtfully in individualising support depends on effective professional education. Yet, cuts in government funding as a result of the ongoing adverse economic conditions will almost inevitably lead to pressure to train staff as cheaply as possible within the shortest time frames. This could leave the academic component of the programme – which already appears somewhat diluted in the new arrangements – increasingly vulnerable and its range of enquiry further narrowed under the guise of financial expediency (Burke 2010). Moreover, the qualifying framework is only available to those working in the Probation Service and there are no equivalent qualifications available to practitioners in private or voluntary organisations. As such, staff undertaking offender management work in other sectors will require the same level of qualifying training in order to foster some consistency in the specialist skills required to work with particular types of offences.

In recent years, probation practitioners have been under political and managerial pressure to enforce orders more rigorously. As we noted previously, the toughening up of enforcement practice may have been a contributory factor in relation to prison growth. But aside from that systemic problem, the emphasis on enforcement arguably also skewed the nature of probation practice, effectively requiring practitioners to value formal compliance with conditions over substantive engagement in the process of change. Rather than using their skills to support engagement and compliance in this deeper sense, practitioners were required to follow strict procedures that were intended to deter non-compliance by making breach or recall more likely. Though further research is urgently needed in this area, the evidence that we have to date suggests that strict enforcement is unlikely to drive up compliance (Ugwudike 2010); people under supervision (perhaps just like the rest of us) are more likely to comply when we anticipate some potential benefits of engagement, when we are drawn into positive relationships with those doing the supervision, when supervisors exercise their authority fairly and reasonably, taking into account our circumstances, and when, for all of these reasons, we are persuaded that it is the right thing to do (McNeill and Robinson 2012; Robinson and McNeill 2008).

Since we know that desistance is a complex process which often involves lapses and relapses, it is critically important for probation staff (and judges) to manage non-compliance constructively – at least where non-compliance represents struggling in the change process rather than refusing to engage in it. Staff involved in public protection are well aware that sometimes merely formal compliance (sticking by the 'letter' but ignoring the 'spirit' of the order) can be much more concerning than the honest struggles involved in trying to change a chaotic and difficult life.

PROBATION STRUCTURES, COMMISSIONING AND COMPETITION

Debates about the development of probation practice may have pre-occupied researchers (and to some extent practitioners), but in recent years the focus of much governmental and managerial effort has been on a series of significant changes to the organisational structures and service delivery arrangements for probation work. Despite all of this recent structural reform, the focus of the second consultation paper is on yet further reform of the Probation Service (Ministry of Justice 2012b).

The creation of the National Offender Management Service (NOMS) was premised on the belief that closer alignment with the Prison Service would increase probation services' credibility and align the custodial and community elements of sentences more effectively. Prison and probation appear to work effectively in Norway and Sweden as single organisations but what seems crucial to their 'success' is that they are both located within the context of broader political support for rehabilitation and lower toleration of prison overcrowding (Ploeg and Sandlie 2011). Other countries or states, such as Western Australia, having amalgamated these services into a single organisation, are now re-establishing probation as a separate entity following a major enquiry into a number of serious incidents and findings that suggested that the region was performing less well than other Australian states in terms of successful completions and recidivism rates (Harker and Worrall 2011). The recent report into the future of the Probation Service by the Justice Affairs Select committee found little evidence to suggest that bringing together prisons and probation in England and Wales had yet had a positive impact (Justice Affairs Select Committee 2011).

The Howard League in its submission to the Committee went further, arguing that the 'changes exacted by NOMS on the Probation Service have led to the systematic fragmentation and demoralisation of a Probation Service, whose purpose has been altered beyond all recognition' (The Howard League 2010). This has been compounded by a lack of inclusivity in terms of an absence of input from service users and practitioners in recent policy developments. Many within the Probation

Service viewed the creation of NOMS as a 'hostile takeover'. This perception is perpetuated by the continuing dominance of Prison Service managers in the upper echelons of the organisation and the lack of a high profile representative for the Probation Service at the national level.

It has also been argued that attempts to manage the Probation Service from the centre have undermined 'localism', which is increasingly seen as a means of increasing community cohesion (Commission on English Prisons Today 2009). The Howard League has called for a shift away from offender management towards a localised 'resolution service' in which probation/resolution officers serve as an individualised gateway to offer individuals access to support on problems such as housing and health. Such an approach would capitalise on probation's position as a counterpoint between the criminal justice, social welfare and local strategic partnership systems (The Howard League 2010). A localised approach would seem necessary in order to yield these potential benefits; national commissioning arrangements create problems for probation trusts seeking to offer responsive services quickly and flexibly. As the Howard League has pointed out, 'appropriately incentivised probation trusts could play a key role in commissioning services from the voluntary and private sectors, close to the point of delivery' (The Howard League 2010).

Though the government maintains that it is committed to localism, it seems that competition is seen as providing the primary and best mechanism to deliver cost-effective community sentences. NOMS has begun the process of competition for community payback with the first contract awarded to Serco to take over the management of community payback in the London area in a four-year contract worth some £37 million. The Justice Select Committee (2011) was critical of the earlier decision made by NOMS to divide England and Wales into six large lots when inviting bids to run community payback. It turned out that these lots were geographical anomalies; Wales found itself linked with the North West of England, South Yorkshire was moved to the Midlands and trusts as far apart as West Mercia and Devon and Cornwall were defined as regional neighbours (Ledger 2012).

Payment by Results is seen by the government as the 'mechanism for harnessing market disciplines to improve the delivery and efficiency of public services, and to enable innovative third-and-private sector providers to compete on an equal footing with the statutory services' (Roberts 2011: 130). The aim is 'to reward positive outcomes with minimal prescription as to how these outcomes will be achieved' (Fox and Albertson 2011: 395). It is claimed that this approach has the potential to bring new money into the system, for example, through greater philanthropic and 'social investment, and to improve performance by providing a greater focus on specified outcomes, potentially yielding cost saving by weeding out inefficiency' (Justice Affairs Select Committee 2011). The pilot Payment by Results programme run at HMP Peterborough is targeted at released prisoners serving sentences of 12 months or less. Investors pay into a Social Impact Bond (SIP) that is used to finance the work of the service providers to reduce reoffending rates amongst the target group. If these services achieve the outcome of reducing reoffending by 7.5 per cent over six years, then the investors receive a return on their initial investment. Service providers are thus shielded from financial risk, all of which is borne by the investors (Clinks 2010: 4). Whilst there is some evidence that the Peterborough SIP has introduced some new funding into the system and thus transferred the risk away from government to non-governmental investors, it has also been claimed that the Peterborough scheme has siphoned off money from organisations which would previously have been given the same money as grants (Gelsthorpe and Hedderman 2012).

The market and application of Payment by Results in criminal justice terms is both complex and untested and its implementation raises a number of issues. First, there is likely to be considerable variation across England and Wales in the work that will be required to establish a stable market. In some areas there will be a local infrastructure of existing organisations but in others this will need to be developed.

HMP Peterborough was selected because it has a high proportion of local releases (Disley *et al.* 2011) but this may not be the case in other areas. The Justice Affairs Select Committee has warned that 'the differences between dealing with prison-based and community-based offenders are not fully appreciated either within NOMS and the MoJ, or by potential new providers' (Justice Affairs Select Committee 2011). The role of sentencers in determining the demands for community sentences will also need to be taken into account. As the Justice Affairs Select Committee again notes, 'the separation of commissioning arrangements between probation trusts and courts/sentencers means that there is an inherent tension between what is demanded of probation services and what can be delivered' (Justice Affairs Select Committee 2011).

It is far from clear whether there will be sufficient interest from potential social investors given the difficulties in making informed investment decisions. In addition, there is a strong likelihood that the economic situation will have a considerable impact in diminishing the range of providers whilst there is an increase in demand (Justice Affairs Select Committee 2011). The government's proposed model for the application of Payment by Results to community sentences is to make an initial payment to providers for the delivery of community orders and a subsequent one for reducing reconviction, yet it does not intend to provide additional resources upfront to finance local incentive schemes. Payment by Results will require significant working capital. Accessing capital from mainstream financial services is easier for larger private organisations, giving them a competitive edge as potential providers. Most local-level voluntary and community sector organisations have little or no reserves and thus cash flow and the levels of financial risk-taking required are likely to be real barriers to engaging in this process.

The current pilot at Peterborough prison has a six-year life span so evaluative evidence of its outcomes will not be available for some time. However, the initial report into the implementation of the Peterborough scheme in its first year suggests that the fact that the project is securely funded for six years means it has time to become fully integrated into local provision and because the project is not subject to onerous monitoring of all its inputs and processes (merely focusing on successful resettlement and reduced reoffending) – clients progress at a speed that suits them to find the support which best meets their needs (Social Finance 2012). It is important that we learn from the lesson of the 'What works?' initiative in which interventions were rolled out nationally before being fully evaluated due to political pressures to achieve set targets.

If the recent experience of the Department of Work and Pensions is applied to the provision of community sentences, subcontracting to smaller organisations by the 'prime provider' is likely to be an important delivery mechanism. Subcontracting models of course pose risks to autonomy and accountability for the smaller voluntary and community organisations. Operating beneath a prime contractor will inevitably mean a change in strategic direction for many organisations, and potentially restrain innovation, given the imperative to demonstrate outcomes in order to receive a financial return. There have been warnings 'that levels of competition will squeeze out VCS agencies' (Clinks 2010: 6) and there is already some evidence that this is happening (Senior 2011). The risk therefore is that marketisation has the paradoxical effect of *reducing* both the range of providers and their local connectedness, concentrating provision in the hands of a small number of large corporations.

The government clearly believes that Payment by Results will achieve worthwhile cost savings, yet, as Fox and Albertson (2011) point out, it does not necessarily follow that reductions in reconvictions will accrue significant savings when the costs of existing services are largely fixed. Achieving significant savings is likely to need substantial economies of scale involving large cohorts. Evidence from other sectors suggests that whilst Payment by Results enabled potential savings in terms of lower costs in negotiating prices and volumes, these were more than offset by increased expenditure involved in the recruitment of additional staff; higher costs of data collection; higher monitoring costs; and higher enforcement costs. Research by Hudson *et al.* (2010, cited in Roberts 2011) also found little evidence that outcome-based contracting was driving innovation and instead was largely focused on reducing operational costs and achieving performance efficiencies (cited in Roberts 2011). According to the Young Foundation (2010), experience suggests that the model supporting Social Impact Bonds works best where there is a reasonably short gap between interventions and measurable results; the number of players is small; and there are agreed baselines and metrics that are not vulnerable to economic downturns or national policy changes. Worryingly, none of these conditions would appear to prevail in the current criminal justice environment.

The application of Payment by Results in the NHS would suggest that it works best when you have a comparatively straightforward problem that requires a single intervention from a single provider (Roberts 2011: 17). However, many of those subject to community sentences will have complex needs that often require services from multiple providers. Having different providers responsible for different elements of a community order could seriously undermine the overall coordination of the sentence (Justice Affairs Select Committee 2011). Moves to develop Payment by Results as part of the government's fading 'rehabilitation revolution' need to ensure that they result in a coherent experience for service users and are connected in ways that make sense to local communities and stakeholders. Fragmenting responsibility for offender management among different providers could jeopardise existing public protection arrangements. Perhaps one of the most worrying aspects of the consultation paper on the future of the Probation Service (Ministry of Justice 2012b) is the artificial division created between 'high' and 'low' offenders with the latter outsourced to other providers – according to government estimates about 60 per cent of current provision. This ignores the fluctuating nature of risk and that circumstances can change abruptly. Andrew Bridges (the former head of the Probation Inspectorate) has calculated that approximately 80 per cent of serious further offences are committed by those classified as medium or low risk (Bridges 2006).

There would be sensitive issues of legitimacy and accountability if statutory responsibilities were given to profit-making organisations or to an organisation whose lines of accountability to the court and public were less clear. As Geoff Dobson has remarked, 'If a judge or magistrate has concerns about the supervision of a contracted-out court order, with one or more organisations involved, who do they ask to appear before them?' (Dobson 2012). At present there is currently no independent organisation to safeguard professional standards and establishing a robust system of accountability, though necessary, could add further costs and bureaucracy. Yet, if the experience of Payment by Results in other sectors is any kind of guide, there are many real concerns that require such scrutiny. The list of Work Programme prime contractors for example is dominated by private sector companies including G4S, Serco and A4e, who all also have involvement in the criminal justice market. However, at least two of these companies have been involved in highly publicised scandals centring on claims that they were manipulating results in order to meet targets for payment (*Guardian* 2012a, 2012b). The high profile failure of G4S to provide sufficient security for the London 2012 Olympics has also brought into question the assumed efficiency of the private sector (Orr 2012). Working with large private sector contractors clearly brings financial, reputational and quality of practice risks (Dominey 2012).

It could be argued that the idea of Payment by Results is predicated on a notion of cause and effect that does not fit well with what is known about the nature of desistance. Interventions do not 'cause' people not to offend. Despite the progress made by the research into effectiveness it remains unclear which interventions are most likely to deliver the desired results (Fox and Albertson 2011). Even well-executed programmes often achieve only modest change and impact tends to lessen between pilot projects and wider scale roll-outs. An important lesson from the desistance literature is that change (in terms of reoffending) could increase or reduce due to factors outside of the proposed intervention.

More generally, the principal measure for Payment by Results – reconviction – is not an adequate measure of desistance. As many criminologists have noted, reconviction is not a straightforward measure of behaviour change, it is the result of a series of social interactions and processes in which a range of actors make discretionary judgements about how to react to information, whether in witnessing, reporting, detecting, prosecuting or sentencing a crime. In other words it is a measure of social and professional reactions; and these reactions are vulnerable to a wide range of influences. Leaving these technicalities aside, a binary measure of reconviction also fails to recognise the differences between formal and substantive compliance noted above; in essence, implicitly it risks rewarding services who cherry-pick those considered to be low risk, or who process as 'successes' those who simply keep their heads down for long enough. By contrast, it risks penalising those who opt to work with those in the greatest need and at the greatest risk of reoffending, ignoring their possible successes in slowing down or reducing the seriousness of offending while someone makes real but imperfect progress towards desistance. In this respect it would not appear to matter to the Payment by Results model 'if people cease to offend, or merely become less easy to catch' (Fox and Albertson 2012: 361).

CONCLUDING THOUGHTS

Given the inadequacies of reconviction as a measure, we need to get better at assessing, measuring and evaluating both progress towards compliance and progress towards desistance; and that will require work to develop a range of intermediate measures that help us understand the distance that people have travelled under supervision, and whether their progress has been accelerated or impeded due to criminal justice interventions. Capitalising on the work that NOMS has already commissioned on Quality in Probation Practice and on the Offender Management Feedback Questionnaire, we need to develop a much sharper sense of what matters most to practitioners and to probationers. Only then will we be able to explore the relationships between the quality of supervision and its outcomes. Such research needs to find ways to develop measures that are sensitive to diversity; that recognise that pathways towards desistance will be different for different people in different circumstances, and to find out what different kinds of support work with and for different people. More generally, we need to recognise that quality supervision and effectiveness in reducing reoffending are not the only important measures of probation's success. It is at least as important to develop better ways of assessing the credibility and legitimacy of probation – both for its public audiences and for its judicial audiences. What sorts of reparation and redemption signals can probation send to communities that might foster community support for reintegration? To what extent can probation's successes curb the excessive use of imprisonment? These remain key questions for a service that should be as much about justice as it is about crime reduction. But as Andrew Neilson (2012) has argued, justice should not be treated as a commodity to be 'priced and transacted' (2012: 422).

Despite the ideologically driven and radical nature of the proposals contained within the two review documents, ultimately they are undermined by a lack of political ambition to address the underlying causes of offending and to promote social as well as criminal justice. The misplaced policies which have led to record levels of imprisonment with all the attendant problems and human costs that this invariably brings are unlikely to be rectified through the proposed reforms. The approach taken in the consultations is one primarily based on punishment rather than one that emphasises constructive encouragement towards desistance, reparation and rehabilitation. As Nacro has noted:

> much more could and should be done to a) involve ordinary people (as mentors, volunteers, employee outreach schemes); b) engage employers and social enterprises (in creating work placements, apprentice schemes and real jobs); c) explore the potential to 'mainstream' restorative approaches; and d) link community payback to hard-edged community problems such as crime and community safety.
>
> (2012: 3)

Somewhat predictably, the proposals in the consultation documents look to the criminal justice system for answers to wider social problems in contemporary society that draw many individuals into the criminal justice system. But as Richard Garside (2012) has noted, reforms that are internal to the criminal justice process are unlikely by themselves to have an impact on the underlying prison population.

Those countries that have achieved significant reductions in the use of imprisonment have done so by implementing a broader framework of reforms, involving: differential arrangements for children and young adults; options to divert even relatively serious cases from prosecution and restrictions on remand; the existence of milder sentencing tariffs; better treatment options for people with drug dependency and psychiatric problems, targeting community sentences as alternative to imprisonment; the application of higher thresholds to breaches of suspended sentences and recalls to prison; and attempts to shield sentencers from populist public and political opinion (Allen 2012). Instead the two consultation documents present a narrower vision around the privatisation of punishment and reform, but as the title of this chapter suggests, when it comes to reforming community sentences, 'the devil is in the detail'. Developments such as Payment by Results may be politically attractive on a superficial level – who after all could defend paying for failure (Neilson 2012) – but ultimately they fail to address the deeper questions of penal politics, values and approaches on which progressive reform depends.

FURTHER RESEARCH

1. Existing research on 'what works' to reduce reoffending has led to a narrow focus on the technical effectiveness of intervention programmes. Important though this question is, we know far too little about what supervision 'is'; developing understanding of supervision as a socially constructed practice and as a lived experience is crucial to opening up a richer and more critical examination of its effects and impacts.
2. More generally, evaluation research needs to develop a broader engagement with the multiple and often contested purposes of community sanctions, for example, exploring the impact of supervision as a means of protecting the public, reducing reoffending, delivering punishment in the community, reducing the use of imprisonment, or promoting the social integration of ex-prisoners.
3. Bearing in mind this broader range of purposes, a more diverse research and knowledge exchange agenda is needed to support the development of a range of intermediate measures that will help us understand how far people have travelled under supervision, and what effect criminal justice interventions have on their progress

towards desistance and social integration. In this connection, further research into what really matters to practitioners and probationers should be undertaken, so that the relationships between quality of supervision and its outcomes can be explored. Such research would need to be sensitive to issues of diversity.

4. Research on what supports and frustrates initial engagement and ongoing compliance with supervision is urgently required. Such research needs to look beyond mere formal compliance, exploring how and why people become committed to changing their lives, and how they sustain that commitment.

5. Bearing in mind again the diverse and contested purposes of community sanctions, more research is needed to explore the credibility and legitimacy of probation, and what enhances and undermines it. More broadly, research should also look at how probation can encourage community support for reintegration.

Notes

1   See www.cost.eu/domains_actions/isch/Actions/IS1106.

References

Allen, R. (2012) *Reducing the Use of Imprisonment: What Can We Learn From Europe?* London: Criminal Justice Alliance.

Annison, J., Eadie, T. and Knight, C. (2008) 'People First: Probation Officer Perspectives on Probation Work'. *Probation Journal* 55 (3) pp. 259–71.

Bradley, Rt Hon. (2009) *Lord Bradley's Review of People with Mental Health Problems or Learning Disabilities in the Criminal Justice System.* Report No. 294278. London: Department of Health.

Bridges, A. (2006) *Speech by Andrew Bridges, HM Chief Inspector of Probation at the Home Secretary's Public Protection Event for Probation Service Middle Managers, 24 April 2006.* Available at: www.justice.gov.uk/downloads/about/hmiprob/speech.pdf/ [accessed August 2011].

Bottoms, A. (2008) 'The Community Dimension of Community Penalties'. *The Howard Journal of Criminal Justice* 47 (2) pp. 146–69.

Bottoms, A.E. and Costello, A. (2010) 'The Phenomenon of Victim-Offender Overlap: A Study of Offences against Households' in A.E. Bottoms and J. Roberts (eds) *Hearing the Victim.* Cullompton: Willan pp. 104–40.

Burke, L. (2010) 'Probation Qualifications Framework: Getting the Right Balance'. *Probation Journal* 57 (1) pp. 3–8.

Clinks (2010) *Payment by Results: What Does it Mean for Voluntary Organisations Working with Offenders?* Available at: www.clinks.org [accessed 10 September 2011].

Cohen, S. (1985) *Visions of Social Control*. Oxford: Blackwell.

Commission on English Prisons Today (2009) *Localism: A Consultation Paper*. Available at: www.howardleague.com [accessed 1 September 2011].

COST (2012) *Memorandum of Understanding for the Implementation of a European Concerted Research Action designated as COST Action IS1106: Offender Supervision in Europe, 8 December 2011, COST 4178/11, European Cooperation in Science and Technology (COST)*. Available at: http://w3.cost.eu/fileadmin/domain_files/ISCH/Action_IS1106/mou/IS1106-e.pdf [accessed 20 December 2012].

Criminal Justice Alliance (2012) *Response to the Ministry of Justice Consultation 'Punishment and Reform: Effective Community Sentences'*. London: Criminal Justice Alliance.

Deering, J. (2010) 'Attitudes and Beliefs of Trainee Probation Officers: A "New Breed"'. *Probation Journal* 57 (1) pp. 9–26.

Deuchar, R. (2012) 'The Impact of Curfews and Electronic Monitoring on the Social Strains, Support and Capital Experienced by Youth Gang Members and Offenders in the West of Scotland'. *Criminology and Criminal Justice* 12 (2) pp. 113–28.

Disley, E., Rubin, J., Scraggs, E., Burrows, N. and Culley, D. (2011) *Lessons Learned From the Planning and Early Implementation of the Social Impact Bond at HMP Peterborough*. Research Series 5/11. London: Ministry of Justice.

Dobson, G. (2012) 'The Problem with Privatising Probation Services'. *Guardian*, 22 May. Available at: www.guardian.co.uk/society/2012/may/22/problem-with-privatising-probation-services? [accessed 17 December 2012].

Dominey, J. (2011) 'A Mixed Market for Probation Services: Can Lessons from the Recent Past Help Shape the Near Future?' *Probation Journal*, December 2012, 59 (4) pp. 339–54.

Durnescu, I. (2011) 'Pains of Probation: Effective Practice and Human Rights'. *International Journal of Offender Therapy and Comparative Criminology*, 55 (4) pp. 530–45.

Fox, C. and Albertson, K. (2011) 'Payment by Results and Social Impact Bonds in the Criminal Justice Sector: New Challenges for the Concept of Evidence-Based Policy?'. *Criminology and Criminal Justice* 11 (5) pp. 395–413.

Fox, C. and Albertson, K. (2012) 'Is Payment by Results the Most Efficient Way to Address the Challenges Faced by the Criminal Justice Sector?'. *Probation Journal* December 2012, 59 (4) pp. 355–73.

Garside, R. (2012) *Downsizing Prison*. Available at: www.worksforfreedom.org [accessed 21 June 2012].

Gelsthorpe, L. and Hedderman, C. (2012) 'Providing for Women Offenders: the Risks of Adopting a Payment by Results Approach'. *Probation Journal* December 2012, 59 (4) pp. 374–90.

Gregory, M. (2007) 'Probation Training: Evidence from Newly Qualified Officers'. *Social Work Education* 26 (1) pp. 53–68.

Guardian (2012a) 'DWP "Did Not Do Enough to Stop Fraud Among Welfare-to-Work Companies"', 16 May. Available at: www.guardian.co.uk [accessed 30 June 2012].

Guardian (2012b) 'Serco Investigated Over Claims of "Unsafe" Out-of-Hours GP Service', 25 May. Available at: www.guardian.co.uk [accessed 30 June 2012].

Harker, H. and Worrall, A. (2011) 'From "Community Corrections" to "Probation and Parole" in Western Australia'. *Probation Journal* 58 (4) pp. 364–71.

The Howard League for Penal Reform (2010) *A Howard League for Penal Reform Submission to the Justice Affairs Select Committee's Inquiry on the Role of the Probation Service*. Available at: www.howardleague.org [accessed 10 September 2011].

Humberside Probation Trust (2012) *Response to Punishment and Reform: Effective Community Sentences* (Consultation Paper CP8/2012). Humberside: Humberside Probation Trust.

Justice Affairs Select Committee (2011) *The Role of the Probation Service*. Available at: www.publications.parliament.uk [accessed 1 September 2011].

Ledger, J. (2012) 'Probation and Contracting Out: The Case Against' in V. Helyar-Cardwell (ed.) *Delivering Justice: The Role of the Public, Private and Voluntary Sectors in Prisons and Probation*. London: Criminal Justice Alliance pp. 46–50.

Mair, G. (2011) 'The Community Order in England and Wales: Policy and Practice'. *Probation Journal* 58 (3) pp. 215–32.

Make Justice Work (2011) *Community or Custody*. Available at: makejustice-work.org.uk [accessed 21 October 2011].

Malloch, M. and McIvor, G. (2011) 'Women and Community Sentences'. *Criminology and Criminal Justice* 11 (4) pp. 325–44.

Maruna, S. (2001) *Making Good: How Ex-Convicts Reform and Rebuild Their Lives*. Washington, DC: American Psychological Books.

Maruna, S. and King, A. (2004) 'Public Opinion and Community Penalties' in T. Bottoms, S. Rex and G. Robinson (eds) *Alternatives to Prison: Options for an Insecure Society*. Cullompton: Willan pp. 83–113.

Maruna, S. and King, A. (2008) 'Is a Conservative Just a Liberal Who Has Been Mugged? Exploring the Origins of Punitive Views'. *Punishment and Society* 20 (1) pp. 129–34.

McCulloch, T. and McNeill, F. (2007) 'Consumer Society, Commodification and Offender Management'. *Criminology and Criminal Justice* 7 (3) pp. 223–42.

McNeill, F. (2011) 'Probation, Credibility and Justice'. *Probation Journal* 58 (1) pp. 9–22.

McNeill, F. (2012a) 'A Copernician Correction for Community Sentences'. *The Howard Journal* 51 (1) pp. 94–9.

McNeill, F. (2012b) *Not Big, Not Tough, Not Clever*. Available at: http:// blogs.iriss.org.uk/discoveringdesistance/2012/06/16/not-big-not-tough-not-clever/ [accessed 8 August 2012].

McNeill, F. and Robinson, G. (2012) 'Liquid Legitimacy and Community Sanctions' in A. Crawford and A. Hucklesby (eds) *Legitimacy and Compliance in Criminal Justice*. Abingdon: Routledge pp. 116–37.

McNeill, F. and Whyte, B. (2007) *Reducing Reoffending: Social Work and Community Justice in Scotland: Social Work with Offenders in Scotland*. Cullompton: Willan.

Mills, H. (2011) *Community Sentences: A Solution to Penal Excess*. Available at: www.crimeandjustice.org.uk [accessed 15 October 2011].

Ministry of Justice *Probation Qualifications Framework Review*. London: Ministry of Justice.

Ministry of Justice (2010a) *Offender Management Caseload Statistics 2009 – Ministry of Justice Statistics Bulletin*. London: The Stationery Office.

Ministry of Justice (2010b) *Breaking the Cycle: Effective Punishment, Rehabilitation and Sentencing of Offenders*. London: The Stationery Office.

Ministry of Justice (2012a) *Punishment and Reform: Effective Probation Services* – Consultation Paper CP7/2012. London: Ministry of Justice.

Ministry of Justice (2012b) *Punishment and Reform: Effective Community Sentences* – Consultation Paper CP08/2012. London: Ministry of Justice.

Ministry of Justice (2012c) *Consultation on Sentences in the Community and the Future Shape of Probation Services Impact Assessment 4 January 2012*. Available at: https://consultjustice.gov.uk [accessed 8 August 2012].

Nacro (2012) *Response to Punishment and Reform: Effective Community Sentences June 2012*. Available at: www.nacro.org.uk/ [accessed 15 July 2012].

Napo (2012) *Punishment and Reform: Effective Community Sentences – A Response from Napo*. London: Napo.

National Audit Office (2008) *National Probation Service: The Supervision of Community Orders in England and Wales*. London: NAO.

Neilson, A. (2012) 'Counterblast: Putting a Price on Rehabilitation: Payment by Results and the March of the Market in Prisons and Probation'. *The Howard Journal of Criminal Justice* 51 (4) pp. 419–22.

Nellis, M. (2010) 'Electronic Monitoring: Towards Integration into Offender Management' in F. McNeill, P. Raynor and C. Trotter (eds) *Offender Supervision: New Directions in Theory, Research and Practice*. Cullompton: Willan pp. 509–33.

Orr, D. (2012) 'Private Sector Efficiency? This Lie has to Stop', *Guardian*, 14 July. Available at: www.guardian.co.uk [accessed 8 August 2012].

Ploeg, G. and Sandlie, J.L. (2011) 'Mapping Probation Futures: Norway'. *Probation Journal* 58 (4) p. 38.

Prison Reform Trust (2012) *Prison Reform Trust Response to the Ministry of Justice Consultation, Punishment and Reform: Effective Community Sentences*. London: Prison Reform Trust.

Roberts, M. (2011) *By Their Fruits ... Applying Payments by Results to Drugs Recovery*. Available at: www.ukdpc.net [accessed 1 September 2010].

Robinson, G. and McNeill, F. (2004) 'Purposes Matter: Examining the "Ends" of Probation' in G. Mair (ed.) *What Matters in Probation*. Cullompton: Willan pp. 227–304.

Robinson, G. and McNeill, F. (2008) 'Exploring the dynamics of compliance with community penalties'. Theoretical Criminology, 12 (4) pp. 431–49.

Scottish Prisons Commission (2008) *Scotland's Choice: Report of the Scottish Prisons Commission*. Edinburgh.

Senior, P. (2011) 'The Voluntary and Community Sector: The Paradox of Becoming Centre-Stage in the Big Society'. *British Journal of Community Justice* 9 (1/2) pp. 37–54.

Smith, D. (2010) *Public Confidence in the Criminal Justice System: Findings from the BCS 2002/2003 to 2007/8* – Ministry of Justice Research Series 16/10. London: Ministry of Justice.

Social Finance (2012) *The One Service. One Year On: Reducing Reoffending Among Short Sentenced Male Offenders from Peterborough Prison*. London: Social Finance Ltd.

Ugwudike, P. (2010) 'Compliance with Community Penalties: The Importance of Interactional Dynamics' in F. McNeill, P. Raynor and C. Trotter (eds) *Offender Supervision: New Directions in Theory, Research and Practice*. Cullompton: Willan pp. 325–43.

Young Foundation (2010) *What does Ken Clarke's Rehabilitation Revolution Mean for Justice Innovation?* Available at: www.youngfoundation.org/justice [accessed 7 January 2010].

7

MENTAL DISORDER AND IMPRISONMENT

UNDERSTANDING AN INTRACTABLE PROBLEM?

JILL PEAY

Determining the contribution made by those with mental health problems[1] to the size of the prison population is not easy. Those who offend who coincidentally have a mental health problem are subject both to all the normal alternative sanctions to imprisonment and are also candidates for diversion into the mental health system under the Mental Health Act 1983. Indeed even after remand or prison sentence there are options for transfer to hospital. Understanding this web of possibilities and the problems associated with correctly placing those with mental health problems is central to any proposal to reduce the flow of this group into prison.

This chapter will examine briefly the factors that underpin the scale of the current prison population, assess the contribution made by those with mental health problems to this and then pose a series of questions about what is not known or not sufficiently understood about the relationship between mental health problems and the prison population. This is intended to help identify viable lines for research.

FACTORS CONTRIBUTING TO THE CURRENT
PRISON POPULATION

One of the best summaries of the factors underpinning the rise in the prison population can be found in the Ministry of Justice's *Story of the Prison Population 1995–2009 England and Wales*:

> Between 1995 and 2009, the prison population in England and Wales grew by 32,500 or 66 per cent. Almost all of this increase took place within two segments of the prison population – those sentenced to immediate custody (78% of the increase) and those recalled to prison for breaking the conditions of their release (16%).
>
> The immediate custodial sentenced population increased after 1995 because the courts sentenced more offenders to prison each year between 1995 and 2002, and because offenders have been staying in prison for longer.
>
> (Ministry of Justice 2009a)

Whilst the recall population makes a significant contribution (attributable both to higher recall rates and longer periods spent in custody) the vast bulk of the increase is due to those sentenced to immediate imprisonment. The remand population has remained fairly stable, albeit large, at around 12–13,000; the fine defaulter population has all but vanished since 2001. Although those in breach of non-custodial penalties and the population of non-criminals has grown rapidly, they both remain small in proportion to the total. Since 2009 the population has grown to 85,400 in March 2011 (Berman 2011). By March 2011 a fifth of the sentenced prison population were serving indeterminate sentences (life sentences or IPPs) (Berman 2011).

Questions remain as to why the courts sentenced more people to immediate imprisonment (up until 2002) and why people then stayed for longer periods in prison (which may be attributable to longer initial sentences, the frequency of use of indeterminate sentences, and policies on release).

With respect to recall, the Ministry of Justice summary asserts that:

> The higher recall rate was caused by changes to the law making it easier to recall prisoners, and changes introduced in the Criminal Justice Act 2003 which lengthened the licence period for most offenders. Recall prisoners

have stayed in custody for longer, partly reflecting the increase in licence periods and also because, prior to the introduction of Fixed Term Recalls in 2008, the Parole Board were required to review all recall cases.

(Ministry of Justice 2009a)

Key questions here include the level of contribution (if any) that a person's mental health status has made to these developments. Accordingly, what interventions in this field might contribute to reducing the current prison population?

THE EXTENT OF THE PROBLEM

A number of official documents and reports assert the mental health make-up of the prison population is disproportionate and unjustifiable:

There is a growing consensus that we are sending some people to prison who should not be there. Short prison sentences are not appropriate for all the offenders who currently receive them; and too many people with severe mental illness are in prison rather than secure treatment facilities. All of this contributes to the problem of overcrowding, which in turn limits the capacity of prisons, probation and other services to work effectively to reduce reoffending.

(Social Exclusion Unit 2002: 17)

Notions of disproportionality derive from the sense that prisoners (compared with the general population) display greater levels of mental (and physical) health problems. As the Social Exclusion Unit report observes '72 per cent of male and 70 per cent of female sentenced prisoners suffer from two or more mental health disorders; 14 and 35 times the level in the general population respectively' (Social Exclusion Unit 2002: 10.2). The evidence cited for this is the Singleton *et al.* study (1998). Figures with respect to young people are the most concerning – '95 per cent of young prisoners aged 15 to 21 suffer from a mental disorder. 80 per cent suffer from at least two. Nearly 10 per cent of female sentenced young people reported already having been admitted to a mental hospital at some point'. Comparable figures with the general population are not given here.

It is difficult to know how robust these figures remain given the passage of time since Singleton *et al.* conducted their study and given all of the original caveats about what the term 'mental health disorder' included. However, it is worth noting that incarcerated populations are overpopulated by those with 'mental disorders' – 90 per cent have one of five diagnosable disorders – psychosis; neurosis; learning disability; personality disorder; and/or drug or alcohol dependence. Most worryingly, 7–10 per cent displayed functional psychotic disorders (Singleton et al. 1998; see also Melzer et al. 2002). Undoubtedly prisoners with dual diagnoses (Crome 2001) – having both a diagnosis of mental illness and substance abuse – contribute markedly to the figures and face the particular problems of being eligible to be rejected by both addiction and mental health programmes. Similarly, the tautological association between some definitions of personality disorder and offending behaviour will make for inevitable high levels of personality disorder amongst custodial populations.

How broad a definition is adopted of what constitutes a 'mentally disordered offender' is also critical. The recent *Report of the Criminal Justice Joint Inspection* by the assorted Inspectorates for the Police, Probation Service and CPS (Criminal Justice Joint Inspection 2009) recommended the adoption of a common definition of the term 'mentally disordered offender' by the Department of Health, Department of Education, Ministry of Justice, Youth Justice Board and the Home Office. This definition asserts:

> Those who come into contact with the criminal justice system because they have committed, or are suspected of committing, a criminal offence, and who may be acutely or chronically ill. It also includes those in whom a degree of disturbance is recognised even though it may not be severe enough to bring it within the criteria laid down by the Mental Health Act 1983 (now 2007).
>
> (Criminal Justice Joint Inspection 2009)

Using this definition would draw much of the offending population within its ambit. Thus it would be surprising if the figures had changed radically. Indeed, a more recent appraisal of the mental health status of prisoners (albeit nothing like as systematic as the Singleton et al. study) reports the findings of a survey of some 1,435 prisoners (see Table 7.1).

In addition to this there has been a raft of policy documents and reviews dealing with the issues raised by 'mentally disordered offenders'

Table 7.1 Proportion of sample reporting mental health issues

Said they needed help for an emotional or mental health problem at the time of interview	20%
Treated/counselled for a mental health or emotional problem in the year before custody	17%
Suicidal thoughts in the year before custody	16%
Mental health illness or depression as a long-standing limiting illness	12%
Attempted suicide in the year before custody	9%
Heard voices saying 'quite a few words or sentences' when there was no one around to account for it	9%
Prescribed anti-psychotic medication in the year before custody	2%

Source: Ministry of Justice (2010a: 134).

in the prison population. Undoubtedly the most important of these is the *Bradley Report* (2009), which made 82 recommendations in a 173-page report, all but four of which were accepted by the then government in whole or in principle.[2] Following the report a Health and Criminal Justice National Programme Board (chaired by David Behan) was established. A National Advisory Group to support ministers was also set up. Professor Louis Appleby has been appointed National Director for Health and Criminal Justice. It is too early to tell what difference, if any, the institution of these oversight arrangements is making in the field with respect to the implementation of Bradley's proposals.

Amongst the most important of the recommendations was the establishment of a national network of criminal justice mental health teams to divert people at various stages in the criminal justice process towards support services and away from a penal outcome, or to give support after release if a penal outcome transpires. Recommendations on training and awareness for criminal justice personnel, the 14-day maximum wait period for transfer from prison to hospital (not initially accepted by the government), and the need for the NHS to take on the provision of health services in police stations (see IPCC 2008) were also important.

There are also numerous other relevant reports including the *Corston Report* (2007) on vulnerable women; NACRO (2007 and 2010) – the latter with a focus on foreign nationals; the RCN, NACRO and the Centre for Mental Health (2010); the Sainsbury Centre (2008) on IPPs, (2009) on diversion and (2010) on the convergence of policy between mental health and criminal justice; HMIP (2007); Prison Reform Trust (2009); Ministry of Justice (2010b) – the Green Paper *Breaking the Cycle*, which makes 'mentally disordered' prisoners a focus for renewed attention.

The Report by Lennox, Senior and Shaw (2009) on *Offender Health* for the Department of Health also constitutes a valuable resource. As a scoping study it usefully identifies the knowledge gaps and research priorities across the criminal justice system as they relate to health issues generally, but with mental health being the major component of the review. Similarly, albeit on the 'single issue' of pathways into medium secure care, the work of Melzer et al. from 2004 (see generally Melzer *et al.* 2004a, b; Grounds *et al.* 2004) reveals some fascinating insights on the fine detail of admission policies (for example, those without a primary diagnosis of mental illness being generally excluded from admission to Medium Secure Units (MSUs)) and waiting times. It may be that there is a gulf between recognising what needs to be done and achieving its implementation. Mentally disordered offenders may present peculiarly irresolvable dilemmas.

Many of these documents observe that the principle of equivalence – the notion that prisoners should receive the same quality of health care as those outside prison – has been in place for over a decade, together with the establishment of in-reach teams. Accordingly, there is an argument that prisoners should be receiving at least as good care for their mental health in prison as outside; for some prisoners, attention will be given where outside they may have not accessed services. However, the documents also all agree that prison is no place for those with acute or severe mental illness. Again, in principle, criminal justice liaison and diversion schemes, health screening on reception and comprehensive screening within a week should be identifying these individuals and transferring them to appropriate services (Huws *et al.* 1997; Mackay and Machin 2000). So why is there a persistent perception that there are too many mentally disordered offenders in prison?

TOO MANY IN PRISON? PERSPECTIVES

There is a persistent perception that there are too many people with mental health issues in prison. One approach takes as its starting point the combination of an increased sensitivity to mental health issues and the notion that the large number of people sent to prison each year on sentences of under 12 months[3] will make inevitable the identification of many with diagnosable mental disorders. Indeed, the very definition of what constitutes mental disorder (Peay 2010a: 3) is critical here. The Mental Health Act 1983 (as amended by the 2007 Act) states 'mental disorder means any disorder or disability of the mind'; whilst dependence on drugs and alcohol alone is insufficient, disorders related to their use can be included. The Act's Code of Practice (Department of Health 2008: para 3.3) notes:

> Clinically recognised conditions which could fall within the Act's definition of mental disorder:
> - affective disorders, such as depression and bipolar disorder
> - schizophrenia and delusional disorders
> - neurotic, stress-related and somatoform disorders, such as anxiety, phobic disorders, obsessive compulsive disorders, post-traumatic stress disorder and hypochondriacal disorders
> - organic mental disorders such as dementia and delirium (however caused)
> - personality and behavioural changes caused by brain injury or damage (however acquired)
> - personality disorders
> - mental and behavioural disorders caused by psychoactive substance use...
> - eating disorders, non-organic sleep disorders and non-organic sexual disorders
> - learning disabilities...
> - autistic spectrum disorders (including Asperger's syndrome) ...
> - behavioural and emotional disorders of children and adolescents.
>   (Note: this list is not exhaustive.)

Thus what is disproportionate depends upon what might be expected. Certainly the UK prison population is not unique in attracting comment for the numbers of prisoners with mental health problems. Fazel and Danesh's study (2002) of 62 surveys in 12 countries involving some 23,000 prisoners found 'prisoners were several times more likely to have psychosis and major depression, and about ten times more likely to have antisocial personality disorder, than the general population' (Fazel and Danesh 2002: 545). This would, at first sight, imply that prisoners are not representative of the general population in terms of their mental health status.

However, given that prisoners in the remand population are more likely than sentenced prisoners to suffer from personality and neurotic disorders and to have had contact with mental health services before entering custody, are these enhanced incidences of mental disorder a consequence of some selection effects amongst those thought inappropriate for remand on bail? Similarly, both young adults and black and minority ethnic people suffer from higher rates of some forms of disorder (perhaps because of reduced engagement with mental health services) and yet these groups are disproportionately represented in the prison population. This may account in part for raised levels of mental illness – or is it that prison itself promotes the development of mental disorder in those who are vulnerable?

> High proportions of prisoners spend significant amounts of time in their cells. It has been found that 28 per cent of male sentenced prisoners with evidence of psychosis reported spending 23 or more hours a day in their cells – over twice the proportion of those without mental health problems.
>
> (Social Exclusion Unit 2002: 10.21)

Whilst the solution of diversion elsewhere seems attractive and relatively easy it remains an enigma as to why so many people with mental health problems remain within custodial penal populations. Perhaps diversion is neither attractive nor easy to those who would have to accommodate these people and for those who would be subject to such diversion.

On 14 October 2011 the prison population stood at 86,751 with a further 796 people held in NOMS operated immigration removal centres. Figures on mental health detained patients in England on 31 March 2010 amounted to 16,622 (12,832 detained patients in NHS facilities and a further 3,790 individuals in independent hospitals). The bulk of these patients had not committed offences but a limited number of patients had committed less serious offences and received hospital orders – only 3,937 were on section 37/41 hospital orders with a restriction order attached where the court was satisfied that the restriction order was necessary to protect the public from serious harm. Clearly, there is a very obvious problem of capacity within the health sector to receive people who have committed offences. Diversion from the criminal justice sector into mental health services may be easier in theory than in practice.

It is equally the case that alternative pressures may result in more people being diverted to prison when they might otherwise be dealt with in the community, either because of perceptions relating to risk (hence the misconceived Dangerous and Severe Personality Disorder (DSPD) initiative) or because of a need for therapeutic endeavours – of assessment or treatment – to occur within a secure environment. Prison then becomes the default setting for these people, particularly for those deemed 'risky'. The key issue here is where else might these people be diverted and, in turn, are those destinations enthusiastic or willing to accept as patients people who have committed such offences?

FURTHER RESEARCH

1. Is the mental health make-up of the increased prison population similar to that encountered by Singleton *et al.* (1998)? Have any particular factors influenced it in particular ways (veterans; foreign nationals; the age range; homelessness; alcohol and drugs; the offence types; the growing proportion of those serving sentences for violence, etc.)? Repeating the Singleton *et al.* (1998) study was also recommended by the *Bradley Report*.

2. What has been the effect of the Criminal Justice Act 2003 and its provisions on psychiatric reports? Similarly, are those with mental health problems dealt with according to the Act's six principles (section 142(1)), or under the exception in section 142(2)(d) for those dealt with under the Mental Health Act 1983? Why has there been a shift away from the use of the hospital order without restrictions (in 2008 there were only 343 hospital orders with restrictions and 392 hospital orders without restrictions made by the courts: compare this with the 926 prisoners transferred before or after sentence to hospital under the Mental Health Act 1983). These numbers are low both in

comparison and as a proportion of the overall sentenced population. Moreover, why are alternatives to custody not used and in particular, why are community penalties with a mental health order attached used so very infrequently?

3. Is mental health a factor that makes release more difficult (with respect to either early release (end of custody licence before its abolition on 12 March 2010 or home detention curfew – both by executive discretion) or discretionary conditional release/parole, discretionary life sentences, release from IPPs etc. – see, for example, Asthana 2010)? The role of both those involved in executive release and by parole boards and their attitudes to mental disorder as a factor affecting release is uncertain. Work with the mental health unit (Boyd-Caine 2010) with respect to the release of restricted patients indicated that attributed risk was a key factor. (See also Royal College of Psychiatrists (2008) for a measured approach to the issues associated with assessing risk.) Little is known about the influence of mental health factors in the work of the Early Release and Recall Section, part of the Sentencing Policy and Penalties Unit in the National Offender Management Service (NOMS), but there is a Public Protection and Mental Health Group at NOMS (see also Seddon 2008).

4. What accounts for the disproportionate use of indeterminate sentences for those with mental health problems, e.g. IPPs, 'discretionary' life sentences, mandatory life (see Sainsbury Centre for Mental Health 2008)? What accounts for the marked reduction in the successful use of diminished responsibility defences? Has the situation been exacerbated by the substantial amendment of this defence under the Coroners and Justice Act 2009 (see Mackay 2010)?

5. Why has recall for breach of licence increased? Is it used disproportionately for those with mental disorder? Longer periods on recall (hence a greater period at risk) because of longer sentences and indeterminate sentences and easier recall provisions answer in part the former question but what part, if any, does mental disorder play here? What role does MAPPA play in sustaining this (see Multi-Agency Public Protection Arrangements Annual Report, Ministry of Justice 2010c)?

6. Failure to use non-custodial options – community penalties with mental health treatment requirements (see Seymour et al. 2008 and Seymour and Rutherford 2008). In 2006 there were 725 MHTRs in 2006 for England and Wales – compared with 11,261 community

orders with drug treatment requirements – why are they so comparably neglected? This was also an issue identified by the *Bradley Report* as critical. Also is the fine (which has declined) seen as peculiarly inappropriate for those with mental health problems? If so, why?

7. Delay in release once recalled due to backlog with Parole Board – what part does mental health play?

8. Breach of non-custodial options and the non-criminal population (that is, persons held under the Immigration Act plus those held for civil offences such as contempt of court and non-payment of child maintenance) have grown disproportionately but are small in absolute numbers. Is mental health a factor here?

9. The remand population – of the approximately 12–13,000 detainees how many of them are there to enable psychiatric reports to be prepared? Why are the remand to hospital provisions under the Mental Health Act 1983 (sections 35, 36 and 38) not used as envisaged? What accounts for the recent increase in use of section 38 – is this indicative of the scope for change? Why are hybrid orders (the hospital and limitation direction, Eastman and Peay 1998) not an option for young adults (given that they have now been extended from psychopathic disorder to all forms of mental disorder)? Should they be?

10. How do mandatory minimum sentences impact on those with mental health problems where they are not eligible for disposal under the Mental Health Act 1983 (see point 2 above).

11. If more serious offence groups are coming before courts does this imply less use of diversion into the mental health system? Moreover, whilst the use of unfitness to plead has increased (see Mackay appendix in Law Commission 2010) has it increased as much as it perhaps ought to have given the levels of disorder within the prison population (Peay 2010b)? Why does the special verdict of not guilty by reason of insanity remain so rare? (The Law Commission issued a Scoping Report on this and on the subject of automatism in July 2012.)

12. Since offences of violence against the person represent the highest proportion of offence groups for all sentenced prisoners (adult male/female/juvenile male and young adult male) to what extent does the presence of mental disorder make alternative disposals not viable? Similarly, for women, offences of violence now outnumber drug offences (historically the most common offence group). Again, does mental disorder make a difference here?

13. The use of suspended sentences has increased dramatically. Are these sentences much used with those with mental health problems (if not, why not?). What happens at breach?

14. The Crime and Disorder Act 1998 introduced executive recall for those on sentences of up to four years (previously 12 months – four years recall by courts on recommendation of Probation Service). Is mental health a factor in the increased use of recall?

15. Do the figures on the transfer of prisoners, and in particular the recent increase in the transfer of sentenced prisoners (as opposed to those on remand) to hospital, suggest that the system is working better (more responsive to need) or that the courts are inappropriately sending acutely mentally disordered people into custody when they ought to be given hospital disposals in the first instance? In 2008 there were 442 transfers of sentenced prisoners (up from 258 in 1998) and 484 transfers of remand prisoners (481 in 1998).

16. There is a central paradox at the heart of diversion issues (James 1999; James *et al.* 2002). Diversion is regarded as 'a good thing'; a number of opportunities arise for diversion during the 'process' of criminal justice (police, CPS, courts, probation, prison, hospital, community, licence and recall; place of safety, arrest, charge, pre-trial, plea, trial, conviction, sentence or disposal). Yet many people continue to come before the courts, the vast bulk of whom receive conventional sentences without their mental disorder playing any significant part in their disposal. Why is this? At every stage similar questions can be asked in respect of why the facility and power to divert are not used – indeed, how is the Bradley recommendation that all courts should have access to liaison and diversion services progressing? To take just one example of a failure to use existing powers, why do magistrates not make more use of section 37(3) of the Mental Health Act 1983 – is it due to some unawareness of the existence of the provision or that the provision is regarded as inappropriate? Is this just yet another example across all pre-trial provisions of a form of 'professional carelessness' (Rumgay and Munroe 2001)?

17. Following the *Bradley Report* there have been a number of developments in service delivery (see, for example, the screening programme run by Dr Andrew Forrester for the South London and Maudsley NHS Foundation Trust, which endeavours to identify defendants

with mental disorder and learning disability at courts, in prison and in police stations in the Lambeth area of London). Whether all of these developments also include a research arm is unclear but questions can be asked generally about how many Bradley 'criminal justice mental health teams' are in place and providing effective diversion?

18. Since learning disability in some of its guises (acute vulnerability) can be brought under the broader definition of 'mental disorder' advocated above by the CJJI Report, and falls under the Mental Health Act where it is associated with abnormally aggressive or seriously irresponsible conduct, to what extent does learning disability (rife in the prison population) contribute to our perception of who should and should not be in a custodial population?

19. Is reception screening in prisons effective?

20. Implementing *Bradley* – it is hard to achieve an overview on progress – one way forward might be some focused interviews with the three named parties above who have been given responsibility for this in their various guises.

21. Are all the opportunities for work with mentally disordered prisoners fully exploited during imprisonment? If there is any kind of relationship between disorder and offending (itself not straightforward), it would be regrettable to fail to take the opportunities that present themselves in prison, particularly the opportunities for 'talking therapies'. Reoffending is already a too common pattern following release, yet the view persists that those with mental health problems are 'not suitable' for such interventions. Can this be justified? Is it true?

Notes

1 Those with mental health problems in the criminal justice system are referred to as 'mentally disordered offenders'. This term has been jointly adopted by the Department of Health, Department of Education, Ministry of Justice, Youth Justice Board and the Home Office.

2 A good briefing on the *Bradley Report* can be found in Sainsbury Centre for Mental Health (2009b). The Sainsbury Centre is now known as the Centre for Mental Health.

3 64,985 in 2008 (Ministry of Justice 2009b, table 6.1).

References

Asthana, A. (2010) 'Prisoners on indeterminate sentences "left in limbo" over parole dates'. *Observer*, 31 October.

Berman, G. (2011) *Prison Population Statistics Standard Note SN/SG/4334*. London: House of Commons Library.

Boyd-Caine, T. (2010) *Protecting the Public? Detention and Release of Mentally Disordered Offenders*. Cullompton: Willan.

Rt Hon Lord Bradley (2009) *Lord Bradley's Review of People with Mental Health Problems or Learning Disabilities in the Criminal Justice System*. London: Department of Health.

Corston, J. (2007) *Review of Women in the Criminal Justice System with Particular Vulnerabilities*. London: Home Office.

Criminal Justice Joint Inspection (2009) *A Joint Inspection on Work Prior to Sentence with Offenders with Mental Disorders*. Available at: www.scie-socialcareonline.org.uk/profile.asp?guid=9f9b620e-5fb7–458a-8807-bof2be27abca [accessed July 2012].

Crome, I. (ed.) (2001) *Co-existing Problems of Mental Disorder and Substance Misuse ('Dual Diagnosis'): A Review of Relevant Literature*. London: Royal College of Psychiatrists Research Unit.

Department of Health (2008) *Code of Practice, Mental Health Act 1983 published pursuant to s.118 of the Act*. London: The Stationery Office.

Eastman, N, and Peay, J. (1998) 'Sentencing psychopaths: is the hospital and limitation direction an ill-considered hybrid?'. *Criminal Law Review* pp. 93–108.

Fazel, S. and Danesh, J. (2002) 'Serious mental disorder in 23,000 prisoners: a systematic review of 62 surveys'. *Lancet* 359 pp. 545–50.

Grounds, A., Gelsthorpe, L., Howes, M., Melzer, D., Tom, B., Brugha, T., Fryers, T., Gatward, R. and Meltzer H. (2004) 'Access to medium secure psychiatric care in England and Wales. 2: A qualitative study of admission decision-making'. *Journal of Forensic Psychiatry and Psychology* 15 (1) pp. 32–49.

HM Inspectorate of Prisons (2007) *The Mental Health of Prisoners: A Thematic Review of the Care and Support of Prisoners with Mental Health Needs*. London: HM Inspectorate of Prisons.

Huws, R., Longson, D., Reiss, D. and Larkin, E. (1997) 'Prison transfers to special hospitals since the introduction of the Mental Health Act 1983'. *Journal of Forensic Psychiatry* 8 pp. 74–84.

Independent Police Complaints Commission (2008) *Police Custody as a Place of Safety: Examining the use of Section 136 of the Mental Health Act 1983*. Available at: www.ipcc.gov.uk/en/Pages/mh_polcustody.aspx [accessed July 2012].

James, D. (1999) 'Court diversion at 10 years: can it work, does it work and has it a future?'. *Journal of Forensic Psychiatry* 10 pp. 507–24.

James, D., Farnham, F., Moorey, H., Lloyd, H., Hill, K., Blizard, R. and Barnes, T.R.E. (2002) *Outcome of Psychiatric Admission through the Courts RDS Occasional Paper no. 79*. London: Home Office.

Law Commission (2010) *Unfitness to Plead: A Consultation Paper, No. 197*. Available at: http://lawcommission.justice.gov.uk/docs/cp197_Unfitness_to_Plead_consultation.pdf [accessed 20 December 2012].

Law Commission (2012) *Insanity and Automatism: A Scoping Paper*. 18 July. Available at: http://lawcommission.justice.gov.uk/docs/insanity_scoping.pdf [accessed July 2012].

Lennox, C., Senior, J. and Shaw, J. (2009) *Offender Health: Scoping Review and Research Priorities within the UK, Report for Offender Health at the Department of Health*. Available at: www.ohrn.nhs.uk [accessed July 2012].

Mackay, R. (2010) 'The new diminished responsibility plea'. *Criminal Law Review* pp. 290–302.

Mackay, R. and Machin, D. (2000) 'The operation of Section 48 of the Mental Health Act 1983: an empirical study of the transfer of remand prisoners to hospital'. *British Journal of Criminology* 40 (4) pp. 727–45.

Melzer, D., Brian, T., Brugha, T., Fryers, T., Grounds, A., Johnson, T., Meltzer, H. and Singleton, N. (2002) 'Prisoners with psychosis in England and Wales: a one-year national follow-up'. *Howard Journal* 41 (1) pp. 1–13.

Melzer, D., Tom, B., Brugha, T., Fryers, T., Gatward, R., Grounds, A., Johnson, T. and Meltzer, H. (2004a) 'Access to medium secure psychiatric care in England and Wales. 1: A national survey of admission assessments'. *Journal of Forensic Psychiatry & Psychology* 15 (1) pp. 7–31.

Melzer, D., Tom, B., Brugha, T., Fryers, T., Gatward, R., Grounds, A., Johnson, T. and Meltzer, H. (2004b) 'Access to medium secure psychiatric care in England and Wales. 3: The clinical needs of assessed patients'. *Journal of Forensic Psychiatry and Psychology* 15 (1) pp. 50–65.

Ministry of Justice (2009a) *Story of the Prison Population 1995–2009 England and Wales Statistics Bulletin*. London: Ministry of Justice.

Ministry of Justice (2009b) *Offender Management Caseload Statistics 2008*. London: Ministry of Justice.

Ministry of Justice (2010a) *Compendium of Reoffending Statistics and Analysis Statistics Bulletin 4 November 2010*. London: Ministry of Justice.

Ministry of Justice (2010b) *Breaking the Cycle: Effective Punishment, Rehabilitation and Sentencing of Offenders*. London: Ministry of Justice.

Ministry of Justice (2010c) Annual statistics on Multi-Agency Public Protection Arrangements (MAPPA) eligible offenders for 2009–10. Available at:

www.justice.gov.uk/statistics/prisons-and-probation/mappa/mappa-2010 [accessed July 2012].

NACRO (2007) *Effective Mental Healthcare for Offenders: The Need for a Fresh Approach*. London: Nacro.

NACRO (2010) *Foreign National Offenders, Mental Health and the Criminal Justice System*. London: Nacro.

Peay, J. (2010a) *Mental Health and Crime*. Abingdon: Routledge.

Peay, J. (2010b) 'Civil admission following a finding of unfitness to plead' in B. McSherry and P. Weller (eds) *Rethinking Rights Based Mental Health Legislation*. Oxford: Hart Publishing, pp. 231–54.

Prison Reform Trust (2009) *Too Little, Too Late: An Independent Review of Unmet Mental Health Need in Prison*. London: Prison Reform Trust.

Royal College of Nursing, NACRO, Centre for Mental Health (2010) *Prison Mental Health: Vision and Reality*. London: Royal College of Nursing.

Royal College of Psychiatrists (2008) *Rethinking Risk to Others in Mental Health Services – Final Report of a Scoping Group*. Available at: www.rcpsych.ac.uk/files/pdfversion/CR150.pdf [accessed July 2012].

Rumgay, J. and Munroe, E. (2001) 'The lion's den: professional defences in the treatment of dangerous patients'. *Journal of Forensic Psychiatry* 12 (2) pp. 357–78.

Sainsbury Centre for Mental Health (2008) *In the Dark: The Mental Health Implications of Imprisonment for Public*. Available at: www.centreformentalhealth.org.uk/publications/in_the_dark.aspx?ID=584 [accessed July 2012].

Sainsbury Centre for Mental Health (2009) *Diversion: A Better Way for Criminal Justice and Mental Health*. Available at: www.centreformentalhealth.org.uk/publications/diversion.aspx?ID=593 [accessed July 2012].

Sainsbury Centre for Mental Health (2009b) *Briefing 38: The Bradley Report and the Government's Response: The Implications for Mental Health Services for Offenders*. Available at: www.centreformentalhealth.org.uk/pdfs/briefing38_Bradley_report.pdf [accessed July 2012].

Sainsbury Centre for Mental Health (2010) *Blurring the Boundaries on the Convergence of Mental Health, Criminal Justice Policy, Legislation, Systems and Practice*. Available at: www.centreformentalhealth.org.uk/pdfs/blurring_the_boundaries.pdf [accessed July 2012].

Seddon, T. (2008) 'Dangerous liaisons: personality disorder and the politics of risk'. *Punishment and Society* 10 (3) pp. 301–17.

Seymour, L. and Rutherford, M. (2008) *Report by the Sainsbury Centre into the Use of Community Penalties with a Mental Health Order Attached*. Available at: www.centreformentalhealth.org.uk/pdfs/scmh_mental_health_treatment_requirement_paper.pdf [accessed July 2012].

Seymour, L., Rutherford, M., Khanom, H. and Samele, C. (2008) 'The community order and the mental health treatment requirement'. *Journal of Mental Health Law* 2008 pp. 53–65.

Singleton, N., Meltzer, H. and Gatward, R. (1998) *Psychiatric Morbidity Among Prisoners in England and Wales*. London: The Stationery Office.

Social Exclusion Unit (2002) *Reducing Reoffending by Ex-Prisoners*. London: Office of the Deputy Prime Minister.

8

MINORITY GROUPS AND THE PENAL LANDSCAPE

CHALLENGES FOR RESEARCH AND POLICY

NEIL CHAKRABORTI AND CORETTA PHILLIPS

This chapter outlines the key issues and challenges surrounding minority groups within the penal system in England and Wales. Particular focus has been given to identifying the main pressure points which contribute to and exacerbate the problems facing minority groups caught up in the penal system, highlighting areas which should be prioritised by researchers and policy-makers as a way of minimising prison use and its associated problems in the context of minority groups.

DISPROPORTIONALITY IN THE PRISON POPULATION

Ever since the first ethnic monitoring exercise was undertaken by the Prison Service in 1984–5 there has been evidence of racial disproportionality in the prisons of England and Wales (Home Office 1986). In the 1980s those of black origin comprised only 1 per cent of the national population but made up 8 per cent of the male and 12 per cent of female prison populations. In June 2010, 14 per cent of the prison population was of black origin. When those of foreign nationality are excluded,

11 per cent of the prison population was black, a further 6 per cent was of Asian origin, 4 per cent was mixed, and less than 1 per cent was of 'Chinese/other' and unknown ethnic origins. Thus, while 80 per cent of the prison population of England and Wales is of majority white origin, black people make up 11 per cent of the prison population but only 3 per cent of the general population (Ministry of Justice 2011a).

CURRENT PENAL LANDSCAPE: PRESSURE POINTS

Much criminological attention has focused on whether disproportion-ality reflects higher rates of offending among minority ethnic groups or is the result of discrimination by the police and courts (Bowling and Phillips 2002; Webster 2007). This is a rather vexed question given the inherent flaws in the various data sources which shed light on this (see Phillips and Bowling 2012). Official arrest and imprisonment statis-tics, for example, reflect the outcomes of decisions by criminal justice agents and do not represent an independent account of offending per se. Victim and witness descriptions can sometimes reveal ethnicity but according to the British Crime Survey such information is only available for around 40 per cent of incidents, typically in 'contact offences' such as assault, robbery and theft (Clancy *et al.* 2001). Self-report offending surveys escape the biases of official statistics but they rely on the honesty and accuracy of interviewees to admit their offending behaviour. While seen as a valid and reliable measure, they may tell us more about offend-ing in the general population than amongst those who have committed serious offences.

Despite these methodological limitations it is possible to come to the following general conclusions which indicate current pressure points which contribute to minority ethnic over-representation in the prison and probation systems.

- Victims' descriptions and other data indicate that in certain less fre-quent offences, namely robbery, fraud and forgery and homicide, black people appear to be more often involved as suspects than might be expected from their representation in the general population (Clancy *et al.* 2001; Harrington and Mayhew 2001; Ministry of Justice 2009).
- Minority ethnic groups may be cumulatively disadvantaged in the criminal justice process by practices reliant on their cooperation with

police officers or prosecutors (Phillips and Bowling 2012). Research conducted in the 1980s and 1990s showed that minority ethnic suspects were more likely to opt for legal advice and to exercise their right of silence, but less likely to admit offences during police interview or before trial (Phillips and Brown 1998; Bucke and Brown 1997). These actions precluded the issuing of cautions or sentencing discounts and may have reflected a distrust of the police amongst minority ethnic individuals.

- There is some evidence of direct racial discrimination in the criminal justice process. 'Over-charging' by the police has been indicated in studies by Phillips and Brown (1998) and Mhlanga (1999) where minority ethnic suspects have been significantly more likely to have their cases terminated by the Crown Prosecution Service (CPS) even once previous convictions and the type and seriousness of the offence have been taken into account. The recent and methodologically robust studies of youth justice practice support claims of direct racial discrimination at various points in the criminal justice process (pre-court disposals; case termination; remands; acquittals; committals to crown court; pre-sentence reports (PSR) recommendations and sentencing) but these findings are complex and seem to vary by suspect ethnicity, gender and area (Feilizer and Hood 2004; May *et al.* 2010).

- The sentencing of drug importation offences along similar lines to violent offences and based on drug weight brings a significant number of minority ethnic male and female 'drug mules' into the prisons of England and Wales (Fleetwood 2011). Mitigating factors and PSRs are not taken into account in sentencing despite the fact that research has consistently shown low culpability among drug mules (Sudbury 2005; Agozino 2000). Notwithstanding public opinion may support lesser sentences than actually passed where the 'drug mule' is a Nigerian single mother involved in the medium scale importation of cocaine, for example (Jacobson *et al.* 2011).

MINORITY GROUPS INSIDE PRISON

In principle, the Prison Service appears to recognise not only the presence of large numbers of minority prisoners within domestic prisons but also the importance of safeguarding minority prisoners from prejudice and harassment. Indeed, as a way of demonstrating its commitment to diversity, the Prison Service (HMPS) pledges to 'promote diversity, equality of opportunity and combat unlawful discrimination' (HMPS 2011a). Furthermore 'irrespective of ... race, colour, religion, sex or sexual orientation' prisoners are guaranteed that their 'safety' and 'decency' will be protected (HMPS 2011b).

However, there are a number of pressure points evident within wider academic literature which suggest that there are significant problems associated with minority groups' lived experiences of the prison environment, and these have yet to be fully explored, contextualised or addressed. The following discussion focuses upon a range of identity characteristics (including ethnicity and faith, sexuality and disability) to illustrate the heightened vulnerabilities of minority group members within a prison setting and how prisons, in many respects, fail to provide an appropriate environment for prisoners from a minority background.[1] It outlines the case for stemming the flow of people incarcerated for committing offences against minorities, and suggests that the current over-reliance on punitive sanctions for hate crime perpetrators has little or no benefit in terms of encouraging desistance.

Ethnicity and faith

The Prison Service's record on race equality in prisons has been under considerable scrutiny in recent years. A formal investigation conducted by the Commission for Racial Equality (CRE) in 2003 concluded that the Prison Service had committed unlawful racial discrimination by failing to protect prisoners and staff from racist abuse, by not meeting the religious and cultural needs of Muslim prisoners and by not providing equal access to services and facilities within prisons. The elevated vulnerability of ethnic minorities in prison has been poignantly illustrated by the brutal murder of young Asian prisoner Zahid Mubarek by his former cellmate in 2000. The subsequent *Keith Inquiry* (2006) suggested that the Prison Service should have been aware of the violently racist mentality of Zahid's cellmate, Robert Stewart, and should have acted to prevent Zahid's exposure to him. Recent research by Phillips (2008) and Phillips and Earle (2011) suggests that social relations between white and minority ethnic prisoners are complex (often vacillating between the convivial and the conflictual) but must be understood within the context of broader societal race and faith relations (see also Liebling *et al.* 2012).

Despite an impressive reform programme in prisons to promote race equality, the Ministry of Justice (2008) *Race Review* still reported black prisoners as 30 per cent more likely than white prisoners to be on the basic prison regime. Equally concerning was the ethnic monitoring data which showed that black prisoners were 50 per cent more likely to be held in segregation and 60 per cent more likely to have force used against them. The *Race Review* also reported prison staff utilising negative stereotypes of minority ethnic prisoners which resulted in discrimination, and noted that constant yet 'subtle' and 'hidden' forms of racist discrimination amplified ethnic minority prisoner vulnerability, thereby creating a climate of fear within an already claustrophobic environment (Ministry of Justice 2008).

The national picture using SMART ethnic monitoring data for 2010–11 indicates that black prisoners experience disadvantage compared with their white counterparts in accessing Release on Temporary Licence (ROTL), in being categorised as higher security, and in their rate of adjudications and the use of segregation (for cellular confinement, good order and discipline and awaiting adjudication). Significantly, the use of force was also markedly higher for black prisoners (double the rate used against white prisoners). However, there were also proportionate or more advantageous outcomes for black prisoners' security recategorisation downwards, for Home Detention Curfew (HDC), and enhanced IEP status (Ministry of Justice 2011b).

HM Inspectorate of Prisons' (2010c) recent thematic review of the experience of Muslim prisoners indicated they held more negative perceptions of their treatment inside prison than their non-Muslim counterparts. Particular concerns centred on feelings of being negatively stereotyped as religious extremists by prison staff. At the same time, staff emphasised the need for specific training to assist Muslim prisoners as their needs were not met within existing diversity training. Recognising the often problematic dynamics of minority ethnic prisoner–prison officer relations, the Prison Service has recently funded research on evaluating the effects of structured communications to improve legitimacy and procedural justice in staff–prisoner relations (Tyler 2010; Jackson *et al.* 2010).

Allied to the general concerns about the levels of prejudice directed towards minority ethnic and faith prisoners are the more specific challenges facing the Prison Service that come with housing an ever diversifying range of ethnicities and faiths – each of whom will have their own needs, their own vulnerabilities, and their own prejudices. Therefore developing effective and sustainable responses to racist and faith-based discrimination within the prison environment cannot be achieved through the all too common 'one size fits all' approach to diversity strategising (Chakraborti 2010a) but instead is contingent upon research which identifies how best to respond to the differences that exist within and between minority prisoners.

Foreign national prisoners

Between 1999 and 2008 the number of foreign nationals imprisoned within the UK rose by 113 per cent. This compares to a 20 per cent rise in the number of British nationals sentenced to prison (Ministry of Justice 2010b: 78). Approximately 11,135 foreign national prisoners are housed in UK prisons, with around 1,500 prisoners held on 'non-criminal' sentences (Ministry of Justice 2010b, 2011a). Of particular note is the increase in the number of foreign national women imprisoned for drug trafficking offences. The prevalence of this specific minority group within prison is reflective of a punitive governmental stance towards drug offences designed to encourage desistance (Joseph 2006; Allen *et al.* 2003). Unfortunately little merit has resulted from such an initiative with the number of imprisoned 'drug mules' remaining high (HMIP 2009a: 8).

Unlike most British minority ethnic prisoners, foreign nationals in the UK often face the added vulnerability of a 'language barrier' which leaves them exposed to feelings of 'stress, anxiety, shock and confusion' (Coffey and Church 2002: 3). Alongside these stress factors, it is often the case that foreign national individuals residing in the UK are displaced from their families, and this sense of isolation from close loved ones and native culture can exacerbate their vulnerability. Moreover, foreign national prisoners simultaneously bring with them vulnerabilities derived from outside of the UK, which can include physical and psychological scars as a result of torture in their home country (Coffey and Church 2002).

The lack of basic communication between foreign national prisoners, fellow prisoners and prison staff further compounds the vulnerabilities of the former. In 2010 the Inspectorate of Prisons discovered instances of Race Equality Officers doubling up as Foreign National Liaison Officers (HMIP 2010a). This inappropriate attempt to conjoin two distinctly diverse groups has resulted in foreign national prisoners receiving such little information that many are completely unaware that they even possess the right to make a telephone call home (HMIP 2009b). Similarly, educative material and resettlement information within prison is typically solely printed in English (HMIP 2010a), while sporadic 'drug importer courses' within prison tend only to be available in English, excluding most, if not all, of the foreign national traffickers the government have targeted through the deployment of penal sanctions (Singh Bhui 2004).

Despite the Prison Service's pledge to offer prisoners the opportunity to 'reform' (HMPS 2011b), it is clear that foreign national prisoners reside in UK prisons with the sole purpose of punishment, and often deportation. There is very little evidence to suggest that the causes of foreign national criminality are addressed within a prison environment or that foreign national prisoners are provided with resettlement advice and services (Jacobson *et al.* 2010). Stemming the flow of foreign national prisoners into current UK prison conditions and developing alternatives to 'punitive warehousing' are important pressure points worthy of urgent enquiry if the Prison Service is to move away from what Fekete and Webber describe as a 'separate penal policy' for foreign national prisoners:

> [The current prison system] creates discrimination ... as foreign prisoners have fewer rights than citizen prisoners and are subjected to greater punishments. It is a system that smacks of xeno-racism ... it seems that we are going back in time, to the time of the aliens' laws – not integration or even immigration policy.
>
> (Fekete and Webber 2010: 13)

Sexuality

The UK's population at large includes an estimated 3.6 million gay people, one in five of whom has been the victim of homophobic hate crime (Dick 2008). Reliable estimates of the number of gay people in prison are virtually non-existent. One prison survey has suggested that around 4 per cent of the inmate population within England and Wales classes themselves as homosexual (HMIP 2010b: 55). The following comment from a serving prisoner, writing for the prison newspaper *Inside Time*, is illustrative of the lack of awareness surrounding the numbers and needs of the gay prison population:

> The subject of homosexuality in prison seems to me to be one that is permanently kept under wraps, swept under the carpet, ignored and regarded as unmentionable in the hope that it will somehow disappear on its own volition. Unfortunately this stance is not helping prison management, officers and staff to come to terms with what is becoming quite a sensitive, troublesome and irksome prison-specific issue.
>
> (Hanson 2007)

Among the features that make the prison environment an especially challenging one for gay people is the prevalence of homophobic stereotyping and prejudice on the part of both staff and prisoners. An inspection of Dartmoor prison in 2010, for instance, discovered that staff overtly referred to gay prisoners as 'girls' or 'ladies', while one prisoner requesting a copy of the *Gay Times* received his request within a paper bag as the member of staff was unwilling to physically touch the magazine for fear of contamination (HMIP 2010b). Moreover, prison inspections have revealed that scant information or publicity exists in the context of homosexuality (HMIP 2010b), serving to marginalise this minority group of prisoners more than they would be ordinarily. Equally problematic is the issue of homophobic violence within prisons, described in some reports as 'endemic' (Hanson 2007). Ultimately, the factors that are known to contribute to gay people's sense of vulnerability outside of prison – verbal abuse, bullying and a fear of physical attack, being 'outed' or unwanted sexual contact (Chakraborti and Garland 2009) – are all factors which are equally and arguably significantly more evident within the context of prison life.

DISABILITY

The harrowing cases of individuals such as Brent Martin, Francesa Hardwick and Michael Gilbert (all targeted on the basis of their disabilities) act as potent reminders of the vulnerability of disabled people in the community to physical attacks and degrading behaviour (Sherry 2010). Equally, the abuses directed towards vulnerable adults with learning disabilities at Winterbourne View residential hospital near Bristol, captured through covert filming as part of a 2011 BBC *Panorama* documentary, have given greater prominence to problems of disablist prejudice within closed environments (Kenyon 2011). Issues surrounding disabled prisoners are also a major cause for concern. Whilst the prison system itself reports that 5 per cent of prisoners are disabled, prisoner surveys suggest that this figure is in reality closer to 15 per cent at a minimum (HMIP 2009c).

It is perhaps unsurprising that large numbers of disabled prisoners go unnoticed by the prison system given that only two-thirds of prisons possess Disability Liaison Officers with specific disability training (HMIP 2009c: 8). As a result extreme occurrences, such as physically disabled prisoners sleeping in their own faeces, being deserted in cold bath tubs and being granted no access to purposeful activities, have been allowed to take place (Travis 2010). Despite the fact that disabled prisoners report significant levels of victimisation there are few firm policies and procedures in place to combat such an issue (HMIP 2009c), although the public sector Equality Duty introduced in April 2011 as part of the Equality Act 2010 provides prison establishments with an added impetus to develop policy that affords disability the same level of priority as other equality strands.

It is important also to acknowledge that within the minority group of disabled prisoners lie those whose minority status as a disabled person might not be readily recognised. For example, prisoners suffering from HIV – although they may not appear physically impaired – are classified as disabled, and yet despite the fact that HIV prevalence is significantly higher in prison than in the general population, 36 per cent of prisons possess no HIV policies (Prison Reform Trust and National AIDS Trust 2005: 29). Prisoners suffering from Asperger's Syndrome can find themselves similarly marginalised. Asperger's Syndrome is known to leave some sufferers appearing unremorseful and uncaring, and in view of the prison system's failure to consistently identify disabled prisoners, these unsympathetic traits could result in refusal of parole and elongated periods of imprisonment where prisoners with Asperger's Syndrome go undetected (Browning and Caulfield 2011).

PUNISHING CRIMES AGAINST MINORITY GROUPS: SHOULD PUNISHMENT MEAN PRISON?

In addition to highlighting pressure points relating to minority groups in prison, reference should also be made to the problems associated with using imprisonment as a default response to crimes committed against minority groups. The hate crime policy framework in the UK surrounding offences directed towards minority groups because of their identity characteristics – be it their ethnicity, faith, sexuality, disability or transgender status – allows for perpetrators of such crimes to be punished through the imposition of extended sentences. However, there is now an established body of literature to suggest that penalty enhancement legislation does little to promote desistance in this context (Jacobs and Potter 1998; Iganksi 1999; Chakraborti 2010b). Dixon and Gadd (2006) refer to the hypersensitivity of the former Labour administration to hate crime perpetration which in turn has led to the highly punitive ways in which those who commit such offences are dealt with. Without attempting to minimise the impact that incidents of hate crime can have on associated victims, some scholars question whether an overtly punitive sanction is necessarily the appropriate response in cases where the expression of 'hate' or prejudice may commonly occur in the context of a highly individualised trigger situation or as a departure from the perpetrator's standard norms of behaviour. In this sense, the current UK approach to the punishment of perpetrators of hate crime is arguably creating a revolving door of people who have committed hate crime offences, benefiting neither the perpetrator nor the victimised minority group.

In this context, the development of restorative interventions is likely to have greater potential as a mechanism for encouraging desistance amongst perpetrators of crimes against minorities. Relatively little research has been done in this area but that which exists suggests that prisons lack the capacity to get to grips with the root cause of hate perpetration, whereas the engagement that restorative justice offers could well provide the deterrence and desistance that prison fails to implement (Walters and Hoyle 2010, 2012). In the restorative justice scenario, victim–perpetrator mediation serves to provide hate crime perpetrators with recognition of the damage their offence has caused, not only to a single victim, but also to a wider minority group. Consequently the dialogue between perpetrator and victim challenges stereotypes potentially held by those who have committed hate crimes and demands that they confront the impact of their hatred.

FURTHER RESEARCH

1. Criminal offending
   There is little understanding of why certain offence types are more attractive to people of particular ethnic origins. While robbery, homicide, fraud and forgery and drug importation are less common than volume crimes, their serious nature means that those convicted of such offences (a disproportionate number of whom are of minority ethnic origin) are more likely to move up the sentencing tariff. Better knowledge about decision-making could illuminate this significant pressure point.

2. Discrimination in youth justice
   Further detailed qualitative case research on police, CPS and sentencers' actual decisions and actions is required to understand why minority ethnic young people experience, in some cases, more severe outcomes in the youth justice process. This would supplement the quantitative studies which have used multivariate analysis.

3. Indirect discrimination
   Earlier research on cooperation with the police and prosecutors suggests that minority ethnic groups may be subject to harsher outcomes because they do not assist the investigative and court process. This research could usefully be updated to see whether such practices are still prevalent. Such work also needs to consider whether indirect racial discrimination plays a part in prison disproportionality. Historically, minority ethnic groups have often been remanded in custody because of housing inequalities and a perceived lack of 'community ties' which is linked to a heightened risk of absconding. In turn, if convicted, an individual who has been remanded is more likely to face prison. Current evidence on this is needed to assess its impact on prison disproportionality.

4. Drugs stop and searches
   Whilst perhaps not a pressure point in terms of volume, it is worth noting that less than 10 per cent of stop and searches led to arrest by the police in 2008–9 (Ministry of Justice 2010a). Forty-three per

cent of stops and searches in England and Wales were for suspected drug offences in the case of white suspects but this was higher at 51 per cent for black suspects. This is significant because since the early 1990s at least nine Home Office self-report surveys of drug use have consistently shown that drug use is similar among black and white people, but lower amongst those of Asian origin. Sharp and Budd (2005) reported that young men of 'mixed' ethnicity were most likely to have used drugs, typically cannabis. This was true of 27 per cent, while rates were lower among black and white survey respondents (16 per cent), 'other' ethnic groups (13 per cent) and Asians (5 per cent). Class A drug use in the last year was similar for males of 'white', 'mixed', and 'other' ethnic origins (6 per cent) and much lower for Asian and black males (1 per cent and 2 per cent respectively).

5. Prisoner diversity

   Currently, prison policy is failing to ensure that staff engage fully or consistently with prisoner diversity. Indeed, throughout this chapter, the shortcomings of the prison environment in terms of its capacity to engage effectively with diversity have been apparent. Examples of staff intolerance towards prisoners from a minority background – whether in relation to their ethnicity, faith, sexuality or disability – are commonplace and illustrative of a pressing need for renewed training, fresh policies and improved practice. The Prison Service has a duty of care to every prisoner within the system, and it is therefore imperative that research uncovers the true extent of diversity within prisons and continues to monitor staff engagement with minority prisoners.

6. Generic approaches to diversity

   Diversity is regarded too generically within the prison system and in many instances knowledge and understanding of diversity inside prison is very poor. Current policy and practice is indicative of a homogenous blanket approach to diversity which pays insufficient regard to the differences in need, perception and experience amongst minority prisoners. In view of the increasing diversification of the prison environment in terms of the range of different ethnicities, faiths and other markers of identity that make up its population, research must identify ways in which prisons can respond more effectively to 'difference', and to acts of prejudice directed towards those who are perceived to be 'different'.

7. Foreign nationals

Perhaps one of the most troubling areas highlighted in the preceding discussion – and one which demands further research – relates to the imprisonment and subsequent treatment of foreign national prisoners. In particular, whilst tough sentencing policies on foreign national drug couriers have been designed with one eye on deterring future criminality, foreign national prisoners are in reality afforded what arguably amounts to the most inadequate and inhumane provision of all minority prisoners with little in place to facilitate desistance.

8. Punishing crimes against minorities

Current penal sanctions for perpetrators of crimes against minorities commonly fail to encourage desistance. Although imprisonment may be the most appropriate option for some hate crime perpetrators, using prison as a default response to punish crimes against people from a minority background is unlikely to deter future criminality. Greater use of alternative non-custodial pathways, including restorative interventions for hate crime perpetrators, could address the roots of prejudicial behaviour much more effectively whilst also significantly stemming the flow of individuals sentenced to imprisonment.

Note

1   Since the time of writing, research supported by the Howard League for Penal Reform has examined the experiences of deaf prisoners and trans prisoners in England and Wales. Further information can be found in *Not hearing us: an exploration of the experience of deaf prisoners in English and Welsh prisons* by Daniel McCulloch (2013) and in *Rethinking gendered prison policies: impacts on transgender prisoners* by Sarah Lamble (2012). Both are available from the Howard League for Penal Reform: www.howardleague.org.

References

Agozino, B. (2000) 'Theorizing Otherness, the War on Drugs and Incarceration'. *Theoretical Criminology* 4 (3) pp. 359–76.

Allen, R., Levenson, J. and Garside, R. (2003) *A Bitter Pill to Swallow: The Sentencing of Foreign National Drug Couriers*. London: Rethinking Crime and Punishment.

Bowling, B and Phillips, C. (2002) *Racism, Crime and Justice*. London: Longman.

Browning, A. and Caulfield, L. (2011) 'The Prevalence and Treatment of People with Asperger's Syndrome in the Criminal Justice System'. *Criminology and Criminal Justice* 11 (2) pp. 165–80.

Bucke, T. and Brown, D. (1997) *In Police Custody: Police Powers and Suspects' Rights Under the Revised PACE Codes of Practice, Home Office Research Study 174.* London: Home Office.

Chakraborti, N. (2010a) 'Crimes against the "Other": Conceptual, Operational and Empirical Challenges for Hate Studies'. *Journal of Hate Studies* 8 (1) pp. 9–28.

Chakraborti, N. (ed.) (2010b) *Hate Crime: Concepts, Policy, Future Directions.* Cullompton: Willan.

Chakraborti, N. and Garland, J. (2009) *Hate Crime: Impact, Causes and Responses.* London: Sage.

Clancy, A., Hough, A., Aust, R. and Kershaw, C. (2001) *Crime, Policing and Justice: The Experience of Ethnic Minorities: Findings from the 2000 British Crime Survey,* Home Office Research Study 223. London: Home Office.

Coffey, E. and Church, E. (2002) *Health Needs Assessment of Immigration Detainees.* Liverpool: HM Prison Service.

Commission for Racial Equality (2003) *Race Equality in Prisons: A Formal Investigation by The Commission for Racial Equality into HM Prison Service of England and Wales.* London: Commission for Racial Equality.

Dick, S. (2008) *Homophobic Hate Crime: The Gay British Crime Survey.* London: Stonewall.

Dixon, B. and Gadd, B. (2006) 'Getting the Message? "New" Labour and the Criminalisation of "Hate"'. *Criminology and Criminal Justice* 6 (3) pp. 309–28.

Equality Act 2010 (c15). London: HMSO.

Feilizer, M. and Hood, R. (2004) *Difference or Discrimination?* London: Youth Justice Board.

Fekete, L. and Webber, F. (2010) 'Foreign Nationals, Enemy Penology and the Criminal Justice System'. *Race and Class* 51 (4) pp. 1–25.

Fleetwood, J. (2011) 'Five Kilos: Penalties and Practice in the International Cocaine Trade'. *British Journal of Criminology* 51 (2) pp. 375–93.

Hanson, K. (2007) *Prison and Homosexuality.* Available at: www.insidetime. org/articleview.asp?a=147 [accessed July 2012].

Harrington, V. and Mayhew, P. (2001) *Mobile Phone Theft, Home Office Research Study 235.* London: Home Office.

Her Majesty's Inspectorate of Prisons (2009a) *Race Relations in Prison: Responding to Women from Black and Minority Ethnic Backgrounds.* London: HMIP.

Her Majesty's Inspectorate of Prisons (2009b) *Report on an Unannounced Full Follow up Inspection of HMP Parkhurst.* London: HMIP.

Her Majesty's Inspectorate of Prisons (2009c) *Disabled Prisoners: A Short Thematic Review on the Care and Support of Prisoners with a Disability.* London: HMIP.

Her Majesty's Inspectorate of Prisons (2010a) *Thematic Report by HM Inspectorate of Prisons: Women in Prison: A Short Thematic Review.* London: HMIP.

Her Majesty's Inspectorate of Prisons (2010b) *Report On An Unannounced Full Follow Up Inspection of HMP Dartmoor.* London: HMIP.

Her Majesty's Inspectorate of Prisons (2010c) *Muslim Prisoners' Experiences: A Thematic Review.* London: HMIP.

HM Prison Service (2011a) *Organisations.* Available at: www.justice.gov.uk/about/hmps/index.htm [accessed July 2012].

HM Prison Service (2011b) *Decency.* Available at: http://webarchive.nation-alarchives.gov.uk/20110206184958/http://www.hmprisonservice.gov.uk/abouttheservice/decency/ [accessed July 2012].

Home Office (1986) *The Ethnic Origins of Prisoners: The Prison Population on 30 June 1985 and Persons Received, July 1984–March 1985.* London: Home Office.

Iganski, P. (1999) 'Why Make "Hate" A Crime?'. *Critical Social Policy* 19 (3) pp. 386–95.

Jackson, J., Tyler, T.R., Bradford, B., Taylor, D. and Shiner, M. (2010) 'Legitimacy and Procedural Justice in Prisons'. *Prison Service Journal* 191 pp. 4–10.

Jacobs, J. and Potter, K. (1998) *Hate Crimes: Criminal Law and Identity Politics.* Oxford: Oxford University Press.

Jacobson, J., Kirby, A. and Hough, M. (2011) *Public Attitudes to the Sentencing of Drug Offences.* London: Sentencing Council.

Jacobson, J., Phillips, C. and Edgar, K. (2010) *'Double Trouble?' Black, Asian and Minority Ethnic Offenders' Experiences of Resettlement.* York: Clinks.

Joseph, J. (2006) 'Drug Offences, Gender, Ethnicity and Nationality: Women in Prison in England and Wales'. *The Prison Journal* 86 (1) pp. 140–57.

Keith Inquiry (2006) *Report of the Zahid Mubarek Inquiry.* London: HMSO.

Kenyon, P. (Reporter) (2011) 'Undercover Care: The Abuse Exposed (TV series episode)' in M. Chapman (Producer) *Panorama.* London: BBC.

Lamble, S. (2012) *Rethinking gendered prison policies: impacts on transgender prisoners.* London: Howard League for Penal Reform.

Liebling, A., Arnold, H. and Straub, C. (2012) *An Exploration of Staff-Prisoner Relationships At HMP Whitemoor: 12 Years On – A Revised Final Report.* London: Ministry of Justice.

May, T., Gyateng, T. and Hough, M with the assistance of Isabella Boyce, Bina Bhardwa and Juan-Carlos Oyanedel (2010) *Differential Treatment in the Youth Justice System, Equality and Human Rights Commission Research Report 50*. London: EHRC.

McCulloch, D.(2013) *Not Hearing Us: An Exploration of the Experience of Deaf Prisoners in English and Welsh Prisons*. London: Howard League for Penal Reform.

Mhlanga, B. (1999) *Race and Crown Prosecution Service Decisions*. London: The Stationery Office.

Ministry of Justice (2008) *Race Review 2008: Implementing Race Equality in Prisons – Five Years On*. London: Race and Equalities Action Group.

Ministry of Justice (2009) *Statistics on Race and the Criminal Justice System 2007/8*. London: Ministry of Justice.

Ministry of Justice (2010a) *Statistics on Race and the Criminal Justice System 2008/9*. London: Ministry of Justice.

Ministry of Justice (2010b) *Offender Management Caseload Statistics 2009*. London: Ministry of Justice.

Ministry of Justice (2011a) *Statistics on Race and the Criminal Justice System 2009/10*. London: Ministry of Justice.

Ministry of Justice (2011b) *Equalities Annual Report 2010–11*. London: Ministry of Justice.

Phillips, C. (2008) 'Negotiating Identities: Ethnicity and Social Relations in a Young Offenders' Institution'. *Theoretical Criminology* 12 (3) pp. 313–31.

Phillips, C. (2012) *The Multicultural Prison: Ethnicity, Masculinity and Social Relations among Prisoners*. Oxford: Oxford University Press.

Phillips, C. and Bowling, B. (2012) 'Ethnicities, Racism, Crime and Criminal Justice' in M. Maguire, R. Morgan and R. Reiner (eds) *The Oxford Handbook of Criminology* (fifth edition). Oxford: Oxford University Press pp. 370–97.

Phillips, C. and Brown, D. (1998) *Entry into the Criminal Justice System: A Survey of Police Arrests and Their Outcomes* Home Office Research Study No. 185. London: Home Office.

Phillips, C. and Earle, R. (2011) 'Cultural Diversity, Ethnicity and Race Relations in Prison' in B. Crewe and J. Bennett (eds) *The Prisoner*. Abingdon: Routledge pp. 117–30.

The Prison Reform Trust and National AIDS Trust (2005) *HIV and Hepatitis in UK Prisons: Addressing Prisoners' Healthcare Needs*. London: Prison Reform Trust.

Sharp, C. and Budd, T. (2005) *Minority Ethnic Groups and Crime: Findings from the Offending, Crime and Justice Survey 2003 (2nd Edition)* Home Office Online Report 33/05. London: HMSO.

Sherry, M. (2010) *Disability Hate Crimes: Does Anyone Really Hate Disabled People?* Farnham: Ashgate.

Singh Bhui, H. (2004) *Going the Distance: Developing Effective Policy and Practice with Foreign National Prisoners*. Available at: www.prisonreform-trust.org.uk/Portals/0/Documents/going%20the%20distance%20-%20%20foreign%20national%20prisoners.pdf [accessed July 2012].

Sudbury, J. (2005) '"Mules", "Yardies" and Other Fold Devils: Mapping Cross-Border Imprisonment in Britain' in J. Sudbury (ed.) *Global Lockdown: Race, Gender, and the Prison-Industrial Complex*. Abingdon: Routledge pp. 167–82.

Travis, A. (2010) *Disabled Prisoner to be Paid £20,000 for Discrimination at Belmarsh*. Available at: www.guardian.co.uk/society/2010/nov/08/disabled-prisoner-20000-compensation-belmarsh?INTCMP=SRCH [accessed November 2010].

Tyler, T. R. (2010) '"Legitimacy in corrections": policy implications'. *Criminology and Public Policy* 9 (1) pp. 127–34.

Walters, M. and Hoyle, C. (2010) 'Healing Harms and Engendering Tolerance: The Promise of Restorative Justice for Hate Crime' in N. Chakraborti (ed.) *Hate Crime: Concepts, Policy, Future Directions*. Cullompton: Willan Publishing, pp. 228–48.

Walters, M. and Hoyle, C. (2012) 'Exploring the Everyday World of Hate Victimisation through Community Mediation'. *International Review of Victimology* 18 (1) pp. 7–24.

Webster, C. (2007) *Understanding Race and Crime*. Buckingham: Open University Press.

9

RAW DEAL

THE CURIOUS EXPANSION OF PENAL CONTROL OVER WOMEN AND GIRLS

LIZZIE SEAL AND JO PHOENIX

This chapter highlights key issues from recent research on the entry of women and girls into the criminal justice system in England and Wales. It discusses the recent policy context, considers the reasons for the flow of women and girls into the criminal justice system and suggests what research could be carried out to gain the knowledge necessary to stem this flow.

WHAT IS THE CURRENT PENAL LANDSCAPE FOR WOMEN AND GIRLS?

Key facts

- Women and girls accounted for 4,324 out of a total prison population in England and Wales of 86,980 as of 25 May 2012 (Howard League 2012).
- There were 110 girls and 1,694 boys in the under-18 secure population in March 2012 (Ministry of Justice 2012).

- The use of imprisonment for women has accelerated since the early 1990s with a 106 per cent rise in women received into custody 1995–2005. The comparative figure for the male prison population was a rise of 24 per cent.
- During the same period there was a 69 per cent increase in women sentenced to immediate custody (Gelsthorpe *et al.* 2007: 6).
- The female prison population doubled between 2000 and 2005 (Player 2005).
- Recently there has been a flattening out of the numbers of women in prison but this stabilisation is of an imprisoned female population much larger than it was 20 years ago.

Seventy per cent of women sentenced to custody receive sentences of less than one year and the majority are in prison for non-violent offences (Cabinet Office 2009; Gelsthorpe and Sharpe 2009). Imprisonment exacerbates the already high levels of social exclusion experienced by women who offend, which include insecure accommodation and employment; mental health and substance abuse problems; experience of physical and sexual violence; low levels of educational attainment and lone parenting responsibilities (Carlen and Tombs 2006; Cabinet Office 2009; Gelsthorpe and Sharpe 2009). The use of community sentences for women has also increased, mainly at the expense of lesser disposals such as the fine,[1] rather than as an alternative to imprisonment (Patel and Stanley 2008). This amplification of the penal control of women has taken place even though the pattern of women's offending has remained fairly consistent over the last 30 years, accounting for around one-fifth of known offending and mainly relating to property-based crimes (Carlen and Tombs 2006; Gelsthorpe 2006; Gelsthorpe *et al.* 2007).

Rather than a change in women's offending behaviour, there have been changes in criminal justice policy and in how the courts perceive women's offending which account for the enhanced use of penal measures against them (Gelsthorpe *et al.* 2007). The overall picture since the 1990s has been one of the disproportionately heightened use of penal measures against women despite no corresponding rise in the seriousness of women's offending.

HOW THE RECENT CRIMINAL JUSTICE POLICY CONTEXT HAS AFFECTED THE USE OF PENAL MEASURES AGAINST WOMEN AND GIRLS

In order to comprehend the current penal landscape as it pertains to women and girls it is necessary to examine the recent policy context in England and Wales and the trends that can be identified within it. There have been two trends in recent criminal justice policy and practice in relation to women's offending. These are a trend towards 'punitiveness' and a trend towards gender responsiveness.

Punitiveness

Changes in criminal justice legislation enhanced penalties for less serious offending and disproportionately caught women in the net of penal control.[2] Amendments to the Criminal Justice Act 1991, enacted in 1993, were significant because they increased the use of immediate custody for summary offences (Patel and Stanley 2008). The Criminal Justice Act 2003 had a panoply of effects that further swelled the female prison population, such as a decline in the use of cautions, a rise in custodial sentencing by magistrates and the use of longer sentences by the crown courts. This Act also led to the heightened use of community sentences over fines, subjecting more women to penal control (Player 2005).

Player (2005) argues that recent years have also seen a shift in terms of how women's offending is perceived by sentencers, with greater emphasis being placed on the need for public protection and the risk caused than on the welfare needs of those appearing before the courts. Women had traditionally been perceived as particularly suitable for and in need of 'welfarist' responses which emphasised treatment and rehabilitation rather than punishment. Therefore a wider penal shift away from welfarism and towards the greater use of prison has especially impacted on them (Gelsthorpe 2005). Coupled with this, increased enthusiasm for using penal measures such as imprisonment and community sentences as a means of meeting women's social needs also helps to explain the disproportionate rise in women's subjection to the criminal justice system (Carlen 2002; Gelsthorpe 2005).

Gender responsiveness

In contrast with the punitive trend which resulted in the rocketing of the female prison population, the early twenty-first century saw the emergence of a gender-responsive trend in criminal justice policy in England and Wales. This trend has been characterised by a recognition that the 'pains of imprisonment' are felt more keenly by women and that alternatives to prison should be used for women where possible (Hedderman 2010). The gender-responsive trend also includes the acknowledgement in relation to community penalties that women often benefit from female-only provision.

In 2001, the Labour government recognised the especially deleterious effects that imprisoning women had on families and resolved to develop a strategy that would establish further alternatives to imprisonment for women (Player 2005). In 2004 it launched the three-year Women's Offending Reduction Programme (WORP) to support projects aimed at diverting women from custody, aiding resettlement after release from prison and providing community-based non-custodial supervision (Corcoran 2011). The WORP was intended to address the particular disadvantages experienced by women on release from prison, many of whom were not eligible for statutory supervision due to serving sentences of less than one year (Gelsthorpe and Sharpe 2009). Women were less likely than men to have accommodation, employment or access to training after leaving prison (Hedderman 2010).

In late 2006 and early 2007, Together Women, an initially three-year programme of multi-agency provision for women who had offended or were at risk of offending was launched across five sites in northern England (Gelsthorpe *et al.* 2007; Hedderman *et al.* 2008, 2011). Together Women incorporated a variety of centres that provided 'one-stop-shop' services to women and were designed to help prevent women from entering the criminal justice system or to aid their resettlement in the community following a conviction or release from prison (Gelsthorpe *et al.* 2007; Hedderman *et al.* 2008). The services offered through Together Women included help with managing mental health, training for parenting, thinking skills, life skills and addressing offending behaviour (Hedderman *et al.* 2008). There was also an emphasis on multi-agency working, for example with housing and employment services (Hedderman *et al.* 2011). Centres offered designated advice surgeries as well as drop-in times and crèche facilities. The programme continues as an independent charity (Together Women 2011).

The need for criminal justice policy to respond to gender differences and inequalities was stepped up by section 84 of the Equality Act 2006, which established a gender duty in equality legislation (Jones 2011). After the deaths of six women at Styal Prison within one year, the *Review of Women with Particular Vulnerabilities in the Criminal Justice System* was launched in 2006 and the subsequent *Corston Report* was published in 2007. Baroness Corston argued that there were many women in prison for whom it was 'disproportionate and inappropriate' (2007: i) due to the minor nature of their offending; their problems with mental and physical health and substance abuse; their experiences of violent and sexual abuse and difficult childhoods and their parenting responsibilities. She called for a 'radical change' in the criminal justice system and for it to take a 'woman-centred approach' (Corston 2007: 2).

The *Corston Report* emphasised that the harms experienced by vulnerable women were compounded by imprisonment. It recommended that community penalties should be the norm for women (with custody reserved only for serious offences) and that a holistic approach should be taken through the provision of services to support women's complex needs. It also stressed that equality did not mean treating women and men in the same way. Women's needs were distinct and female prisoners had been disadvantaged through subjection to a system designed for men. The *Corston Report* raised the profile of the issue of the needs and treatment of women in the criminal justice system (Hedderman 2010).

Both the Together Women programme and the *Corston Report* (2007) bore the traces of the findings and arguments of the criminological literature from the 1980s and 1990s on women's offending and punishment (Gelsthorpe *et al.* 2007). This literature highlighted the link between social disadvantage and women's offending and stressed the disproportionate and damaging effects of imprisonment on women (Carlen 1983 and 1985; Morris and Wilkinson 1995; Rumgay 1996). It also suggested the use of community-based, woman-centred alternatives to imprisonment for women (Carlen 1985; Heidensohn 1986; Carlen 1990). The organisation Women in Prison was founded in 1983 to highlight and campaign on these issues (Carlen 2005), and indeed, Labour's 1983 manifesto pledged to '[e]xamine the additional problems faced by women prisoners, especially those with young children' (Labour

Party 1983). The twenty-first century recognition that gender-specific approaches could be beneficial for women who offend was not new knowledge but rather discovery and rediscovery of these ideas in the government's policy-making occurred during this time.

In 2009, in response to the *Corston Report*, the Ministry of Justice announced £15.6 million funding for the provision of additional community-based services for women who had offended and women at risk of offending, £9 million of which was allocated to third sector providers (Malloch and McIvor 2011a). This Strategy for Diverting Women Away from Crime had a narrower agenda than the *Corston Report*, and was focused on diverting women away from custody and reducing the risks of reoffending, rather than the influence of wider social factors such as poverty (Corcoran 2011). This represented a blunting of the *Corston Report*'s radicalism in terms of its translation into policy and also a loss of concentration on the importance of gaining a holistic understanding of women's offending. Arguably this has limited the reach of the gender-responsive trend and stymied the aspiration to significantly reduce the number of incarcerated women. Certain key recommendations from the *Corston Report* that showed the influence of a 'woman-centred' penology (Carlen 1990) were not implemented, such as establishing small, community-based units as an alternative to the use of imprisonment (Hedderman 2010).

CURRENT YOUTH JUSTICE POLICY REGARDING GIRLS

The policy context for girls has some parallels with that of adult women but has many significant differences. Like adult women, most crimes committed by girls are minor and property-based, although for girls within the youth justice system violence against the person is the most frequent offence (Youth Justice Board 2009). The punitive trend in criminal justice and youth justice has affected girls who come into contact with the youth justice system. There has been a large increase in the use of short detention and training orders, and coupled with an increase in the conditions attached to community penalties, this has led to a growth in the female youth custodial population (Sharpe 2011).

Most girls who encounter the criminal justice system receive a pre-court disposal rather than conviction (Youth Justice Board 2009). Between

2002 and 2005–6 there was a 38.7 per cent rise in disposals for girls (Sharpe and Gelsthorpe 2009), although disposals have declined since 2008 (All Party Parliamentary Group on Women in the Penal System 2012). The use of cautions has fallen in the past ten years with a rise in girls receiving the more serious disposals of reprimand and final warning (Youth Justice Board 2009). The trend in the early twenty-first century has been for girls' offending to be processed through the criminal justice system whereas in the past it would more frequently have been dealt with via welfare-based measures (O'Neill 2005; Gelsthorpe and Sharpe 2006). As well as greater entry into the youth justice system, girls are being convicted at earlier ages. This is despite the fact that, as with adult women, there has not been a proportionate rise in girls' offending to warrant this (Youth Justice Board 2009). Unlike for adult women and men, there is parity in patterns of sentencing severity between girls and boys even though girls' offending is less frequent and less serious than that of boys (Youth Justice Board 2009).

An increasingly gender-neutral approach to youth justice in the 1990s onwards has meant that more girls have come before the courts and received custodial sentences than previously (Worrall 2001; Gelsthorpe and Worrall 2009). The *Corston Report* was mainly concerned with adult women and made few recommendations on girls. In terms of youth justice, innovations have been made with boys rather than girls in mind (Matthews and Smith 2009). Therefore gender-focused policy and services in relation to girls who offend have not developed in the same way that they have for adult women. However, there have been examples of female-only provision for girls, such as projects run in Nottingham (Matthews and Smith 2009) and Birmingham (Sharpe and Gelsthorpe 2009).

WHAT CAN BE LEARNED FROM THE EXAMPLES OF THE IMPLEMENTATION OF THE GENDER-RESPONSIVE TREND?

The gender-responsive trend in recent criminal justice policy offers some positive lessons about using community-based approaches with women who offend or are at risk of offending. One of these concerns the potential mixed-use services have for reducing stigma (Gelsthorpe and Sharpe 2009; Hedderman 2011). Whereas women frequently report finding probation a stigmatising experience (Malloch and McIvor 2011a) services such as the Together Women programme integrate those who have offended alongside non-offenders and can overcome this problem. This provides women who have offended with the opportunity to interact with 'pro-social' peers (Hedderman 2011), something which has been identified as significant to encouraging women's desistance from crime (Rumgay 2004). This 'normalising strategy' has also been identified as holding potential for working with girls, by involving them in community projects not specifically targeted at those who have offended (Sharpe 2011).

Interventions and services aimed specifically at women help to address the problem of the male-centred nature of criminal justice responses. That women's offending, their pathways into offending and their needs are distinct from those of men has been an important and consistent message from the research on women and crime (Carlen 1985; Morris 1987; Worrall 1990; Gelsthorpe 2004; Hedderman 2004). It is well understood that women who offend often have complex needs related to experiences of poverty and abuse, mental health problems and motherhood responsibilities (Hedderman 2004; Gelsthorpe and Sharpe 2009; Loucks 2010; Sheehan *et al.* 2011). Their explanations of their offending tend to stress necessity due to poverty over thrill seeking (Hedderman 2004; Martin *et al.* 2009). Working successfully with women and girls requires gender-specific training for staff (Matthews and Smith 2009; Sheehan *et al.* 2011) and the use of approaches that suit women's learning styles, such as role-modelling and mentoring, which favour collaboration (Gelsthorpe 2011). Research suggests that girls can also benefit from involvement in activities based on mutual support and which build solidarity (Sharpe 2011).

An important aspect of female-only centres and services is that they can offer a safe space to their users. For some women, these become the only places where they can avoid abusive men (Hedderman *et al.* 2008; Vickers and Wilcox 2011). Up to half of women prisoners have experienced abuse (Hayes 2007) and mixed programmes frequently mean that women must associate with men who have displayed abusive behaviour or with men who have abused them (Vickers and Wilcox 2011). A safe, female-only environment is also beneficial for girls (Matthews and Smith 2009). Gender-specific services can provide women and girls with the option of interacting solely with female staff if experience of abuse or other factors mean that they do not feel that they can relate to male workers (Hedderman 2011; Sharpe 2011). Contact with services via the criminal justice system often becomes the primary means through which women who offend can begin to get their complex needs addressed, in relation to involvement in sex work, alcohol and substance abuse and experiencing abuse in violent relationships (Corcoran 2011).

Additionally, gender-specific services with multi-agency links can offer support and training tailored to meet women's individual needs enabling them to participate in a wide range of activities (Hedderman *et al.* 2008). This also offers the potential for women to be involved in the design of their own support – something which is argued to improve services' effectiveness and to help empower women to desist from offending (Cabinet Office 2009). The need for services to foster empowerment is stressed as particularly important to women's desistance (Gelsthorpe and Sharpe 2009; Gelsthorpe 2011). Other valuable features that community-based programmes such as Together Women can offer include practical help for women to maintain improvements and flexibility to offer continued support even after a designated period of contact has ended (Gelsthorpe 2011). The voluntary sector seems to be especially well suited to offering this type of provision because it 'enjoy[s] a greater degree of flexibility and freedom to meet women's real needs' (Gelsthorpe 2011: 136).

WHAT IS CAUSING THE FLOW OF WOMEN AND GIRLS INTO THE CRIMINAL JUSTICE SYSTEM?

Over the past 20 years, the scholarship on women who offend[3] has analysed relevant social, cultural and political shifts, the policy environment and processes of policy implementation in order to understand why policies and approaches have failed to: (1) stem the flow of women into the criminal justice system; and (2) reduce the negative effects this system has on them. This is despite attempts to introduce policies that seem to be intended to do both of these things. This scholarship exists in the context of a body of knowledge that, as explained above, has been consistent in its identification of the needs of women who have offended as being distinct from those of men, and as being complex and strongly related to social disadvantage. This pattern has varied little over the last 30 years

(Carlen and Tombs 2006). We possess a sound knowledge from a range of studies of the context in which women offend and the effects that criminal justice interventions have on their lives.

Although researchers have commended the efforts of the previous Labour government to fund appropriate gender-sensitive, community-based services for women (Gelsthorpe 2011), they also highlight that this has not had the effect of reducing the number of imprisoned women, most of whom still serve short sentences, and that this punitive trend further accelerated during Labour's tenure (Hedderman 2010, 2011). The increased use of community orders and suspended sentences for women does not appear to have led to a reduction in the use of custody (Patel and Stanley 2008), and alternatives to imprisonment such as these have gone down the tariff, catching more women in the net of the criminal justice system (Hedderman 2010). What in theory could (or should) be alternatives often do not operate as such in practice. This has also been a recurrent message from the criminological literature, not only in relation to women (Cohen 1985; Carlen 2002; Worrall and Gelsthorpe 2009).

A key problem in the recent policy context is that the punitive trend in criminal justice policy counters and works against the gender-responsive trend which acknowledges the particularly harmful effects of imprisonment for women. There has been an expectation on judges to use custodial penalties more frequently and for longer amounts of time (Kruttschnitt 2006). The *Corston Report*'s (2007) recommendation that flexibility should be exercised in relation to penalties for breach of community sentences was not implemented (Patel and Stanley 2008). Instead, it was accepted that increased information should be provided for sentencers on the negative impacts of imprisonment on women despite the fact that this has not been shown to have an effect on reducing women's custody (Hedderman 2010).

In relation to women and girls, it could be argued that the punitive trend has triumphed over, and trumped, the gender-responsive trend. However, the picture is more complicated than this. Although this chapter has identified two trends in recent criminal justice policy in relation to women (and to an extent girls), in operation these trends do not always compete and contrast. Sometimes they have had the effect of complementing one another and working together to increase the reach of the penal net. It is therefore essential to explore the tensions,

contradictions and hybridisations that coexist within criminal justice policy and to understand their outcomes in terms of the failure
to stem the flow of women and girls into the criminal justice system.
'Hybridisation' refers to the phenomenon whereby more than one justification or guiding principle for sentencing and sanctions is conflated
in the introduction and application of these measures (Robinson 1987;
Brownlee 1998; O'Malley 2000).

Tensions, contradictions and hybridisations in the guiding purpose
of the sentencing of women and girls have had the effect of increasing the use and severity of penalties. Women's identification as having
complex needs can lead them to receive longer sentences, as this can be
seen as an opportunity to use imprisonment to meet these needs (Carlen
and Tombs 2006; Gelsthorpe 2006). Here, what could be understood
as a traditionally gendered welfarist approach, which legitimises criminal justice intervention on the grounds that it will be for the woman's own good, meets a punitive approach that legitimises the utility of
prison. Rather than contradicting or countering one another, they can
also become mixed up (Gelsthorpe 2005). The dual role of prison as a
place of punishment and of welfare has been disadvantageous for women
(Carlen 2002; Carlen and Tombs 2006; Phoenix 2007, 2008a, 2008b).
Welfare and control also get bound up together in the disposal of girls,
with concerns that they are at risk of sexual exploitation or of running
away leading to the use of criminal justice measures under a justice-based
model (Phoenix 2002, 2003, 2009, 2012; O'Neill 2005; Gelsthorpe and
Sharpe 2009; Sharpe 2009).

The focus on risk management and public protection in the contemporary criminal justice system means that factors such as mental health
and addiction problems can be significant in decisions to remand women
in custody (Player et al. 2010) again reflecting how the use of sentencing
to address women's needs can derive from hybridised influences (Player
2005). The prioritisation of criminogenic risk factors has the potential to
be doubly detrimental to women. On the one hand, their complex needs
'may render women offenders more "risky"' (Gelsthorpe et al. 2007: 19),
on the other, welfare-based needs that are not calculated as contributing
to recidivism may be overlooked and remain unmet (Hannah-Moffat
2005; Gelsthorpe et al. 2007). Risk assessment tools such as Offender
Assessment System (OASys), which are based on criminogenic risk factors and were designed with men in mind, do not appear to be good

predictors for women, whose reasons for offending are frequently different from those of men and whose compliance with programmes and services tends to be less instrumental and more normative (Martin *et al.* 2009). Risk management therefore works against the gender-responsive trend in criminal justice policy (Martin *et al.* 2009). Girls who offend have also increasingly been redefined as 'risky', with the consequence that they have been subject to criminal justice intervention, which has also become the means through which they access welfare support (Phoenix 2009, 2012; Sharpe 2009).

The need for attention to the significance of perceptions of gender on the part of sentencers and practitioners remains[4] as these are utilised in sentencing decisions (Player 2005, 2007). Anxiety that women and girls were becoming 'masculinised' in their behaviour and offending emerged in the criminal justice system and in media portrayals (especially of girls) in the late 1990s onwards (Hedderman *et al.* 2011; Sharpe 2011).[5] Where women are perceived to display too much agency, in other words where they seem assertive and/or in control of their actions, they may be seen as masculine and deserving of punishment. Where they are understood to display too little agency and seem passive and/or at the mercy of factors beyond their control, they being seen as in need of intervention for their own good (Player 2005). As Gelsthorpe (2006: 422) argues, these types of gender representation '[cloud] perceptions of seriousness and desert'.

The views of practitioners are also significant as frontline workers are the ones who enact policy in a way that directly affects the women and girls with whom they work (Sharpe 2009). In particular, beliefs that girls are becoming more violent and 'out of control' have been found amongst youth justice practitioners, with the media seemingly influencing these views (Sharpe 2009), alongside a sustained concern about putative 'sexual promiscuity' (Matthews and Smith 2009; Sharpe 2009). In actual fact girls' convictions for violent offences declined between 2006 and 2010 (All Party Parliamentary Group on Women in the Penal System 2012).

Factors beyond the operation of the criminal justice system must also be recognised as important pressure points. Gelsthorpe (2005) argues that the rise in women's imprisonment in the 1990s can be linked to the increased feminisation of poverty that took place at this time. The current economic climate, in which employment opportunities are limited and the cost of living has become more expensive, is therefore a hazard in terms of women's offending, which is frequently linked to poverty. Recent cuts in the public sector workforce have impacted particularly on women and planned reductions in benefits will also disproportionately affect them (Bird 2011). Certain groups, such as women with mental health problems, are especially at risk of being worse off as entitlements for people with disabilities are contracting. Retrenchment in other services (such as mental health) should also be a cause for concern, especially given the overrepresentation of women with mental health problems in the female prison population.

There is uncertainty surrounding the approach that the Coalition government will take towards women in the criminal justice system. The Legal Aid, Sentencing and Punishment of Offenders Act 2012 does not make reference to women in the criminal justice system, seemingly rowing back from the gender-responsive trend established under the previous government. This was despite attempts to add amendments to the Bill for the introduction of a Women's Justice Strategy Commission and a Women's Justice Board (Prison Reform Trust 2012), which were rejected. Future budgetary cuts could also pose a threat to gender-specific, community-based services provided through the voluntary sector, although the second round of the Women's Diversionary Fund in May 2011 awarded £3.2 million of funding to such services (Corston Independent Funders' Coalition 2011).

WHAT ARE THE GAPS IN KNOWLEDGE ABOUT WOMEN, GIRLS AND CRIMINAL JUSTICE?

Knowledge about issues relating to the diversity of the sentenced female population in England and Wales is restricted. 'Women' do not constitute a homogenous group (Goulding 2011) and there are different categories of women about whom we need to know more (Malloch and McIvor 2011b). Girls have frequently been ignored in both policy and scholarship on criminal justice (Sharpe and Gelsthorpe 2009) falling between the youth justice focus on boys and young men and the gender-sensitive lens on adult women (Burman and Batchelor 2009). The research on certain groups of women such as older women (Wahidin 2004) and women with learning disabilities (Hayes 2007), including accurate knowledge of the prevalence of learning disabilities amongst women who offend, remains scanty (Cabinet Office 2009).

The situation regarding minority ethnic women also requires more knowledge and analysis. There is an overrepresentation of British and foreign-born black women in the prison population of England and Wales (Joseph 2006) and foreign nationals constitute a higher proportion of the female incarcerated population than the male (Player *et al.* 2010). Convictions for drugs-related offences are significant to the overrepresentation of foreign-born women and more needs to be known about their experiences and circumstances. The failure to meet the specific needs of minority ethnic women in prison (Joseph 2006) and in terms of resettlement (Gelsthorpe *et al.* 2007) has been noted, as has the need to know more about pathways into crime for women from different minority ethnic groups (Gelsthorpe *et al.* 2007). Minority ethnic women and girls are particularly vulnerable to falling foul of sentencers and practitioners' judgments of gender-appropriate demeanour and behaviour due to the added factor of racial stereotyping and its interaction with perceptions of gender (Player 2005; Toor 2009). Women's perceptions of their own ethnic identity may be significant to how they cope with imprisonment (Kruttschnitt and Husseman 2008). Finally, there is also the issue of the invisibility of minority ethnic women and girls to policy-making and scholarship – a point Toor (2009) makes in relation to British Asian women and girls.

Following the gender-responsive trend in criminal justice policy there is a substantial body of research on community penalties as they apply to women, as well as on the use of community-based services and their greater flexibility for working effectively with women (Gelsthorpe *et al.* 2007; Gelsthorpe 2011; Hedderman *et al.* 2011; Malloch and McIvor 2011a; Sheehan *et al.* 2011). As discussed, some key lessons emerge from this, such as the importance of female-only spaces and multi-agency links, and the role of positive self-esteem and empowerment in aiding desistance. Further knowledge of women's desistance from offending could help to enhance our knowledge of the factors that prevent reoffending.

The gendered dimensions of other alternatives to imprisonment, such as restorative justice, also require further investigation. So far there is very little literature on the potential for the use of restorative justice approaches with women and girls who offend as opposed to female victims. Some authors have argued that restorative justice may be effective with women and girls as it encourages empowerment and personal accountability (Salgado *et al.* 2011) although others caution that the focus on reintegrative shaming is potentially counter-productive (Toor 2009). However, restorative justice does not have to be based on notions of shaming, but can instead emphasise building solidarity between the perpetrator and victim (Rossner 2011).

In England and Wales there has been some attempt to incorporate restorative approaches into the youth justice system although this has been more at the level of rhetoric than of practice (Muncie 2011). Sharpe (2011) found that girls failed to see the benefit of supposedly reparative activities carried out in the form of community payback which were not particularly constructive or linked into the community. How far restorative justice will become embedded in the criminal justice system of England and Wales, and furthermore its suitability for women and girls who offend, is open to question. However, as Daly and Stubbs (2006) argue, it is necessary to engage with new developments in justice in relation to women.

FURTHER RESEARCH

1. Research designed to improve our knowledge of the diversity of women and girls in the criminal justice system and the diversity of their experiences is needed. This will make it possible to explore whether some of the recommendations for and practices of gender-specific approaches end up disadvantaging or failing to meet the needs of certain groups of women and girls.
2. The impact of the recession and current economic stagnation on women and girls' offending and their entry into the criminal justice system, coupled with the austerity measures of the Coalition government, requires investigation. This could be researched both quantitatively and qualitatively.
3. Comprehension of the significance of living in the intensely consumerist society of the early twenty-first century to the conditions in which women and girls offend is needed, especially given the property-based nature of their offending and its connection with poverty.
4. Alongside an appreciation of wider social structural influences, research that uncovers women's narratives about their involvement

in crime or desistance from it and relates this to their construction of offending and post-offending identities would be illuminating.

5. Considering the embryonic state of restorative justice in England and Wales, research in this area would likely be in the form of a review of the domestic and international literature on restorative justice with women and girls who offend.

6. There is an ongoing need to understand the views and 'interpretive behaviour' (Player 2005: 434) of sentencers and practitioners in relation to women and girls who offend and to appreciate how this is shaped by the wider culture and political climate of which they are a part including media and popular culture. This has particular resonance in terms of perceptions of girls as growing more violent on the part of the police and youth justice practitioners, and also relates to media-led anxieties surrounding the emergence of 'girl gangs'. Research on this theme should also attempt to explore the relationship between perceptions of gender and other areas of identity, such as ethnicity, class, age, sexuality and dis/ability.

7. Contextualising criminal justice approaches to women and girls in relation to wider penal trends remains important as is attention to the functions and justifications that are assigned to penal measures. Comprehending the 'broader social, political and ideological factors surrounding the criminalisation and punishment' of women and girls requires continued attention (Malloch and McIvor 2011a: 326). A hazard that must be considered is the continued expansion of the criminal justice system in the face of the retrenchment of social welfare. This is especially so when services are offered on the basis of diverting women and girls from offending rather than as welfare entitlement, or when penal measures become the means of providing welfare (Phoenix 2009).

The research programme suggested above would produce studies that would continue to map penal trends as they pertain to women and girls. As Carlen and Tombs (2006: 357) state, 'there is *no way* that primarily *penal* methods can address primarily *social* injustices' [italics in original].

Notes

1   Fines account for 79 per cent of non-custodial penalties (Cabinet Office 2009).

2   The conceptualisation of the different elements of the criminal justice system as forming a net derives from Cohen (1985: 41), who used this analogy to describe the operation of the 'deviancy control system' as a net 'cast by an army of different fishermen and fisherwomen' to catch the fish deviants.

3   The scholarship has mainly focused on adult women as opposed to girls (Gelsthorpe and Sharpe 2009).

4   The argument about the significance of perceptions of femininity in relation to women who offend has been well-established in the criminological literature over time. See for example Wootton (1959); Carlen (1983); Heidensohn (1985); Eaton (1986); Worrall (1990); Hedderman and Gelsthorpe (1997). For historical analyses see Ballinger (2000) and Seal (2010).

5   The tendency to represent women who have offended as masculine has been historically recurrent (Seal 2010). See also Naffine (1985).

References

All Party Parliamentary Group on Women in the Penal System (2012) *Keeping Girls out of the Penal System*. London: Howard League for Penal Reform.

Ballinger, A. (2000) *Dead Woman Walking*. Aldershot: Ashgate.

Bird, A. (2011) 'The Impact of Cuts on Women'. *Criminal Justice Matters* 85 (1) pp. 32–3.

Brownlee, I. (1998) 'New Labour – New Penology? Punitive Rhetoric and the Limits of Managerialism in Criminal Justice Policy'. *Journal of Law and Society* 25 (3) pp. 313–35.

Burman, M. and Batchelor, S.A. (2009) 'Between Two Stools'. *Youth Justice* 9 (3) pp. 270–85.

Cabinet Office Social Exclusion Task Force (2009) *Short Study on Women Offenders*. London: Cabinet Office.

Carlen, P. (1983) *Women's Imprisonment*. London: Routledge.

Carlen, P. (ed.) (1985) *Criminal Women: Autobiographical Accounts*. Cambridge: Polity Press.

Carlen, P. (1990) *Alternatives to Women's Imprisonment*. Milton Keynes: Open University Press.

Carlen, P. (2002) 'Carceral Clawback: The Case of Women's Prisons in Canada'. *Punishment and Society* 4 (1) pp. 115–21.

Carlen, P. (2005) *Women in Prison: The Early Years*. Available at: www.womeninprison.org.uk/about us.php#25_Years_of_WIP [accessed July 2012].

Carlen, P. and Tombs, J. (2006) 'Reconfiguration of Penality: The Ongoing Case of the Women's Imprisonment and Reintegration Industries'. *Theoretical Criminology* 10 (3) pp. 337–60.

Cohen, S. (1985) *Visions of Social Control*. Cambridge: Polity Press.

Corcoran, M. (2011) 'After Corston, the Rehabilitation Revolution?'. *Criminal Justice Matters* 85 (1) pp. 26–7.

Corston, J. (2007) *The Corston Report*. London: Home Office.

Corston Independent Funders' Coalition (2011) *Women's Diversionary Fund*. Available at cifc/mytechie.co.uk/womens-diversionary-fund [accessed July 2012].

Daly, K. and Stubbs, J. (2006) 'Feminist Engagement with Restorative Justice'. *Theoretical Criminology* 10 (1) pp. 9–28.

Eaton, M. (1986) *Justice for Women? Family, Court and Social Control*. Milton Keynes: Open University Press.

Gelsthorpe, L. (2004) 'Female Offending: A Theoretical Overview', in G. McIvor (ed.) *Women Who Offend*. London: Jessica Kingsley pp. 13–37.

Gelsthorpe, L. (2005) 'Back to Basics in Crime Control: Weaving in Women', in M. Matravers (ed.) *Managing Modernity: Politics and the Culture of Control*. Abingdon: Routledge pp. 76–103.

Gelsthorpe, L. (2006) 'Counterblast: Women and Criminal Justice: Saying it Again, Again and Again'. *The Howard Journal* 45 (4) pp. 421–4.

Gelsthorpe, L. (2011) 'Working with Women Offenders in the Community: A View from England and Wales', in R. Sheehan, G. McIvor and C. Trotter (eds) *Working with Female Offenders in the Community*. Abingdon: Willan pp.127–50.

Gelsthorpe, L. and Sharpe, G. (2006) 'Gender, Youth Crime and Justice', in B. Goldson and J. Muncie (eds) *Youth, Crime and Justice: Critical Issues*. London: Sage pp. 47–61.

Gelsthorpe, L. and Sharpe, G. (2009) 'Women and Resettlement', in A. Hucklesby and L Hagley-Dickinson (eds) *Prisoner Resettlement: Policy and Practice*. Cullompton: Willan.

Gelsthorpe, L. and Worrall, A. (2009) 'Looking for Trouble'. *Youth Justice* 9 (3) pp. 209–23.

Gelsthorpe, L., Sharpe, G. and Roberts, J. (2007) *Provision for Women Offenders in the Community*. London: Fawcett Society.

Goulding, D. (2011) 'Breaking the Cycle: Addressing Cultural Difference in Rehabilitation Programmes', in R. Sheehan, G. McIvor and C. Trotter (eds) *Working with Female Offenders in the Community*. Abingdon: Willan pp. 173–89.

Hannah-Moffat, K. (2005) 'Criminogenic Needs and the Transformative Risk Subject'. *Punishment and Society* 7 (1) pp. 29–51.

Hayes, S.C. (2007) 'Women with Learning Disabilities Who Offend: What do we Know?'. *British Journal of Learning Disabilities* 35 pp. 187–91.

Hedderman, C. (2004) 'The "Criminogenic" Needs of Women Offenders', in G. McIvor (ed.) *Women Who Offend*. London: Jessica Kingsley pp. 82–98.

Hedderman, C. (2010) 'Government Policy on Women Offenders'. *Punishment and Society* 12 (4) pp. 485–500.

Hedderman, C. (2011) 'Policy Developments in England and Wales', in R. Sheehan, G. McIvor and C. Trotter (eds.) *Working with Female Offenders in the Community*. Abingdon: Willan pp. 26–44.

Hedderman, C. and Gelsthorpe, L. (1997) *Understanding the Sentencing of Women*. London: Home Office.

Hedderman, C., Gunby, C. and Shelton, N. (2011) 'What Women Want'. *Criminology and Criminal Justice* 11 (1) pp. 3–19.

Hedderman, C., Palmer, E. and Hollin, C. (2008) *Implementing Services for Women Offenders and those 'At Risk' of Offending: Action Research with Together Women*. Available at: www.justice.gov.uk/publications/research.htm [accessed July 2012].

Heidensohn, F. (1985) *Women and Crime*. Basingstoke: Macmillan.

Heidensohn, F. (1986) 'Models of Justice – Portia or Persephone? Some Thoughts on Equality, Fairness and Gender in the Field of Criminal Justice'. *International Journal of the Sociology of Law* 14 (3/4) pp. 287–98.

Howard League for Penal Reform (2012) *Weekly Prison Watch*. Available at: www.howardleague.org/weekly-prison-watch-archive [accessed July 2012].

Jones, S. (2011) 'Under Pressure: Women Who Plead Guilty to Crimes They Have Not Committed'. *Criminology and Criminal Justice* 11 (1) pp. 77–90.

Joseph, J. (2006) 'Drug Offences, Gender, Ethnicity, and Nationality'. *The Prison Journal* 86 (1) pp. 140–57.

Kruttschnitt, C. (2006) 'The Politics of Confinement: Women's Imprisonment in California and the UK', in A. Liebling and S. Maruna (eds) *The Effects of Imprisonment*. Cullompton: Willan pp. 146–76.

Kruttschnitt, C. and Husseman, J. (2008) 'Micropolitics of Race and Ethnicity in Women's Prisons'. *British Journal of Sociology* 59 (4) pp. 709–28.

Labour Party (1983) *Manifesto*. Available at: www.labour-party.org.uk/manifestos/1983/1983-labour-manifesto.shtml [accessed June 2012].

Loucks, N. (2010) 'Women in Prison', in J.R. Adler and J.M. Gray (eds) *Forensic Psychology: Concepts, Debates and Practice*. Abingdon: Willan pp. 466–86.

Malloch, M. and McIvor, G. (2011a) 'Women and Community Sentences'. *Criminology and Criminal Justice* 11 (4) pp. 325–44.

Malloch, M. and McIvor, G. (2011b) 'Women, Drugs and Community Interventions', in R. Sheehan, G. McIvor and C. Trotter (eds) *Working with Female Offenders in the Community*. Abingdon: Willan pp. 190–215.

Martin, J., Kautt, P. and Gelsthorpe, L. (2009) 'What Works for Women'. *British Journal of Criminology* 49 (6) pp. 879–99.

Matthews, S. and Smith, C. (2009) *The Sustainability of Gender Specific Provision in the Youth Justice System Research Paper 2009/04*. London: The Griffin Society.

Ministry of Justice (2012) *Youth Custody Report March 2012 – Youth Custody Data*. Available at: www.justice.gov.uk/publications/statistics-and-data/youth-justice/custody-data.htm [accessed July 2012].

Morris, A. (1987) *Women, Crime and Criminal Justice*. Oxford: Blackwell.

Morris, A. and Wilkinson, C. (1995) 'Responding to Female Prisoners' Needs'. *The Prison Journal* 75 (3) pp. 295–305.

Muncie, J. (2011) 'Illusions of Difference: Comparative Youth Justice in the Devolved United Kingdom'. *British Journal of Criminology* 51 (1) pp. 40–57.

Naffine, N. (1985) 'The Masculinity-Femininity Hypothesis: A Consideration of Gender-Based Personality Theories'. *British Journal of Criminology* 25 (4) pp. 365–81.

O'Malley, P. (2000) 'Criminologies of Catastrophe? Understanding Criminal Justice on the Edge of the New Millennium'. *Australian and New Zealand Journal of Criminology* 33 (2) pp. 153–67.

O'Neill, T. (2005) 'Girls in Trouble in the Child Welfare and Criminal Justice Systems', in G. Lloyd (ed.) *Problem Girls*. Abingdon: Routledge pp. 111–25.

Patel, S. and Stanley, S. (2008) *The Use of the Community Order and the Suspended Sentence Order for Women*. London: Centre for Crime and Justice Studies.

Phoenix, J. (2002) 'In the Name of Protection: Youth Prostitution Policy Reforms in England and Wales'. *Critical Social Policy* 22 (2) pp. 353–75.

Phoenix, J. (2003) 'Rethinking Youth Prostitution: National Provision at the Margins of Child Protection and Youth Justice'. *Youth Justice* 3 (3) pp. 152–68.

Phoenix, J. (2007) 'Regulating Prostitution: Different Problems, Different Solutions, Same Old Story'. *Safer Communities* 6 (1) pp. 7–10.

Phoenix, J. (2008a) 'ASBOs and Working Women: A New Revolving Door?', in P Squires (ed.) *ASBO Nation*. Bristol: Policy Press pp. 289–306.

Phoenix, J. (2008b) 'Governing Prostitution: New Formations, Old Agendas'. *Canadian Journal of Law and Society* 22 (2) pp. 73–94.

Phoenix, J. (2009) 'Beyond Risk Assessment: The Return of Repressive Welfarism', in M. Barry and F. McNeill (eds) *Youth Offending and Youth Justice*. London: Jessica Kingsley pp. 113–131.

Phoenix, J. (2012) *Out of Place: The Policing and Criminalisation of Sexually Exploited Girls and Young Women*. London: Howard League for Penal Reform.

Player, E. (2005) 'The Reduction of Women's Imprisonment in England and Wales'. *Punishment and Society* 7 (4) pp. 419–39.

Player, E. (2007) 'Remanding Women in Custody: Concerns for Human Rights'. *Modern Law Review* 70 (3) pp. 402–26.

Player, E., Roberts, J., Jacobson, J., Hough, M. and Rebottom, J. (2010) 'Remanded in Custody: An Analysis of Recent Trends in England and Wales'. *The Howard Journal* 49 (3) pp. 231–51.

Prison Reform Trust (2012) *Legal Aid, Sentencing and Punishment of Offenders Bill (House of Lords Committee Stage)*. Available at: www.prisonreformtrust.org.uk [accessed January 2012].

Robinson, P. (1987) 'Hybrid Principles for the Distribution of Criminal Sanctions'. *Northwestern University Law Review* 82 (1) pp. 19–42.

Rossner, M. (2011) 'Emotions and Interaction Ritual: A Micro Analysis of Restorative Justice'. *British Journal of Criminology* 51 (1) pp. 95–119.

Rumgay, J. (1996) 'Women Offenders: Towards a Needs Based Policy'. *Vista* September pp. 104–15.

Rumgay, J. (2004) 'Scripts for Safer Survival: Pathways Out of Female Crime'. *The Howard Journal* 43 (4) pp. 405–19.

Salgado, D.M., Fox, J.B. and Quinlan, K. (2011) 'Community Mentoring in the United States: An Evaluation of the Rhode Island Women's Mentoring Program', in R. Sheehan, G. McIvor and C. Trotter (eds) *Working with Female Offenders in the Community*. Abingdon: Willan pp. 279–97.

Seal, L. (2010) *Women, Murder and Femininity: Gender Representations of Women Who Kill*. Basingstoke: Palgrave Macmillan.

Sharpe, G. (2009) 'The Trouble with Girls Today'. *Youth Justice* 9 (3) pp. 254–69.

Sharpe, G. (2011) 'Beyond Youth Justice: Working with Girls and Young Women who Offend', in R. Sheehan, G. McIvor and C. Trotter (eds) *Working with Female Offenders in the Community*. Abingdon: Willan pp. 151–72.

Sharpe, G. and Gelsthorpe, L. (2009) 'Engendering the Agenda: Girls, Young Women and Youth Justice'. *Youth Justice* 9 (3) pp. 195–208.

Sheehan, R., McIvor, G. and Trotter, C. (2011) 'Introduction', in R. Sheehan, G. McIvor and C. Trotter (eds) *Working with Female Offenders in the Community*. Abingdon: Willan pp. xvii–xxvi.

Together Women (2011) *Who We Are*. Available at: fhg693.demonweb.co.uk/TWP/who_we_are.html [accessed July 2012].

Toor, S. (2009) 'British Asian Girls, Crime and Youth Justice'. *Youth Justice* 9 (3) pp. 239–54.

Vickers, S. and Wilcox, P. (2011) 'Abuse, Women and the Criminal Justice System'. *Criminal Justice Matters* 85 (1) pp. 24–5.

Wahidin, A. (2004) *Older Women in the Criminal Justice System: Running Out of Time*. London: Jessica Kingsley.

Wootton, B. (1959) *Social Science and Social Pathology*. London: Allen & Unwin.

Worrall, A. (1990) *Offending Women: Female Lawbreakers and the Criminal Justice System*. London: Routledge.

Worrall, A. (2001) 'Girls at Risk? Reflections on Changing Attitudes to Young Women's Offending'. *Probation Journal* 48 (2) pp. 86–92.

Worrall, A. and Gelsthorpe, L. (2009) '"What works" with women offenders: the past 30 years'. *Probation Journal* 56 (4) pp. 329–45.

Youth Justice Board (2009) *Girls and Offending Patterns, Perceptions and Interventions*. Available at: www.yjb.gov.uk/publications/Resources/Downloads/Girls_offending_summary.pdf [accessed July 2012].

10

CHILDREN, YOUNG PEOPLE AND THE CONTEMPORARY PENAL LANDSCAPE

REFLECTIONS, PROSPECTS, POLICY AND RESEARCH

BARRY GOLDSON

INTRODUCTION

The guiding rationales underpinning this chapter are to review the impact of the contemporary penal landscape upon children and young people and to begin to explore the prospects for limiting their entry into the youth justice system per se and, in particular, into penal detention. The key implications for youth justice policy are considered and areas for future research are proposed. The chapter is underpinned by a radical evidence-based approach and, as such, it is neither compromised by considerations of pragmatic calculation or any attempt to second-guess what might be politically palatable in the current – or future – period. The jurisdictional emphasis rests with England[1] although, where appropriate, reference is made to comparative analysis and/or to the international literature. The chapter is primarily presented in four inter-related sections as follows:

- contemporary policy and current thinking;
- key areas meriting policy-makers' attention;

- current research developments;
- gaps in knowledge and prospective research projects.

CONTEMPORARY POLICY AND CURRENT THINKING

Throughout much of the Western world in the late modern period, children and young people who offend adult sensibilities, transgress normative boundaries and/or breach the criminal law – the 'disorderly', the 'antisocial', 'young offenders' – are increasingly subjected to disparate, even contradictory, policy responses and practical interventions. In this way, modes of governance appear to comprise uneasy conglomerate formations, embracing multiple and competing priorities whereby:

> discourses of child protection, restoration, punishment, public protection, responsibility, justice, rehabilitation, welfare, retribution, diversion, human rights, and so on, intersect and circulate in a perpetually uneasy and contradictory motion.
>
> (Goldson and Muncie 2009: vii)

More specifically, following the election of the first New Labour government in 1997, the youth justice system in England (and Wales) became a site of near-permanent reform. Fundamental tensions, characterised by seemingly incongruous logics, lay at the very heart of such reforms and extended over three terms of office (1997–2010). On one hand notions of rationality were privileged, most commonly expressed as 'evidence-based policy'. On the other hand an impatient emotive punitivity, emphasising 'toughness' and 'no excuses' sentiments, was apparent (Goldson 2010). It follows that the wide-ranging policies implemented during this period expressed little by way of coherent narrative. Indeed, Fergusson (2007: 180 and 192) astutely detected the 'ambivalent and ambiguous character of New Labour's copious youth justice policies … [a] melting-pot of contending, competing or directly contradictory measures' and cautioned against 'over-ready classification of policies as falling within a single discursive framework' (2007: 181). So whilst a 'toughening up [of] every aspect of the criminal justice system' (Blair 2004) was clearly discernible, it was underpinned neither by unified jurisprudential foundations nor any sense of consistent or coherent principles. Rather, New Labour's youth justice comprised a hybrid and uneasy mix of impulses and rationales; the 'melting pot' to which Fergusson (2007) referred. Even a schematic overview illuminates the intrinsic tensions characteristic of New Labour policy reform including:

- actuarialist logics, a calculus of 'risk' and the so-called 'scaled approach' premising constructions of early (often intensive) intervention, including 'pre-emptive' intervention;
- awkward linkages/slippages between civil and criminal jurisdiction, together with the tenuous conflation of 'anti-social behaviour', 'disorder' and 'crime', seemingly underpinned by varying interpretations of communitarianism;
- derivations of *restorative* justice bolted on to otherwise *retributive* powers and statutory orders;
- the intensification of community-based supervision and surveillance that accompanied, rather than substituted, processes of repenalisation and the significant escalation of custodial detention (although the child prisoner population has dipped since 2007–8, see below);
- the 'triple track' policy emphasis on 'better and earlier prevention', 'non-negotiable support' and 'enforcement and punishment', perhaps best encapsulated the incongruous drivers underpinning New Labour's youth justice policy programme (Home Office *et al.* 2008, 2009).

Although it is difficult to distinguish intelligible coherence within New Labour's youth justice programme, its ultimate effect authenticated the 'toughness' rhetoric with which it was shrouded. At the 'shallow end' of the system, distorted actuarial constructs, risk-based priorities and interventionist strategies gave rise to substantial 'net widening'. At the system's midriff, modes of intensive supervision and correctional regulation were bolstered by surveillance and electronic monitoring technologies. At the 'deep end' more and younger children were detained in penal custody for longer periods. In short, between 1997 and 2010 the youth justice apparatus extended its reach and deepened its penetration ultimately representing the antithesis of knowledge and evidence (for a fuller discussion see Goldson 2010).

With the election of the Conservative–Liberal Democrat Coalition government in May 2010 and a policy context dominated by financial crisis, youth justice has been afforded significantly less attention and it is difficult to identify anything resembling an evolving and/or distinctive policy trajectory. Notwithstanding this, four key developments are noteworthy: the Green Paper 2010; the Independent Commission on Youth Crime and Antisocial Behaviour; the Police Reform and Social Responsibility Act 2011; and the continued existence of the Youth Justice Board. Each merits further comment.

The Green Paper 2010

In December 2010, the Coalition government published a Green Paper entitled *Breaking the Cycle: Effective Punishment, Rehabilitation and Sentencing of Offenders* (Ministry of Justice 2010). Chapter 5 of the Green Paper focuses exclusively on youth justice and five key objectives are set out to:

- prevent more young people from offending and divert them from entering into a life of crime, including by simplifying out-of-court disposals;
- protect the public and ensure that more is done to make young offenders pay back to their victims and communities;
- ensure the effective use of sentencing for young offenders;
- incentivise local partners to reduce youth offending and reoffending using payment by results models; and
- develop more effective governance by abolishing the Youth Justice Board and increasing freedoms and flexibilities for local areas.

(Ministry of Justice 2010: 67)

In essence, the Coalition government's stated priorities are to:

1. reduce the number of first time entrants to the youth justice system;
2. reduce reoffending;
3. extend the application of (a particular variant of) restorative justice;
4. reduce the numbers of children and young people entering penal custody.

The Independent Commission on Youth Crime and Antisocial Behaviour

In July 2010, the Independent Commission on Youth Crime and Antisocial Behaviour published its principal findings in a report entitled:

Time for a Fresh Start: The Report of the Independent Commission on Youth Crime and Antisocial Behaviour. The Commission's report has been subjected to detailed critique elsewhere (Goldson 2011a, 2011b) but three key points are noteworthy here:

1. the Commission's principal recommendations are entirely consistent with the Coalition government's four core priorities as listed immediately above;
2. the emphasis that the Commission places on a specific form of 'responsibilising' restorative justice appears to have been received positively by policy-makers;
3. the Commission controversially claimed that 'a more effective and humane response to youth crime in England and Wales can be achieved without raising the minimum age of criminal responsibility' (Independent Commission on Youth Crime and Antisocial Behaviour 2010: 91).

The Police Reform and Social Responsibility Act 2011

The Act provided for the replacement of Police Authorities by Police and Crime Commissioners (PCCs). Police and Crime Panels – the agencies charged with responsibility for monitoring the activities of PCCs – were established before 41 PCCs were elected in November 2012. Elections for PCCs are to be held every four years.

The introduction of PCCs is likely to make a major impact on criminal justice in general and Youth Offending Teams (YOTs) in particular. The locally elected Commissioners will ultimately be responsible for the delivery of all crime and policing functions and, as such, they will be vested with substantial commissioning power. From April 2013 the funding that has, until then, been administered by the Home Office and allocated to Community Safety Partnerships will instead be allocated to, and be managed by, the PCCs. Similarly, youth crime prevention funding that has previously been channelled directly to YOTs via the Youth Justice Board (YJB) grant will also be managed by the PCCs. A YJB bulletin states:

> as the plans for the creation of Police and Crime Commissioners (PCCs) develop, it is becoming clear that they are going to be an important new player in the youth justice community.
>
> (Youth Justice Board 2011a)

The Youth Justice Board

On 14 October 2010, the government announced its plans to abolish the Youth Justice Board for England and Wales (YJB) – as part of a wider culling of specified public bodies – and to transfer its functions to the Ministry of Justice (Ministry of Justice 2010). This proposal – originally contained within the Green Paper 2010 – has since been withdrawn following stern opposition in the House of Lords.

The Public Bodies Bill was introduced into the House of Lords on 28 October 2010 and completed its stages following significant amendment. The Bill was then introduced into the House of Commons on 10 May 2011 and received its second reading on 12 July 2011. The Bill was considered in a Public Bill Committee between 8 September 2011 and 11 October 2011, followed by the report stage and third reading on 25 October 2011. The Bill was then sent to the House of Lords for consideration of Commons Amendments. The Lords insisted on their amendments to the Bill, which were considered by the Commons on 29 November 2011. The Lords amendments were approved, including Amendment 47A: 'it is not desirable for the Youth Justice Board for England and Wales to be subject to the provisions of the Bill' (that is, to be abolished). The Bill received Royal Assent on 14 December 2011, thus becoming the Public Bodies Act 2011. Further to the above reprieve, the YJB's Chief Executive reported that:

> the YJB are now working with Government to establish the future priorities and 'modus operandi' ... the Government's first concern is to increase ministerial accountability, to increase the involvement of the youth justice minister, Crispin Blunt MP, in the main issues with which the YJB is engaged ... It is the best way to ensure that youth justice is a high priority for ministers and Government.
>
> (Drew 2011)

KEY AREAS MERITING POLICY-MAKERS' ATTENTION

At least ten key areas – in respect of contemporary youth justice policy – either merit, or are receiving, focused attention (although the form that such attention is taking is not necessarily welcome).

The age of criminal responsibility

The age of criminal responsibility in England (and Wales) – ten years – is the lowest in the European Union. Other European countries manage youth justice systems where the age of criminal responsibility is substantially higher than it is in England (and Wales) and where it can be shown that there are no negative consequences to be seen in terms of crime rates (Goldson 2009).

Furthermore, in immediately neighbouring jurisdictions, the modern trend is moving in the direction of raising the age of criminal responsibility. In March 2009, the Scottish Parliament announced:

> The age of criminal responsibility at which children can be prosecuted in adult criminal courts will be raised to twelve. This will bring Scots law into line with jurisdictions across Europe ... In raising the age of criminal responsibility from eight to 12, ministers have taken on board the views of the United Nations, but have ruled out suggestions the age should be raised to 14 or even 16.The new measures [are] to be included in the Scottish Government's forthcoming Criminal Justice and Licensing Bill.
> (www.scotland.gov.uk/News/Releases/2009/03/27140804)

In Ireland, the age of criminal responsibility is covered by the Children Act 2001 (section 52) as amended by the Criminal Justice Act 2006 (section 129), which served to raise the age of criminal responsibility from 7 years to 12 years of age. There is an exception, however, for children aged ten or 11 who can be charged with murder, manslaughter, rape or aggravated sexual assault. In addition, where a child under 14 years of age is charged with an offence, no further proceedings can be taken without the consent of the Director of Public Prosecutions. In Northern Ireland, a major review of the youth justice system was launched in 2010 by the Minister of Justice, David Ford, in furtherance of the Hillsborough Castle Agreement (Graham *et al.* 2011). The final report of the review team states:

> The minimum age of criminal responsibility, which is 10 in Northern Ireland, is an emotive issue. Age 10 is low by comparison with most other countries. International treaties have suggested it should be higher, and certainly not lower than 12. Scotland and the Republic of Ireland have recently raised the age (with some minor provisos) to 12. We suggest it should also be raised to 12 in Northern Ireland with consideration given after a period of time to raising it further to 14.
> (Graham *et al.* 2011: 14)

Accordingly, Recommendation 29 of the Review provides:

> The minimum age of criminal responsibility in Northern Ireland should be raised to 12 with immediate effect, and that following a period of review of no more than three years, consideration should be given to raising the age to 14.
>
> (Graham *et al.*: 118)

Early indications suggest that this recommendation is being seriously considered at Stormont.

A case for raising the age of criminal responsibility in England (and Wales) has been made elsewhere (Goldson 2009). For present purposes, suffice to note that given both the comparatively low age of criminal responsibility and the unmitigated exposure of children to the full weight of criminal law, the jurisdiction is manifestly out-of-sync with the norms of European youth justice law, policy and practice in general, and at odds with recent developments in its immediately neighbouring jurisdictions in particular. Bearing this in mind, the reluctance of the Independent Commission on Youth Crime and Antisocial Behaviour to recommend raising the age of criminal responsibility (see above) was particularly disappointing and, to date, there appears to be no political appetite in England for following the examples set by Scotland, Ireland and (potentially at least) Northern Ireland.

Antisocial behaviour orders

Table 10.1 presents the number of Antisocial Behaviour Orders (ASBOs) imposed on children and young people, the number of ASBOs breached for the first time and the proportion of ASBOs imposed that led to breach action over the period 2003–10 inclusive.

Table 10.2 presents the proportion of breached ASBOs that led to custodial detention over the period 1 June 2000 to 31 December 2010 inclusive.

Since 2005–6 the number of ASBOs imposed on children and young people reveals a pattern of year-on-year decline with the exception of 2010, which marked a 7 per cent increase over 2009. The incidence of breach – averaging at 72 per cent over the 2003–10 period – indicates a fundamental failure of the Order, and the high proportion of breaches

Table 10.1 ASBOs and first time breaches 2003–10 in England and Wales – children and young people aged 10–17 years

Year	No. of ASBOs imposed	No. of ASBOs breached for the first time	Per cent of ASBOs imposed that were breached
2003	629	314	50
2004	1,340	700	52
2005	1,581	1,036	66
2006	1,053	871	83
2007	920	737	80
2008	719	559	78
2009	501	448	89
2010	536	404	75
Totals (means)	7,785	5,264	(72)

that result in the custodial detention of children manifests profound injustice.

The Coalition government has indicated that it will maintain a firm line in addressing antisocial behaviour, declaring: 'Reducing anti-social behaviour is a government priority' (Home Office 2011b: 5). However, it has also stated its intention to reform what it terms the 'antisocial behaviour toolkit' (2011b: 9) by introducing two new sanctions, a Criminal Behaviour Order (2011b: 14) and a Crime Prevention Injunction (2011b: 16). The former applies to criminal offences (in much the same way as the 'criminal' ASBO), whereas the latter is intended to be available only in civil courts (in much the same way as the ASBO made on application). The Coalition government is also apparently intent on introducing a 'Community Trigger that gives victims and communities the right to require agencies to deal with persistent antisocial behaviour' (2011b: 6).

In effect, such proposals are remarkably reminiscent of New Labour's antisocial behaviour sanctions. The Coalition goverment is proposing,

Table 10.2   ASBO breaches leading to custodial detention 2000–10 in England and Wales – children and young people aged 10–17 years

Age of children and young people	Per cent of ASBOs breached leading to custodial detention
10–11 years	0
12–14 years	35.6
15–17 years	40.0

Source: Home Office (2011a).

for example, that breach of a Criminal Behaviour Order might result in a two-year custodial sentence in the case of a child (as with the ASBO). On the other hand, it is proposed that non-compliance with a Crime Prevention Injunction will, in the case of an adult, be treated as contempt of court. Given that children cannot generally be held in contempt of court an alternative sanction will be required. In such cases, the government is indicating a preference for the courts to be given powers to impose supervision with a range of requirements, including detention. Informed by the failings of New Labour's antisocial behaviour agenda and the injustices that ensued – both of which were disproportionately felt by children and young people – such proposals merit close scrutiny by policy-makers.

Breach proceedings

A hardening of attitudes and a mood of intolerance characterise contemporary youth justice policy in England where: the courts exploit expanded powers; practitioners are bound more tightly by centrally imposed national standards; the professional 'contract' with children and young people has become more technical, more unbalanced and more demanding (on children); practice is increasingly managerialised, target-driven, audit-conscious and performance-indicator oriented; and the interface between child welfare and youth justice has become progressively distanced at both central and local government levels (Goldson 2010).

This is the context within which the breach action, considered immediately above, is located. Moreover:

> Data published by the Ministry of Justice (MoJ) and Youth Justice Board (YJB) suggests that breach of statutory order now constitutes 6 per cent of all proven offences, double the proportion in 2002/03 ... Most likely to be returned to court for breach of a statutory order are older boys, and those of mixed ethnicity. Breach offences, however, account for a disproportionate number of younger children, girls and those of white ethnicity in custody. There are also regional variations in the use of breach proceedings ... in 2009/10 an average of 9 per cent of children were in custody solely for breach of a statutory order, usually a community sentence.
>
> (Hart 2011: iv–v; see also Bateman 2011a).

To treat children in this way not only represents a travesty of justice, it is likely to subject them to harm and will almost certainly increase any proclivity that they may have to offend. Both the *general policy context* that appears to have given rise to an increased incidence of breach and the *specific practical consequences* of such actions require urgent attention.

Intervention effect

According to data published by the Youth Justice Board and Ministry of Justice (2011), the number of substantive disposals – grouped into four types: pre-court; first-tier; community; custodial – imposed on children and young people fell from 184,850 in 2008–9 to 155,857 in 2009–10, a reduction of 16 per cent. The same data reveals that levels of detected reoffending have also fallen. Considerable variation is evident, however, contingent upon the precise nature of disposal (see Table 10.3). Apparent reductions in actual reoffending are substantially greater for pre-court measures and first-tier disposals – involving significantly lower levels of intervention – than community and custodial sanctions. In actual fact, reoffending following a community sentence has increased and custodial sentences continue to be the least effective form of intervention.

There are, of course, a number of ways of reading and interpreting such data but at least two propositions merit policy-makers' consideration:

1. Lower levels of youth justice intervention might be taken to imply higher levels of desistance and, should this be so, the practices of

Table 10.3 Intervention effect – nature of disposal and detected reoffending rate within 12 months: 2000 and 2009

Nature of disposal	Detected reoffending rate 2000	Detected reoffending rate 2009
Out-of-court disposal	28%	23.7%
First-tier penalty	51%	45.3%
Community penalty	63.7%	66.9%
Custodial penalty	75.7%	71.9%

Source: adapted from Bateman (2011b) and Youth Justice Board and Ministry of Justice (2011).

   diversion and/or 'down-tariff' sentencing will serve to optimise crime reduction imperatives (see below).

2. The spectacular failure of custodial intervention – as a measure of crime reduction and community safety – requires policy-makers to introduce legislation to limit, if not abolish, its use (see below).

Child imprisonment

Statistics provided by Crispin Blunt, Minister for Prisons and Probation – in answer to a Parliamentary Question in March 2011 – confirm that the imposition of both custodial remands and sentences began to diminish from 2007–8 (see Table 10.4).

A similar pattern of penal reduction is evidenced by recent data published by the Youth Justice Board (see Table 10.5).

Not unlike the 'intervention effect' data presented immediately above, there are different ways of comprehending such patterns, but at least four issues merit policy-makers' attention:

1. There is no evidence that the reductions in child imprisonment have been accompanied by an increase in youth crime, implying that a more concerted and ambitious strategy of penal reduction would not impose any deleterious effect with regard to crime reduction and community safety imperatives.

Table 10.4 Child (10–17 years) imprisonment (remands and sentences) – 2001/2–2009/10

Year	Penal remands	Custodial sentences	Total
2001/2	5,277	5,828	11,105
2002/3	5,693	5,439	11,132
2003/4	5,796	5,140	10,936
2004/5	5,720	4,917	10,637
2005/6	5,757	5,278	11,035
2006/7	6,098	5,479	11,577
2007/8	5,625	5,563	11,188
2008/9	5,221	5,491	10,712
2009/10	4,740	4,261	9,001

Source: Hansard, House of Commons, column 761W, 7 March 2011.

2. The reductions indicated above are principally due to diminishing custodial sentences. Conversely, custodial remands have remained relatively stable. This is particularly troubling given all that is known regarding the particular vulnerabilities of child remand prisoners and the evidence that many children held on penal remand do not attract custodial sanctions when sentenced.

3. Whilst the reductions in custodial sentences for children are welcome, they also appear to rest on fragile foundations. Increases in the number of child prisoners in both May and June 2011 comprise the first rise in consecutive months since March–April 2008. Furthermore, following the disturbances in England in August 2011 (see below), the emerging evidence is suggestive of further significant increases of child prisoners.

4. Justice (or injustice) by geography also persists within the more general context of penal reduction. Statistics provided by Crispin Blunt, Minister for Prisons and Probation – in answer to a Parliamentary Question in May 2011 – reveal significant differences in penal remand

Table 10.5 Average number of child
(10–17 years) prisoners (remands and
sentences) – 2001/2–2010/11

Year	Average number of child prisoners
2001–2	2,801
2002–3	3,029
2003–4	2,771
2004–5	2,745
2005–6	2,830
2007–7	2,914
2007–8	2,932
2008–9	2,881
2009–10	2,418
2010–11	2,067

Source: Youth Justice Board (2011b).

and sentencing behaviour in 2009–10, across Youth Offending Team (YOT) areas. The Minister provided a breakdown of the average child prisoner population per 1,000 children and young people in each YOT area. For 12–15 year olds, for example, the numbers ranged from 0 in Ceredigion, Pembrokeshire, South Gloucestershire and Sutton, to 0.78 in Wandsworth. For children aged 16–17 years, figures ranged from 0.14 in Wokingham to 7.71 in Merthyr Tydfil (Hansard, House of Commons, Column 210W, 18 May 2011).

The care–custody relation

Her Majesty's Chief Inspector of Prisons, Nick Hardwick, recently stated:

> In my view, the state has few responsibilities greater than its statutory responsibility towards looked after children. Even allowing for the damage

they have sustained before coming into the state's care and the challenging behaviour they may present when they do, that so many end up in custody is a cause for real concern.

(Her Majesty's Inspectorate of Prisons 2011b: 10)

Following a thematic review of the care of 'looked after children' in penal custody, however, the Chief Inspector concluded:

Children in the care of the local authority, or 'looked after children', are overrepresented within the custodial population ... With no central record held by the Prison Service or Youth Justice Board, our survey data is one of the best estimates of the overall proportion of looked after children in custody ... [Young Offender Institutions] seemed largely to rely on information arriving with the child to identify whether he/she was looked after ... It is perhaps unsurprising that ... those who said they had spent time in care reported more vulnerability and greater need than those who had not ... the involvement of local authorities was often dependent on the commitment of individual social workers and, worryingly ... some social workers tried to end their involvement while the young person was in custody ... many looked after young people leave custody with inadequate support.

(2011c: 9, 10)

Such observations echo a wealth of previous research indicating: the overrepresentation of 'looked after children' in prisons and other custodial institutions; a complete absence of centrally collated and reliable data on the care–custody relation; the multiple complex vulnerabilities that 'looked after children' import into penal settings; the neglect of such children's manifest needs whilst imprisoned; the near abdication of responsibility by some social services authorities and the inadequate nature of 'resettlement' support for children in the care of the state. Each of these issues – together with the enduring presence of such phenomenon over time – require urgent attention from the policy-making community.

Resettlement

A further thematic review of resettlement, conducted by Her Majesty's Inspectorate of Prisons (2011b), found that 39 per cent of the boys surveyed reported that they did not expect to return to their family home after release from prison custody. Most of these boys simply did not know where they would live once discharged from detention.

In conclusion the Chief Inspector reflected:

> Overall the outcomes for our sample were very disappointing ... Although our recommendations are to the Ministry of Justice, Youth Justice Board and National Offender Management Service we recognise that, to ensure all young people have suitable accommodation and ETE [education, training and employment] on release from custody, a joint approach with other government departments and external agencies is required. The starting point should be an acceptance that vulnerable young people released from custody are children in need.
>
> (Her Majesty's Inspectorate of Prisons 2011b: 10–11)

The provision of adequate post-custodial 'resettlement' clearly requires 'joined-up' strategic initiatives that extend across the policy-making community. This is necessary not only to meet statutory agency responsibilities to such children, but also to 'prevent them from returning to custody and becoming entrenched at an early age in a life of crime' (Ibid.: 11).

'Gangs' and violence

Opinion regarding youth 'gangs' is clearly divided. Questions as to whether or not organised youth 'gangs' actually exist and, if they do, how best to address them are far from settled (Goldson 2011c). Whilst some researchers have gone so far as to argue that youth 'gangs' represent the 'changing face of youth justice' (Pitts 2008), others are significantly more circumspect. Simon Hallsworth and Tara Young (2008: 177), for example, have argued persuasively that:

> [C]onstructing the problem of street violence as essentially a problem of gangs is an exercise flawed on empirical, theoretical and methodological grounds ... there appears to be little evidence to suggest a pervasive and growing gang problem ... 'gang talk', as we label this garrulous discourse, runs the risk of misrepresenting what it claims to represent ... while sanctioning 'solutions' that might be as misdirected as they are misguided.

Within a context characterised by both polarised opinion and public anxiety, carefully measured and dispassionate analysis is clearly required in order to begin to understand – and respond to – the complex worlds that are occupied by some young people. Conversely, 'tough' sounding political rhetoric and pledges from the Home Office (2011c: np) 'to tackle gang and youth violence through prevention and tough punishment' are singularly unhelpful:

> Young people at risk of being drawn into gangs and violence will be targeted at every stage of their lives – from toddlers to teenagers – in a comprehensive approach aimed at preventing the next generation of gang members. Those who refuse help will be met by the full force of strengthened laws to protect local communities from crime and disorder.
>
> (Home Office 2011c: np)

The issues confronting young people involved with and/or afflicted by violent 'street worlds' are unlikely to be resolved by providing the police with extended powers to take out gang injunctions in respect of 14 to 17 year olds, or by implementing custodial sentences for 16 and 17 year olds using a knife to 'threaten or endanger others' (Home Office 2011c). Policy-makers need to exercise more restraint in respect of rhetoric and more rigour with regard to engaging careful analyses and formulating responsible responses.

Gendered and racialised (in)justice

The extent to which the delivery of youth justice is mediated through the structural relations of gender (see, for example, Gelsthorpe and Sharpe 2006, 2009) and 'race'/ethnicity (see, for example, Webster 2006; May *et al.* 2010) has long been researched and debated.

The All Party Parliamentary Group on Women in the Criminal Justice System (2012), supported by the Howard League for Penal Reform, have conducted an independent inquiry on girls and the penal system. The inquiry focused on policy and practice regarding girls and investigated the decisions that route girls away from, or into, the youth justice system. It examined how the police and the courts process girls and young women who come into contact with the system and the different approaches to working with them, both nationally and internationally. The key findings included:

- many magistrates and other professionals appear to lack awareness of the specific needs of girls who tend to be overlooked in the youth justice system owing to their relatively small number;

- girls are being unnecessarily criminalised in cases where diversion would be a more appropriate option;
- girls are treated harshly in the courts if their behaviour is deemed to contradict gender stereotypes;
- magistrates appear to confuse *welfare needs* with *high risk of reoffending* and, as such, increase the severity of the court disposal;
- there is a shortage of gender-specific provision for girls once sentenced;
- prisons – particularly 'special' units for girls in adult prisons – and secure training centres are not appropriate and should be closed in line with the recommendations of the *Corston Report* (Corston 2007);
- contrary to the provisions of the United Nations Convention on the Rights of the Child, penal custody is not being used as a 'measure of last resort' for girls.

Meanwhile, with funding from the Joseph Rowntree Foundation and the Open Society Foundation, the *Guardian*, in collaboration with the London School of Economics and Political Science (LSE), undertook a unique project that brought together investigative journalism and academic research in order to analyse the circumstances that gave rise to a series of major urban disturbances in England in August 2011 (see below). The 'Reading the Riots' initiative focused much of its early attention on questions of policing young people in general and policing black and minority ethnic young people in particular. Tim Newburn (2011: 30) – the lead academic from the LSE – reported that the issues that young people referred to most frequently in relation to policing were 'justice' and 'respect', with their focus fixing on what they perceived to be a lack of each:

> It is the sense that every time they are out on the streets, they face the prospect of being stopped, challenged and, from time to time, abused. Above all, it is stop-and-search that is the focus of the frustrations and anger that many of these young people feel. The practice has been controversial for decades, yet fundamental change appears all but impossible ... Those interviewed ... had two complaints. First, they felt they were deliberately targeted, and that this targeting is discriminatory, unfair or unjust. Rather than having 'reasonable suspicion', as the law generally requires, they believe that officers simply assumed their guilt. Longstanding monitoring of stop-and-search has shown its heavily disproportionate impact on minority youth. Neither the Scarman report in the early 1980s nor the

Stephen Lawrence inquiry in the late 1990s, both highly critical of police practice, have substantially changed the picture. Second, all too often – even when stop-and-search is carried out in circumstances where there appears just cause – the method and style in which it is undertaken are felt to be disrespectful. As is widely recognised, the impact of such discourtesy is dramatic. A growing body of research evidence on 'procedural justice' in policing illustrates how important 'fairness' is, both to police legitimacy and to public willingness to comply with the law and co-operate with the police.

The independent inquiry on girls and the penal system conducted by the All Party Parliamentary Group on Women in the Criminal Justice System, together with the 'Reading the Riots' initiative, each reveal a wide range of issues pertaining to gendered and racialised (in)justice. There is a pressing need for policy-makers to pay attention to such revelations, to locate them within a wider body of evidence and to act in order to address the myriad injustices that afflict the youth justice system.

Urban disorder

The series of disturbances – 'riots' – in major English cities during the early part of August 2011 raised a range of complex questions. To date the debate has largely been polarised between reductionist constructions of moral breakdown on the one hand, and essentialist notions of material determinism on the other hand. Both, in themselves, are patently inadequate.

As is indicated by the 'Reading the Riots' initiative, there is a pressing need for the research, policy and practice communities to collaborate in: making sense of the circumstances and conditions that produce such outbreaks of urban disorder; engaging with the complex range of aetiological phenomenon; retaining a balanced and open perspective and exercising patience in the formulation of appropriate responses.

CURRENT RESEARCH DEVELOPMENTS

Much of the material presented above overlaps – either directly or indirectly – with current research developments in the youth justice sphere. Additionally, at least five further areas are noteworthy.

Diversion

There is substantial research and practice-informed evidence to validate the concept of diversion. Diversionary principles provide that, whenever possible, children and young people in trouble should be directed away (diverted) from the youth justice apparatus. In cases where absolute diversion is deemed inappropriate, the level of formal criminal/youth justice intervention should be limited to the minimum that is judged to be absolutely necessary.

The most compelling recent research evidence in this respect is provided by Lesley McAra and Susan McVie (2007, 2010). McAra and McVie (2007: 315) contend: 'the key to reducing offending lies in minimal intervention and maximum diversion'. By drawing on their detailed longitudinal research on pathways into and out of offending for a cohort of 4,300 children and young people in Edinburgh, and informed more broadly by a growing body of international studies, they conclude:

> Doing less rather than more in individual cases may mitigate the potential for damage that system contact brings ... targeted early intervention strategies ... are likely to widen the net ... Greater numbers of children will be identified as at risk and early involvement will result in constant recycling into the system ... As we have shown, forms of diversion ... without recourse to formal intervention ... are associated with desistance from serious offending. Such findings are supportive of a maximum diversion approach ... Accepting that, in some cases, doing less is better than doing more requires both courage and vision on the part of policy makers ... To the extent that systems appear to damage young people and inhibit their capacity to change, then they do not, and never will, deliver justice.
>
> (McAra and McVie 2007: 337 and 340)

Mental health and youth justice

There is growing interest in mental health issues pertaining to children and young people in trouble and the interface between Child and Adolescent Mental Health Services (CAMHS) and the youth justice system. Amongst others, Goldson (2002) and Goldson and Coles (2005) have drawn attention to mental health issues in respect of child prisoners. More recently, Lord Bradley's (2009) review of people with mental health problems or learning disabilities in the criminal justice system has addressed a range of generic issues, whilst the Office of the Children's

Commissioner (2011) and the Ministry of Justice and the Department of Health (2011) have each focused more sharply on the youth justice system. Finally, for present purposes, a cross-disciplinary team of senior researchers from the University of Liverpool recently published a substantial research report underpinned by an evaluation of the Department of Health-sponsored youth justice liaison and diversion schemes in various localities in England (Haines *et al.* 2012).

Risk

Constructions of 'risk', 'risk factors', 'risk-based early intervention' and actuarialism have imposed significant purchase over contemporary youth justice policy and practice. The submission here is that such approaches are deeply problematic, a view that is shared by others. Carole Sutton and her colleagues, paradoxically amongst the keenest advocates of the early intervention 'risk factor' paradigm, counsel the need for 'caution':

> In particular, any notion that better screening can enable policy makers to identify young children destined to join the 5 per cent of offenders responsible for 50–60 per cent of crime is fanciful. Even if there were no ethical objections to putting 'potential delinquent' labels round the necks of young children, there would continue to be statistical barriers. Research into the continuity of anti-social behaviour shows substantial flows out of – as well as in to – the pool of children who develop chronic conduct problems. This demonstrates the dangers of assuming that anti-social five year olds are the criminals or drug abusers of tomorrow.
>
> (Sutton *et al.* 2004: 5)

Perhaps the most authoritative critical analysis of 'risk' discourses in the youth justice field, however, has been provided by Stephen Case and Kevin Haines (2009).

Desistance

Stephen Farrall and Shadd Maruna (2004: 358) note:

> The in-depth, social scientific study of desistance from crime began with the Gluecks' ... research in the first part of the 20th century. Yet, it was not until the 1970s and 1980s that formal interest in (and even use of the word) desistance started to emerge in criminology.

In recent years, a research interest in desistance in the youth justice context – or 'growing out of crime' (Rutherford 1992) – has gathered momentum. In particular, the importance of *social context* has been emphasised by a number of researchers. For example, Farrall and Bowling (1999: 261) contend that: 'the process of desistance is one that is produced through an *interplay* between individual choices, and a range of wider social forces, institutional and societal practices which are beyond the control of the individual.'

More recently still, Claire Fitzpatrick (née Taylor) (2011: 231–2) in examining the concepts of 'desistance' and 'resilience' together, observed that:

> Although the two concepts have a different heritage ... they have also tended to develop in very similar ways over time ... researchers are increasingly emphasising the importance of understanding the 'process' of desistance and resilience. Early understandings of desistance as a 'termination event' and resilience as a 'set of qualities' are too simplistic and/or one-sided, and researchers in both fields are now focusing on the need to take account of the wider social context as well as the individual in understanding the capacity to overcome adversity. In addition, the development of desistance and resilience has seen them both emerge in their respective fields as dynamic concepts that may be subject to change at different points in the life-course and in different social environments. Both may be usefully viewed as an 'ongoing work-in-progress' ... which implies a need for continued support and relapse prevention measures where appropriate.

Such research offers valuable insights into the uneven and non-linear nature of 'growing out of crime'. Fundamentally, as McNeill (2006) has demonstrated, a key ingredient of effective youth justice practice comprises the quality of relationships between adult 'supervisors' and children and young people; the prevalence of mutual respect and the preparedness of the former to be patient in guiding the latter through the process(es) of 'desistance'.

Comparative analysis

Conventionally, attempts at comparative analysis in the youth justice sphere essentially amount to *describing* different systems and outlining the formal powers and procedures embedded within specific jurisdictions (see for example, Bala *et al.* 2002; Dunkel *et al.* 2010; Junger-Tas and Decker 2008; Hazel 2008; Junger-Tas *et al.* 2010; Tonry and Doob 2004; Winterdyk 2002). Despite their interest and value, such approaches pay scant regard either to the political, social or cultural conditions that sustain particular system formations whilst undermining others, and/or the actual translation and transmission of statute and policy via the varying (discretionary) mechanisms comprising youth justice practice 'on the ground'.

The principal value of comparative analysis, however, rests not so much with state-by-state descriptive accounts of powers and procedures, but rather with critical analyses of both the contexts within which multiple, overlapping and even contradictory policy impulses are located and the means by which they are realised and expressed in practice. This, of course, necessitates a grasp of the political, social, cultural and professional imperatives that might support or subvert the translation of official policy into operational practice (see, for example, Goldson and Hughes 2010; Goldson and Muncie 2006; Muncie 2005; Muncie and Goldson 2006). Furthermore, recent attempts have been made to examine comparative youth justice through an international human rights lens (Goldson and Muncie 2012).

GAPS IN KNOWLEDGE AND PROSPECTIVE RESEARCH PROJECTS

It is near impossible to provide a comprehensive account of gaps in knowledge or an exhaustive list of prospective research projects and, even if it were possible, it is impractical in a chapter such as this. This said, the following six suggestions give some flavour to a prospective or new research programme with a clear focus on policy translation and practical impact. Each 'category' or 'subject field' contains numerous possibilities and, as such, the emphasis is deliberately broad-based.

The impact of financial crisis and severe austerity measures

Given the current socio-economic context in England (and many other Western states) research is required that engages with the impact(s) of austerity on children and young people in general and youth justice in particular.

The age of criminal responsibility and diversion

There is a pressing need for more comparative research on the implications of a raised age of criminal responsibility and the prioritisation of diversion as a foundational principle of youth justice law, policy and practice.

Restorative justice

With restorative justice assuming the status of a new global orthodoxy, research is required that focuses on the multiple variants of restorative justice and adopts a more critical orientation to its adaptations, applications and outcomes in the youth justice sphere.

Children's and young people's perspectives

There remains a shortage of high quality qualitative research that centres the perspectives of children and young people at *all* stages of the youth justice process and takes appropriate account of diversity issues.

Penal custody and its replacement

Despite recent reductions in the numbers of child prisoners in England (and Wales), the jurisdiction continues to incarcerate far too many children (remanded and sentenced). Furthermore, such children continue to endure neglectful and harmful regimes and practices. There is clearly a need to extend knowledge via further research and, in particular, to interrogate the question of penal reduction if not abolition.

Comparative analysis

Cross-jurisdictional and trans-national research continues to be under-developed. This applies as much within the UK (regarding its three, arguably four, jurisdictions) as it does outwith the UK. There are many untapped potential collaborations that might be opened up through the funding of comparative research.

CONCLUSION

Youth justice has comprised an extraordinarily fast-moving policy environment for almost two decades. As successive governments have opted to 'govern through crime' (Simon 2007) and youth justice has become increasingly politicised, ever-expanding numbers of children have been drawn into the correctional apparatus. Indeed, over this period, the youth justice system in England has grown on an almost industrial scale and its bloated and obese form now represents a morally bankrupt and practically ineffective response to young people in conflict with the law. On top of this, conditions of fiscal crisis, severe austerity and dramatic public sector retrenchment demand more responsible, rational and genuinely evidence based approaches.

As indicated at various points throughout this chapter, the above should not be taken to comprise a fully developed account of any of the four principal areas that it covers: contemporary and current thinking; key areas meriting policy-makers' attention; current research developments; and/or gaps in knowledge and prospective research projects. Rather, along with other chapters in this volume, it aims to offer a starting point from which to begin to imagine an alternative policy and practice framework that might serve to 'stem the flow'. In this particular case, the mission must be to divert children and young people from a system of 'justice' that is frequently harmful and damaging and offers minimal practical comfort to a public desiring of crime reduction and community safety.

Notes

1   The UK is the site of three separate territorial jurisdictions – England and Wales, Northern Ireland and Scotland – and each has produced, to a greater or lesser extent, quite distinctive youth justice systems. Furthermore, the value of continuing to regard England and Wales as a single jurisdiction is itself questionable. Several commentators have observed how processes of political devolution are serving increasingly to define and distinguish discrete approaches to youth justice in both England and Wales in ways that appear to undermine the notion of a unified and monolithic jurisdiction (see for example, Cross et al. 2002; Drakeford 2010; Goldson and Hughes 2010; Haines 2009; Hughes et al. 2009). Accordingly, the primary focus here is the youth justice system in England.

References

All Party Parliamentary Group on Women in the Criminal Justice System (2012) *Inquiry on Girls: From Courts to Custody*. London: The Howard League for Penal Reform

Bala, N., Hornick, J., Snyder, H. and Paetsch, J. (eds) (2002) *Juvenile Justice Systems: An International Comparison of Problems and Solutions*. Toronto: Thompson.

Bateman, T. (2011a) '"We now breach more kids in a week than we used to in a whole year": the punitive turn, enforcement and custody'. *Youth Justice: An International Journal*, 11(2) pp. 115–33.

Bateman, T. (2011b) 'Detected youth crime in England and Wales, reoffending and custodial episodes all fall'. Youth Justice News. *Youth Justice: An International Journal*, 11(2) pp. 185–6.

Blair, T. (2004) 'Foreword', *Confident Communities in a Secure Britain: The Home Office Strategic Plan 2004–08*. London: The Stationery Office.

Bradley, K. (2009) *The Bradley Report: Lord Bradley's Review of People with Mental Health Problems or Learning Disabilities in the Criminal Justice System*. London: Department of Health.

Case, S. and Haines, K. (2009) *Understanding Youth Offending: Risk Factor Research, Policy and Practice*. Cullompton: Willan.

Corston, J. (2007) *The Corston Report: A Report by Baroness Jean Corston of a Review of Women with Particular Vulnerabilities in the Criminal Justice System*. London: Home Office.

Cross, N., Evans, J. and Minkes, J. (2002) 'Still children first? Developments in youth justice in Wales'. *Youth Justice*, 2(3) pp. 151–62.

Drakeford, M. (2010) 'Devolution and youth justice in Wales'. *Criminology and Criminal Justice*, 10(2) pp. 137–54.

Drew, J. (2011) 'The future direction of the YJB'. *YJBulletin*, 2 December, Issue 142. London: Youth Justice Board.

Dunkel, F., Grzywa, J., Horsfield, P. and Pruin, I. (eds) (2010) *Juvenile Justice Systems in Europe*. Mönchengladbach: Forum Verlag Godesberg.

Farrall, S. and Bowling, B. (1999) 'Structuration, human development and desistance from crime'. *British Journal of Criminology*, 39(2) pp. 252–67.

Farrall, S. and Maruna, S. (2004) 'Desistance-focused criminal justice policy research: introduction to a special issue on desistance from crime and public policy'. *The Howard Journal of Criminal Justice*, 43(4) pp. 358–67.

Fergusson, R. (2007) 'Making sense of the melting pot: multiple discourses in youth justice policy'. *Youth Justice: An International Journal*, 7 (3) pp. 179–94.

Fitzpatrick, C. (née Taylor) (2011) 'What is the difference between "desistance" and "resilience"? Exploring the relationship between two key concepts'. *Youth Justice: An International Journal*, 11(3) pp. 221–34.

Gelsthorpe, L. and Sharpe, G. (2006) 'Gender, youth crime and justice' in B. Goldson and J. Muncie (eds) *Youth Crime and Justice*. London: Sage pp. 47–61.

Gelsthorpe, L. and Sharpe, G. (eds) (2009) 'Girls, young women and youth justice'. *Youth Justice: An International Journal* – Special Issue 9(3).

Goldson, B. (2002) *Vulnerable Inside: Children in Secure and Penal Settings*. London: The Children's Society.

Goldson, B. (2009) 'Difficult to understand or defend: a reasoned case for raising the age of criminal responsibility'. *Howard Journal of Criminal Justice*, 48(5) pp. 514–21.

Goldson, B. (2010) 'The sleep of (criminological) reason: knowledge-policy rupture and New Labour's youth justice legacy'. *Criminology and Criminal Justice*, 10(2) pp. 155–78.

Goldson, B. (2011a) 'Time for a fresh start, but is this it? A critical assessment of the report of the Independent Commission on Youth Crime and Antisocial Behaviour'. *Youth Justice: An International Journal*, 11(1) pp. 3–27.

Goldson, B. (2011b) 'The Independent Commission on Youth Crime and Antisocial Behaviour: fresh start or false dawn?'. *Journal of Children's Services*, 6(2) pp. 77–85.

Goldson, B. (ed.) (2011) *Youth in Crisis? 'Gangs', Territoriality and Violence*. Abingdon: Routledge.

Goldson, B. and Coles, D. (2005) *In the Care of the State? Child Deaths in Penal Custody in England and Wales*. London: Inquest.

Goldson, B. and Hughes, G. (2010) 'Sociological criminology and youth justice: comparative policy analysis and academic intervention'. *Criminology and Criminal Justice*, 10(2) pp. 211–30.

Goldson, B. and Muncie, J. (2006) 'Rethinking youth justice: comparative analysis, international human rights and research evidence'. *Youth Justice: An International Journal*, 6(2) pp. 91–106.

Goldson, B. and Muncie, J. (2009) 'Editors' introduction' in B. Goldson and J. Muncie (eds) *Youth Crime and Juvenile Justice*, Volume 2: 'Juvenile Corrections', Sage Library of Criminology. London: Sage pp. vii–xxi.

Goldson, B and Muncie, J. (2012) 'Towards a global "child friendly" juvenile justice?'. *International Journal of Law, Crime and Justice*, 40 (1) pp. 47–64.

Graham, J., Perrott, S. and Marshall, K. (2011) *A Review of the Youth Justice System in Northern Ireland*. Belfast: Department of Justice.

Hallsworth, S. and Young, T. (2008) 'Gang talk and gang talkers: a critique'. *Crime, Media, Culture*, 4(2) pp. 175–95.

Haines, A., Goldson, B., Haycox, A., Houten, R., Lane, S., McGuire, J., Nathan, T., Perkins, E., Richards, S. and Whittington, R. (2012) *Evaluation of the Youth Justice Liaison and Diversion Scheme: Final Report*. Liverpool: The University of Liverpool. Available at: www.dh.gov.uk/en/Publicationsandstatistics/Publications/PublicationsPolicyAndGuidance/DH_133005 [accessed March 2012].

Haines, K. (2009) 'The dragonisation of youth justice' in W. Taylor, R. Earle and R. Hester (eds) *Youth Justice Handbook: Theory, Policy and Practice*. Cullompton: Willan pp. 231–42.

Hart, D. (2011) *Into the Breach: The Enforcement of Statutory Orders in the Youth Justice System*. London: Prison Reform Trust.

Hazel, N. (2008) *Cross-National Comparison of Youth Justice*. London: Youth Justice Board.

Her Majesty's Inspectorate of Prisons (2011a) *The Care of Looked After Children in Custody: A Short Thematic Review*. London: Her Majesty's Inspectorate of Prisons.

Her Majesty's Inspectorate of Prisons (2011b) *Resettlement Provision for Children and Young People: Accommodation and Education, Training and Employment*. London: Her Majesty's Inspectorate of Prisons.

Home Office (2011a) *Anti-Social Behaviour Order Statistics – England and Wales 2010*. London: Home Office.

Home Office (2011b) *More Effective Responses to Anti-Social Behaviour*. London: Home Office.

Home Office (2011c) *Ending Gang and Youth Violence – a Cross-Government Report*. Press release, 21 November. London: Home Office. Available at: www.homeoffice.gov.uk/media-centre/press-releases/Ending-gang-violence [accessed December 2011].

Home Office, Ministry of Justice, Department for Children, Schools and Families (2009) *Youth Crime Action Plan: One Year On*. London: HM Government.

Home Office, Ministry of Justice, Cabinet Office, Department for Children, Schools and Families (2008) *Youth Crime Action Plan 2008*. London: HM Government.

Hughes, G., Case, S., Edwards, A., Haines, K., Liddle, M., Smith, A. and Wright, S. (2009) *Evaluation of the Effectiveness of the Safer Communities Fund 2006–2009: Final Research Report Submitted to the Welsh Assembly Government by Cardiff University, Swansea University and ARCS Ltd*. Cardiff: Welsh Assembly Government.

Independent Commission on Youth Crime and Antisocial Behaviour (2010) *Time for a Fresh Start: The Report of the Independent Commission on Youth Crime and Antisocial Behaviour*. London: The Police Foundation.

Junger-Tas, J. and Decker, S. (eds) (2008) *International Handbook of Juvenile Justice*. New York: Springer.

Junger-Tas, J., Haen Marshall, I., Enzmann, D., Killias, M., Majone, S. and Gruszczynska, B. (eds) (2010) *Juvenile Delinquency in Europe and Beyond*. New York: Springer.

McAra, L. and McVie, S. (2007) 'Youth justice? The impact of system contact on patterns of desistance from offending'. *European Journal of Criminology*, 4(3) pp. 315–45.

McAra, L. and McVie, S. (2010) 'Youth crime and justice: key messages from the Edinburgh Study of Youth Transitions and Crime'. *Criminology and Criminal Justice*, 10(2) pp. 179–209.

McNeill, F. (2006) 'Community supervision: context and relationships matter' in B. Goldson and J. Muncie (eds) *Youth Crime and Justice*. London: Sage pp. 125–38.

May, T., Gyateng, T. and Hough, M. (2010) *Differential Treatment in the Youth Justice System*. Manchester: Equality and Human Rights Commission.

Ministry of Justice (2010) *News Release: Reform of Public Bodies Announced* (14 October). London: Ministry of Justice.

Ministry of Justice and the Department of Health (2011) *Government Response to the Office of the Children's Commissioner's Report: 'I think I must have been born bad' – Emotional Wellbeing and Mental Health of Children and Young People in the Youth Justice System*. London: Ministry of Justice.

Muncie, J. (2005) 'The globalization of crime control – the case of youth and juvenile justice: neo-liberalism, policy convergence and international conventions'. *Theoretical Criminology*, 9(1) pp. 35–64.

Muncie, J. and Goldson, B. (eds) (2006) *Comparative Youth Justice: Critical Issues*. London: Sage.

Newburn, T. (2011) 'The riots and policing's sacred cow'. *Guardian*, 7 December, p. 30. Available at: www.guardian.co.uk/commentisfree/2011/dec/06/policing-sacred-cow-reading-riots [accessed December 2011].

Office of the Children's Commissioner (2011) *'I think I must have been born bad': Emotional Wellbeing and Mental Health of Children and Young People in the Youth Justice System*. London: Office of the Children's Commissioner.

Pitts, J. (2008) *Reluctant Gangsters: The Changing Face of Youth Crime*. Cullompton: Willan Publishing.

Rutherford, A. (1992) *Growing Out of Crime: The New Era*. Winchester: Waterside Books.

Simon, J. (2007) *Governing Through Crime*. Oxford: Oxford University Press.

Tonry, M. and Doob, A. (eds) (2004) *Youth Crime and Youth Justice: Comparative and Cross-National Perspectives*. Chicago: Chicago University Press.

Webster, C. (2006) '"Race", Youth Crime and Justice' in B. Goldson and J. Muncie (eds) *Youth Crime and Justice*. London: Sage pp. 30–46.

Winterdyk, J. (ed.) (2002) *Juvenile Justice Systems: International Perspectives* (2nd edn). Toronto: Canadian Scholars' Press.

Youth Justice Board (2011a) *YJBulletin*, 17 November, Issue 141. London: Youth Justice Board.

Youth Justice Board (2011b) *Youth Custody Data October 2011*. London: Youth Justice Board.

Youth Justice Board and Ministry of Justice (2011) *Youth Justice Statistics 2009/10 England and Wales*. London: Ministry of Justice.

About the Howard League for Penal Reform

The Howard League for Penal Reform is a national charity working for less crime, safer communities and fewer people in prison. It is the oldest penal reform charity in the UK. It was established in 1866 and is named after John Howard, one of the first prison reformers.

We work with parliament and the media, with criminal justice professionals, students and members of the public, influencing debate and forcing through meaningful change to create safer communities.

We campaign on a wide range of issues including short-term prison sentences, real work in prison, community sentences and youth justice.

Our legal team provides free, independent and confidential advice, assistance and representation on a wide range of issues to young people under 21 who are in prisons or secure children's homes and centres.

By becoming a member you will give us a bigger voice and give vital financial support to our work. We cannot achieve real and lasting change without your help.

Please visit www.howardleague.org and join today.

INDEX